# PARTY REALIGNMENT AND STATE POLITICS

# Party Realignment
# and State Politics

EDITED BY MAUREEN MOAKLEY

Ohio State University Press

COLUMBUS

Library of Congress Cataloging-in-Publication Data

Party realignment and state politics / edited by Maureen Moakley.
        p.      cm.
    Includes bibliographical references and index.
    ISBN 0-8142-0571-2 (alk. paper).—ISBN 0-8142-0574-7 (pbk. :
alk. paper)
    1. Party affiliation—United States—States.   2. Political
parties—United States—States.   3. Elections—United States—
States.   4. Voting—United States—States.   I. Moakley, Maureen.
JK2261.P3148   1992
324'.0973—dc20                                          91-40730
                                                             CIP

Text and jacket design by Jim Mennick.
Type set in Optima and Palatino by G&S Typesetters, Austin, TX.

The paper in this book meets the guidelines for permanence and durability of the
Committee on Production Guidelines for Book Longevity of the Council on Library
Resources. ∞

9  8  7  6  5  4  3  2  1

# Contents

# Figures

# Tables

# Preface

THIS book is the joint effort of a group of political scientists involved with research on the role of party systems in the American political process. Most of the contributors share the view that parties are a critical link in our representative system and believe we still have much to learn and teach about the various ways parties can and do function in our system. Many of us also are involved in the study of state politics, a field that has been neglected by political science and one where, given the resurgence of the states, deserves more serious study.

The idea for the book grew out of a roundtable on "Realignment and the States," which was sponsored by the Committee for Party Renewal at the 1987 meetings of the American Political Science Association. The committee is essentially an advocacy group composed primarily of political scientists who are engaged in practical programs for party building and renewal as well as teaching and research on the American party system.

We hope this book contributes to each of these endeavors: research, teaching, and party renewal. The research presented in the state studies should inform the study of change in party systems and address some enduring practical and theoretical questions that have long been of concern to scholars. We also hope to provide instructors and students of American politics with a readable and interesting account of the character of party systems in different states. If we are successful, then we may be able to enhance students' understanding of the potential capacity of those institutions to improve our representative system. Given the heightened individualism of the times and the seemingly inherent tendency of American students to disparage political parties, if we can accomplish any part of our goals, then we will contribute to party renewal.

Any project of this scope involving many case studies and contributors represents an organizational as well as an intellectual challenge, and I'm delighted to acknowledge the many debts I have incurred.

As editor, I would like to acknowledge the support I received at various stages of the project. Gerry Pomper, cochair of the Committee for Party Renewal, invited me to chair the panel at the APSA meetings and encouraged me to turn the reports into a book. Tom Anton and Darrell West of Brown University provided me with a summer research internship at the Taubmann Public Policy Center at Brown, where I was able to outline the project, line up the contributors, and contract for a publisher. Our publisher's representative, Alex Holzman of Ohio State University Press, provided encouragement at all stages of the project, and Constance Wanstreet did a masterful job of editing the manuscript.

To my colleagues and the students at Connecticut College, my thanks for all the support they provided. Wayne Swanson and Marion Doro of the government department arranged for student research assistants. My colleagues Bill Frasure, Patrick Ireland, and Jerry Winter lent a hand with editing and transcribing manuscripts into compatible word processing formats. My thanks for the enthusiastic help of students Jennifer Ahlen, Jon Kozzi, and Andrew Middleton who assisted me at various stages of the project, and a special note of gratitude to Chandra Lantz, whose research skills rival those of any graduate research assistant. Gina Foster and Anita Allen lent their considerable organizational and secretarial skills to put the manuscript together.

Finally, I would like to thank our roster of contributors. An editorial effort of this sort is bound to involve some delays and disappointments, which I expected. I was not prepared for the continuous cooperation, professionalism, and goodwill of the authors in this volume, some of whom took on this project at a late date and came through with wonderful chapters. I would especially like to acknowledge the help of Paul Beck and Samuel Patterson of The Ohio State University. In addition to making outstanding individual contributions they also conducted "seminars by mail" with this author, providing editorial and substantive suggestions on my work and the overall shape of the book all along the way. Their efforts, as well as those of all the other political scientists associated with this project, make it gratifying to be part of this community of scholars.

In the end, a book belongs to the readers. We hope they enjoy reading it. We certainly enjoyed writing it.

# Introduction: Realignment and State Party Systems

MAUREEN MOAKLEY

1

A DECADE ago, a new study of states and the party system might have been considered an anachronism. States were regarded as withering partners in the American federal system, and parties had been declared close to irrelevant in electoral politics. But important changes in the American political landscape suggest that such assessments were premature. Most political observers now concede that the American states represent thriving polities with considerable potential for dealing creatively and efficiently with many of the problems of the public sector. And the place of parties in the American political process appears to have been reaffirmed over the past few years. While there is much debate as to the depth, scope, and meaning of recent partisan changes, there is an emerging consensus that political parties may be assuming renewed importance in American politics.

Speculation about the nature of partisan changes emerged during the Reagan years, as the popularity of the president enhanced the fortunes of the Republican party and his support of New Federalism encouraged a more active role for the states. Yet caution prevailed; there was concern that the changes were short-term shifts that would dissipate after Reagan left office. The

The author would like to acknowledge Paul Beck and Samuel Patterson of The Ohio State University and Gerald Pomper of Rutgers University for their helpful comments on earlier drafts of this chapter.

character of the 1988 presidential election, however, suggested something more enduring. While considerable attention was focused, as usual, on the personal capacities of the candidates, political parties and the role of the states were two critical forces underlying the dynamics of that election.

Polling operations, especially early on in the campaign, continued to question voters on their perceptions about the ability of either the Democrat or the Republican party to address key issues. An added dimension of the media campaigns were ads that touted the ability of the party to keep America strong and prosperous. Such events marked a notable shift from the intensely personalized and antiparty campaigns of the seventies.

During the presidential primaries, the parties' nominating process winnowed a broad field of candidates down to two reasonable and capable representatives of each party's constituency and agenda. In the subsequent general election, while short-term forces were important, they were not critical. There were no overriding, divisive issues; and certainly the election did not turn on the personality or charisma of either candidate. The majority of voters, apparently unwilling to consider new issues, voted on their predisposition toward the parties and their evaluation of the performance of the previous Republican administration.

The election also underscored the critical role of the states in those contests. National election coverage tends to obscure the fact that our representative system is a decentralized federal one anchored in fifty individual states. This is reflected in the structure of the party system and the electoral college. So while the media focused on the candidates' standing in national polls—promoting the idea of a close election—any reasonable count of the state-by-state electoral vote suggested that a Democratic win was a long shot. Long before the election, it was clear that the coalitional and regional support within the party system had been significantly altered. No informed political observer a decade ago would have foreseen the Republicans fighting to keep Texas, the Democrats writing off Florida, or Iowa becoming a partisan battleground. And the cumulative result of shifts in the states added up to an electoral victory for the GOP.

After the inevitable campaign postmortems, evaluations based on the longer term acknowledged that the Bush victory was one more indication that the party system had been transformed. If one considers the cumulative pluralities in presidential races that the Republicans have received from 1968 through 1988, we see a ten-point lead that is matched only by the twelve-point plurality that the Democratic party enjoyed during the dominance of the New Deal party system from 1932–48. Support for the Republican party was based on a growing coalitional commitment among discernable groups and fairly clear perceptions by the voters that the GOP represented a distinct and preferable political agenda (Ladd 1989a). One scholar concluded that the position of the Republican party is "more than the popularity of particular candidates or Presidents. It is the strength of a party that most Americans now believe is better able, as a party, to safeguard their peace, prosperity, and political philosophy." Hence, he argues, the election demonstrates a continuing trend toward secular realignment, a long-term transformation of the party system—at least at the presidential level (Pomper 1989).

The growing consensus on the state of presidential politics, especially in the wake of the 1990 congressional races, raises as many questions as it answers. Despite high levels of voter approval for Bush's first two years, the gains the GOP hoped to realize in the Congress in 1990 failed to materialize. Given historical patterns the GOP losses were less than normal, yet the Democrats continue to enjoy a one hundred-odd seat plurality in the House of Representatives and now appear to be akin to a permanent majority in that body. The Democratic Party also sustained its advantages at the state level where it holds a majority of governorships and overwhelming control of state legislatures throughout the country.

The disparate patterns of party control center debate on the significance of the current shifts in electoral trends. Are we in a period of realignment, which represents significant and durable change in the orientation of the voters toward the parties? Or are we witnessing dealignment, whereby voters continue to abandon any enduring orientation toward the parties? The critical importance of political parties lies in their ability to link the electorate and its policy preferences in a decentralized national and state representative system. Thus, to conclude on the basis of trends in recent presidential elections that the United States has experienced a pro-Republican realignment speaks to a change

> devoid of meaning, based on partisan loyalties that cannot hold together across elections and thereby cease to serve as enduring guides to voting behavior. Surely no realignment has occurred if it is based on new "reconstructed partisans" who do not follow up their Republican presidential

preferences by supporting candidates of the same party for other offices. (Beck 1988, 168)

The picture is far from clear. We know that transformed parties are "firmly in place in the United States" and "we need to get on with a precise charting of the new arrangements and their implications" (Ladd 1989a). We do not know what the transformations mean. It is the central premise of this book that any evaluation of those transformations requires focusing attention on changes in party systems of the American states. Political parties are, after all, a composite of fifty state party systems under the umbrella of national organizations. While the national organizations have grown in visibility and importance over the past two decades, our representative system remains rooted in the states.

But states are and have been the missing link in most discussions about party change and its meaning in American politics. The ongoing focus on national trends in voting behavior has provided some important starting points, but clearly it is time to move on. If the critical questions about contemporary parties relate to the depth and scope of the present changes on the partisan landscape, then we need to map the changes as they manifest themselves in state party systems. Until we know how, when, where, and why the apparent momentum that the Republicans enjoy in national politics does or does not translate into enduring loyalties evident in diverse state party systems, we cannot evaluate the meaning of party change in American politics.

This book represents a start in that direction. By charting the shifts in the partisan environment of fourteen diverse American states over the past two decades or more, we hope to elucidate some of the underlying dynamics of party change. It is, however, only a start. One point of agreement in recent studies of American parties is that the changes we are witnessing are ongoing in that they appear to transcend any one event, leader, or administration and are often linked to demographic, ideological, and economic shifts among voters in various political environments (Shafer 1989; Silbey 1989). Therefore, this study can provide one reading on what appears to be a long-term political course.

But such a reading can have important implications. First, in practical political terms, examining the dynamics of change in individual states in various regions can give us a better understanding of the meaning and direction of those changes for American politics over the next few decades. It has been argued that enduring transformations in the party system occur only when there is a convergence of voters' national, state, and local orientations toward the parties (Sundquist 1983, 229). Moreover, the significance of the transformations depends on the cumulative effect of voters' partisan shifts in various states and regions. Hence, looking at various states to see where and why such convergence has occurred should give us some insights into the depth and direction of change in the party system.

Secondly, a study of present changes may help inform the past. We know that the character of all partisan realignments in American politics has depended on the scope and timing of national changes as they played themselves out in various state party systems. Many states, even during times of rapid national change, displayed a curious resistance to national aligning trends (Clubb, Flanigan, and Zingale 1980). However, because of data limitations, we know very little about how and why such transformations eventually occurred. A systematic exploration of the present shifts in the states, with more sophisticated sources of data, might shed some light on broad theoretical questions related to the nature of partisan change in American politics.

The central question we ask is, To what extent have individual states experienced a realignment of their political party systems? We define realignment as a significant and enduring alteration in the partisan orientations of the voters within a state system. This definition implies a fairly straightforward idea and has worked its way into the vernacular so that some dictionaries now mention political parties in their definitions of the word *realignment*.

The term, however, provokes considerable controversy among academics; and some argue that we should abandon it altogether (Ladd 1989b). Many feel that political scientists during the past two decades read too much into earlier declines in voter loyalty and developed a body of scholarship which was modeled on an inappropriate framework of critical elections originally developed by V. O. Key (1955). Moving beyond that debate, more recent research notes that significant change and new alignments are indeed evident in the electorate and that despite the "cry of alarm that the partisan sky was falling" the "persistence of party identification" is still evident in the American electorate (Miller 1990). In light of this, we offer a framework that addresses some of the ongoing questions and concerns about realignment in the context of individual state studies that explore the process of contemporary party change at the state level. But that requires that

we review the broad changes in American politics over the past decade that have generated expectations about new alignments in the
party system.

## SECULAR TRENDS IN THE 1980s

### THE REAGAN WATERSHED

However political historians assess the Reagan era, it is likely to be
regarded as a watershed in American politics. His presidency articula-
ted and legitimated a distinctly conservative political agenda that has
deep roots in American political culture. Hence, the shape of political
dialogue has changed; most national politicians now discuss political
alternatives within the context shaped during Reagan's tenure or offer
liberal alternatives in disguise. As one political commentator noted,
the core premise is "no taxes, no spending, only investing . . ."
(Krauthammer 1988). There were indications that Americans were
slowly becoming disenchanted with the extended role of government
in the aftermath of the Great Society. But Reagan's attacks on big government, especially after the costs and some of the failures of government programs hit home during the Carter years, had a profound
effect on the way Americans view the political world.

Studies of realignment argue that for fundamental change to affect
voters, political issues must be infused with a moral component
(Sundquist 1983). Certainly Reagan was able to suggest that link so
that his positions on cutting domestic spending and shrinking the
role of government, his arguments for strong national defense and increased military spending, and his conservative stand on social issues
took on the quality of a moral quest. In doing so he was able to re-
inforce the idea among some Americans that he and his party were
the "we" that included most hard-working Americans devoted to
middle-class values aligned against "them," the Democrats, who had
miscast American ideals (White 1988). By the end of Reagan's term,
while moderates remained the largest group in Americans' ideological self-definitions, 34 percent now call themselves conservatives,
while only 23 percent consider themselves liberal (Norpoth and Kagay 1989). Even during the 1990 campaign, while the Democrats got
some mileage out of the fairness issue, more spending or more government was never an issue.

And, of course, during Reagan's tenure the status of the Republican
party has been enhanced. During the 1970s, the notion that the Republicans had been relegated to a permanent minority position in the

Table 1.1. National Trends in Party Identification

| | Democratic Advantage | |
| | Total Population | Age 18–29 |
| --- | --- | --- |
| 1980 | +19 | +21 |
| 1981 | +10 | +5 |
| 1982 | +17 | +10 |
| 1983 | +18 | +13 |
| 1984 | +8 | −1 |
| 1985 | +4 | −6 |
| 1986 | +5 | −6 |
| 1987 | +8 | −4 |
| 1988 | +7 | −1 |
| 1989 | +2 | −10 |
| 1990 | +4 | −14 |

Source: Helmut Norpoth and Michael Kagay, "Another Eight Years of Republican Rule and Still No Realignment?" (Paper presented at the annual meeting of the American Political Science Association, 1989). Data up to 1989 based on seventy-six *New York Times*/CBS News polls that were pooled for the years 1980–89; 1990 update from October 1990 *New York Times*/CBS News poll.

Note: Totals include leaners in the general category of partisans. The question asked is, "Generally speaking, do you usually consider yourself a Republican, a Democrat, an independent or what?" If respondent answers independent or don't know: "Do you think of yourself as closer to the Republican or to the Democratic party?"

party system was given serious attention. Now, as table 1.1 indicates, national polls rate the number of voters who identify with the Republicans within a few points of Democratic identifiers. Estimates do vary, particularly in the classification of leaners, who are alternately classified with partisans or independents. Yet there is a consensus that since 1980, the Democratic plurality has dropped to three or four points (Miller 1990). Particularly notable aspects of that trend are the proclivity of younger voters—socialized into the political system during the Carter and Reagan years—to support the GOP, the decline in the number of independents in the electorate and the movement of some of those voters toward the Republican party. One should note, of course, that patterns in the identification of the voters take on a more complex cast when one considers the frequency with which those partisans split their tickets and vote for candidates of different parties.

The result is mixed electoral patterns. The Republicans enjoy consistent success at the presidential level and have made substantial gains in the U.S. Senate, where they took control from 1980–84 and still remain within striking distance of a majority. Yet the Democrats continue to dominate in the U.S. House of Representatives, where they have held a majority for thirty-six years. Moreover, since 1961 the Democratic party has enjoyed significant pluralities in state government. As we enter the 1990s, they control an overwhelming majority of state legislatures and hold the balance in governorships.

Regional and state trends provide insights into the disparate national trends. Regional patterns of change indicate that Reagan's election and tenure only encouraged shifts in voter loyalty that had long been under way in the political system. A steady erosion of the support for the Democrats in the South, particularly among white Southerners, has been under way since the 1950s (Petrocik 1987). A similar shift in support toward the Republicans has also taken place over the past two decades in the states of the Mountain West (Galderisi et al. 1987), while the Democrats appear to be making gains in the Northeast. Changing voter loyalties have produced significant alterations in the electoral status of the parties in those regions.

A recent analysis of long-term regional shifts in officeholding for the U.S. Congress, state legislatures, and governorships documents a Republican realignment in the Mountain West and the South and charts increased, if less significant, gains for the Democrats in the Northeast and North Central region. "Over the last quarter century, the Mountain West experienced a secular realignment to the GOP which has gained seats at a rate of 1.3 percentage points per election. The South is also marked by persistent GOP growth. In both regions, at all levels, officeholders have become substantially more Republican" (Bullock 1988, 71).

But the diversity goes much further. Within regions, individual states exhibit mixed patterns of change in the status of the parties that are often linked to demographic, economic, and political factors removed from national politics. Patterns in New England provide an example. Since the 1950s, Vermont, a traditionally Republican state, has experienced a steady erosion of GOP support and is now leaning Democratic. The critical factors in its transformation have been internal: significant growth and in-migration of liberal and politically active Democrats, changes in the state's economy, and the disintegration of the existing Republican party organization.

Yet similar demographic patterns in other New England states have yielded different political results. In Rhode Island, economic growth and in-migration have eroded the strength of the Democrats and encouraged continued dealignment among voters. In New Hampshire, which has experienced the greatest population growth in the region, significant demographic changes have only strengthened the role of the GOP in that traditionally Republican state. The boom and bust cycle of the past two decades in Massachusetts has done little to alter the overwhelming dominance of the Democratic party in that state.

Given the decentralized and diverse nature of the American political system, this kind of variation should be expected. One observer notes that realignments are "national events only in aggregate terms. Principally, they have been the work of separate and sometimes even countervailing movements at the state level" (Beck 1982, 421). Even the pronounced transformations of the New Deal system were neither national nor uniform but depended on the institutionalization of voters' approval of the Roosevelt agenda in various states and regions, which eventually gave the Democrats the dominant place in the party system. During that era, marked shifts that occurred in presidential and congressional voting were not matched at the state level (Clubb, Flanigan, and Zingale 1980). While many states fell into the New Deal fold early on, others displayed notable resistance to national trends, as counterrealigning forces within the states prevented unified party control. The examples of diversity, past and present, underscore the need to explore and compare patterns of partisan change in individual states.

## STATES AND THE STUDY OF REALIGNMENT

The focus of our comparative study is to chart shifts in the party systems of fourteen economically, politically, and regionally diverse American states. The individual essays all consider the question of to what extent there has been a realignment in the party system of each state and frame their discussion around issues associated with those changes. Each study adheres to a common framework, which includes a general description of each state's political environment, touching on aspects of the state's political history and culture that affect the development and role of the party system. Using statewide survey data, the studies then go on to track trends in the voters' party affiliation and, where possible, voter registration, paying particular attention to significant variations by group or region. The studies also examine trends in voting behavior in the states, charting patterns in national, state, and local electoral contests. The authors also consider

Table 1.2. State Trends in Partisan Support, 1948–1988

| Strong Republican | No Discernible Trend |
|---|---|
| South Carolina | *Rhode Island* |
| Mississippi | *New Jersey* |
| Georgia | Washington |
| *Texas* | Montana |
| *Alabama* | *Iowa* |
| Arkansas | Nevada |
| *Florida* | Connecticut |
| *Virginia* | Michigan |
| Tennessee | South Dakota |
| North Carolina | Strong Democratic |
| Moderate Republican | Vermont |
| Louisiana | Moderate Democratic |
| Missouri | *Wisconsin* |
| Delaware | Nebraska |
| New Mexico | *New York* |
| *Kansas* | Maryland |
| Indiana | Maine |
| Mild Republican | North Dakota |
| Utah | Mild Democratic |
| Oklahoma | Oregon |
| *Arizona* | West Virginia |
| Wyoming | Kentucky |
| Pennsylvania | Minnesota |
| Idaho | Massachusetts |
| *Colorado* | *California* |
| Illinois | *Ohio* |
| New Hampshire | |

Source: Thomas Kephart, "One Concept, Many Measures" (Paper presented at the annual meeting of the American Political Science Association, Atlanta, 1989). Rankings are based on results of presidential and congressional elections. Alaska and Hawaii not included because of recent statehood.

Note: States in italics are featured in this study.

how the role of leadership and key issues on the state's agenda have altered the fortunes of the party system. And finally they consider prospects for the future.

In the West we focus on Arizona, California, and Colorado. The Midwest states are Kansas, Ohio, Wisconsin, and Iowa, while states in the South include Florida, Texas, Virginia, and Alabama. The Northeast states are New York, New Jersey, and Rhode Island. While no division of the states is entirely satisfactory, we have chosen a sample, noted in table 1.2, that suggests the political diversity of the states included in our study. Based on a series of scores related to electoral trends in state voting for president, U.S. senator, and governor, the table charts the directions of partisan change in the states over the past three decades. Taken together, the data bode well for the future of the Republican party, since more states are moving toward the GOP, and this group of states includes many that are experiencing substantial population growth.

The state grouping in table 1.2 however, tells only part of the story. By using multiple sources of survey and aggregate data and looking at electoral patterns in state legislative and local contests as well as national and statewide contests, a much sharper portrait emerges within each state. For example, a state like Iowa might not show any discernable trend based on voting patterns in statewide elections; yet a look at survey and registration data, demographic trends, and the results of legislative contests suggests a marked drift toward the Democratic party in that state. Likewise, while California appears slightly Democratic based on selected voting results, when one looks at patterns of voter identification and registration, a picture of growing Republican strength emerges.

In fact, the ability to use multiple sources of data, especially statewide polls, permits us to chart changes in state parties that were heretofore impossible. Earlier research on realignment usually relied on aggregate voting data from selective states or counties that charted and compared electoral results. While that level of study provided for detailed and interesting comparisons, the data were inherently limited in that one could only infer the link between behavior and attitude or basic attachment to the parties and not discern the impact of long- or short-term forces on the vote. Moreover, one could only draw the crudest comparisons among various demographic groups based on the general demographic characteristics of the area.

The advent of modern polling methods and the subsequent proliferation of national polls provided a much more accurate source of attitudinal and demographic data on political change. Unfortunately, research using that data shifted the focus of study to the national level. The national emphasis, in turn, limited our ability to make comparisons within and across most state systems, especially those with smaller populations. With the development of statewide polls, we now have the best of both worlds in that we have the ability to make detailed comparisons about party change among key groups at the state level using more reliable sources of data. When V. O. Key did his seminal work on secular realignment in New England, he lamented the fact that until other sources of data become "miraculously available," our ability to define the dynamics of partisan change would be inherently limited (1959). Thirty years later, growing pools of state survey data provide a unique opportunity to chart changes in state party systems and evaluate the process with much greater precision.

The study attempts to match a diverse sample of states with those that have comparable statewide survey data. It is not always a perfect fit. Since state polling operations are relatively new, not all states have extensive data sources. States like Iowa, New Jersey, California, and Ohio have data that goes back for decades, while in Rhode Island and Virginia systematic polling operations are newer and have more limited data bases. Private polling data are available in a few states like Colorado and New York. This is less than ideal because sometimes the wording of questions, sampling methods, and the general comparability of the data provide less reliable results. But some states represent such important party systems we felt they had to be included in any study of party change. All studies use data that go back for at least a decade and include more extensive and inclusive analysis as the data sources permit. By comparing available survey data on party orientations with long-term trends in various levels of voting behavior, the authors address some of the issues associated with party change.

ISSUES OF PARTY CHANGE

*Dealignment.* Scholars agree that dealignment, the disengagement of voters from their long-time party affiliations, was a notable phenomenon during the late 1960s and early 1970s (Nie, Verba, and Petrocik 1976; Norpoth and Rusk 1982; Beck 1984). While some suggest that its importance may have been overemphasized (Miller 1990), many argue this trend created a "window of opportunity" for realignment by mobilizing unaligned voters (Norpoth and Kagay 1989). If we define dealignment as the decline among various groups of voters in their orientation toward the parties, and measure this in terms of the rise of independents in the electorate, how consistent has this phenomena been in various states over the past few decades? Given the trends, what factors have encouraged continued dealignment or a reorientation of groups of voters towards another party in different states?

Most states in the 1980s showed a decline in the proportion of independents and an increase in the number of voters who either identify with or lean toward one of the two major parties. Yet in some states the trend toward dealignment continues. In all states, charges in the orientations of the voters do not translate neatly into firm electoral support for a given party. Statewide polling data can give us a picture of voters' *attitudes* toward the parties, but the link to voting *behavior* is much less clear. One of the ironies of the present situation is that while survey data tells us a great deal more about how voters feel about the parties, given a changing political context the data may tell us less about how people are likely to vote. This leads to a second question, What is the relationship between levels of identification and the vote?

*Attitudes and behavior.*    Studies of realignment posit a period of disengagement or dealignment, followed by a shift in voting behavior *and* commitment to a new political party. But the sequence and timing in the process is unclear. While we know that party registration is a lagging indicator, we know very little about how attitudinal trends evident in survey results fit with changes in voting for different levels of office, and what factors bring about the translation, particularly at the level of state offices.

Several state studies illustrate how attitudinal changes toward the parties do not necessarily manifest themselves in electoral support. Often there is a significant lag that is related either to structural characteristics, party leadership, or weakened party loyalties. Patterns of support in these state studies indicate that whatever the inclinations of the voters—however firm or soft their commitment to a given party—it is probably unrealistic to equate strong parties with monolithic voter support. Given growing levels of party competition in most states and the ubiquitous presence of television in statewide races, voters are not likely to support lackluster or inept candidates in any high-visibility race. This poses recruitment problems, particularly for the Republicans, who often have to field outsiders with little political experience.

*Party elites.*    One of the more fascinating questions to emerge in the recent scholarship on realignment concerns the role of elites in the realignment process. While a good deal of the early literature all but ignored the role of elites in party transformation, some studies pointed to their role in a reactive capacity—that is, as actors responding to the issues and divisions in the mass electorate. Key (1959) and Sundquist (1983) allow that a critical dimension in realignment is the response of elites to the issues that emerge. This view is consistent with Clubb, Flanigan, and Zingale who argue that voting is a retrospective act and that possibilities for realignment are based on the electorate's evaluation of the performance of the party in power (1980). Another perspective portrays elites in a more active capacity. Carmines and Stimson maintain that issues are first polarized among elites who, after creating the relevant divisions in the issue agenda, provide cues to the mass electorate to which the voters do or do not respond. They note:

> Changes in the components of party image, . . . should be temporally bounded between the elite policy reorientation which is the beginning of this process and mass issue alignment which is the end. Time ordering is critical. Redefinition of the link between issue and party, however tentative and perhaps unintended it may be, is a process that must begin with elite actors (1986, 903).

The case studies in this book offer some insight on these questions. Elites at the state level can and do influence voting behavior and can also have an impact on the long-term electoral standing of a party. In the short term they can help maintain the existing regime. Over the long term they can define a party's agenda and, if successful, build long-term coalitional support that sustains a party's electoral position.

Their impact on the orientations of the voters is much less clear. For example, in many states Reagan's tenure had only minor influence on the partisan orientations of the voters, since the logic of change was in place long before his election in 1980. In states of the Mountain West, which in some ways experienced the greatest Republican surge, change was fueled by long-term forces very much removed from national leadership. In Arizona, Democratic dominance, evident since 1910 but fueled by the New Deal, began to unravel shortly after World War II as demographic changes encouraged Republican growth. Likewise, in Colorado a long-term Republican realignment had been occurring for thirty years. In this context, one could say that Reagan was the result, not the cause, of shifting orientation of voters. While his presidency appears to have given a marked boost to Republican fortunes in Florida and Alabama, even in those states other key long-term changes related to in-migration and ideology had long been underway.

The exception, of course, is the growth in Republicanism among young people. In many states, even those that generally are tracking Democratic, young voters tend to favor the Republican party. Such support is not monolithic; survey results often give mixed signals, which is probably linked to the disposition of that group to be economically conservative but socially liberal. Yet it is hard to escape the conclusion that Reagan's presidency, following on the heels of Carter, had a profound impact on the way that generation perceives the political world. In this sense, national leadership appears to be an important factor in influencing the partisan orientations of a given generation.

*Sources of partisan change.* A question related to the role of leadership is, What are the sources of group change, and how do those changes occur? What patterns explain the formation of group support for a given party? Early studies of realignment supported the idea of conversion, which is that groups of voters perceive their party as irrelevant to their social, economic, or political needs, and then switch or convert to another party (Sundquist 1983; Erikson and Tedin 1981; Ladd and Hadley 1975). Another perspective suggests a major source of change is the mobilization of formerly unaligned citizens into the electorate (Andersen 1979). Related to that perspective is the argument that party change is often generational: younger voters, born into a different political environment, perceive existing cleavages and group attachments as irrelevant to them and form new political attachments around the leadership and issues of the day (Norpoth and Kagay 1989; Beck 1976; Jennings and Niemi 1975).

Our state studies indicate that to some extent each of those patterns provides an explanation for recent partisan changes. The distinctiveness of the eighteen- to twenty-nine-year-old vote in terms of its inclination to be more partisan and its tendency to favor the Republican party more than past generations—in very different state systems—indicates that generational replacement, linked to national political trends and leadership, is an underlying dynamic in secular partisan change. In other states defections of key groups in the Democratic coalition, such as Catholics and southern whites, indicate that conversion has occurred. Finally, mobilization, in terms of the inmigration of new voters from different states, also appears as a significant factor in the changing alignments of several state party systems in this study.

The state studies do not provide definitive answers. In fact, the authors do not speak with one voice on the issues and instead provide various interpretations of changes in different states. But certain patterns do emerge, which are discussed in the conclusion. In that chapter Paul Beck provides an insightful summary of the disparate findings evident in various states. After charting cumulative patterns of change in state party systems, he considers two alternative evaluations of recent events. One considers the idea of secular change—slowed by weakened party loyalties—that bears some resemblance to national and state patterns evident during the New Deal. The other suggests a party system so badly decomposed that it is incapable of meaningful realignment.

All of the studies that follow underscore the rich and varied nature of state party systems and suggest future lines of inquiry. The individual portraits presented here, which include very different regional and political types, all illustrate the expanded capacity of states in the federal partnership. A comparative study that focuses on state politics and explores factors that influence the political structure and agenda of states should provide a better understanding of this dynamic arena of American politics. While the full impact of the secular changes in the party system is yet to be realized, as we chart the process we need to keep our attention on the American states.

# Is California Going Republican?

## JAMES FAY AND KAY LAWSON

2

DESCRIBING California to non-Californian Americans is like trying to describe the United States to foreigners. It cannot be done easily, because the variety within the polity is simply too great. But without understanding that variety, we cannot understand California's most recent political history, the increase in Republicanism, and the likelihood that recent trends will endure. We therefore begin this study of political realignment in California with a brief examination of the state's population, wealth, and geography.

### POPULATION

California is the third largest state in land area and has the largest population—more than thirty-one million inhabitants. Over 50 percent of all Californians were born outside the state, and nearly 15 percent were born outside the U.S. Now the fastest growing state in the nation, California is presently acquiring an average of more than 650,000 new residents per year. Despite its vast expanse of productive agricultural land, most Californians cluster together. Over 90 percent of them live in cities, and over 80 percent of the city dwellers inhabit one of the state's four great metropolitan areas: Greater Los Angeles, with a population of 13.5 million; the San Francisco Bay Area, with 6.0 million; San Diego, with

The authors would like to thank Jim Glazer, a graduate student at the University of California, Berkeley, for tabulating assorted California poll data.

2.3 million; or Sacramento, with 1.3 million. California is the second most urbanized state in the nation, with an average population density of 183 inhabitants per square mile, almost three times the national average.

The median age in California is thirty-two, identical to the national median. Of the population, 10.6 percent are over sixty-five and 27 percent are under eighteen, percentages that are very similar to the national averages. Forty-seven percent of all Californian adults have had one or more years of college; 26 percent have had four or more years. The racial breakdown as of 1990 was approximately 57 percent white, 26 percent Hispanic (which is the third largest of all the states in percentage and the largest in absolute numbers), 7 percent black, 9.1 percent Asian and Pacific Islanders (Filipinos, Chinese, and Japanese, in that order), and .06 percent American Indian. The Hispanic and Asian populations are growing so rapidly that if present immigration and birth rates continue, sometime between the years 2000 and 2010 the white population will lose its majority status in the state; and by 2030 it will have dropped to 38.4 percent of the population, with Hispanics at 38.1 percent, a very close runner-up. In keeping with that trend, the settlement of 1.2 million Latinos in California between 1980 and 1985 constituted 46 percent of a population increase in that period (Mireles 1987).

WEALTH

California is an affluent state, contributing 13 percent of the nation's gross national product through its yearly gross state product of $733 billion. As a nation, California would be the sixth richest in the world, just ahead of Great Britain. Its late 1991 unemployment rate was 7.7 percent, which was slightly above the national average. The cost of living in California is high and rapidly getting higher. Four of the nation's five most expensive metropolitan areas for home purchases are in California. The median price of a California house is slightly over $200,000, as opposed to $93,000 in the nation as a whole. In contrast, wage levels are merely 10 percent above the national average. Fifty-seven percent of California women over the age of sixteen work. In 1989, the median California family was earning $43,400, several thousand dollars above the median U.S. family. In 1988 California ranked eighth in per capita income among all the states.

On the whole, then, California is wealthy and growing and its citizens know it. Every year for the past few years a majority of those polled have described the state as being "in good economic times;" only 15 percent to 22 percent say the state is in "bad times" (Field Institute 1987). Even so, almost 14 percent of Californians live below the poverty level, an increase of 2.6 percent since 1979.

## GEOGRAPHY

Geographically, one might argue that California is distinctive from the other states. Its 158,706 square miles include desert, mountains, extraordinarily fertile valleys, a long coastline, and 2,121 square miles of water surface. Nearly half of the land in California is government owned, about nine-tenths of which is controlled by the federal government.

California is so large and diversified that each of its major metropolitan areas, particularly Los Angeles, San Diego, and San Francisco, has developed its own political identity and regional chauvinism. The northern and southern parts of the state developed at different times; have experienced different immigration patterns; and have produced separate and often antagonistic political, media, social, and economic elites.

## POLITICAL OVERVIEW

The Democratic party in California is an emulsion of the interest groups associated with the national Democrats: labor unions, teachers, public employees, blacks, Hispanics, liberal and moderate whites, civil libertarians, feminists, homosexuals, Jews, and peace activists. In California, the Democratic coalition takes on a unique character through the addition of large numbers of celebrities from the entertainment industry, support from the state's potent slow-growth environmental lobby, and backing from the Trial Lawyer's Association, the *Bee* newspaper chain in the Central Valley, and assorted real estate, hotel and high-tech moguls. The party's voting strength is in most of the large cities, particularly Los Angeles and the bigger cities of the San Francisco Bay Area.

The leading lights in the Democratic party who have dominated the statewide political scene are former governors Pat Brown (1958–66) and Jerry Brown (1974–82); the late Jesse Unruh, the legendary assembly speaker; and the current speaker, Willie Brown. Lesser Democratic powers include Los Angeles mayor Tom Bradley; Senator

Alan Cranston; union leader Cesar Chavez; Tom Hayden and his former wife, actress Jane Fonda; and a handful of wealthy men and women who control access to inner circles of campaign contributors. There appear to be no dominant writers, thinkers, or publications that exercise broad influence on the Democratic party faithful and activists.

For the past decade the Democrats have been closely identified with issues such as increased pay and benefits for public employees, particularly teachers; the rights of public employees to organize; the plight of agricultural workers; labor unions in general; increase in social welfare benefits; fierce opposition to offshore and occasionally onshore oil drilling; support for a liberal activist judiciary; increased spending on a variety of environmental issues; support for measures to limit growth; support for abortion; support for alternative sexual life-styles; and active opposition to almost all tax reduction measures.

While abortion has been an important issue in other states, its influence in California may be more limited. Both the Republican and Democratic candidates for governor in 1990, Pete Wilson and Diane Feinstein, opposed restrictions on abortion, effectively neutralizing the issue in the most visible statewide race.

The Republicans find the base of their support in California's prosperous and diversified business and finance community, its huge defense industry, its high-tech concentrations, as well as in the more traditional agribusiness and real estate development sectors. GOP support can also be found among the state's large numbers of military and defense workers. Since the 1970s the Republican Party has been closely identified with the tax revolt movement, with strong opposition to gun control, general cultural conservatism, lukewarm opposition to abortion, and with a hard line toward criminals and the formerly liberal California Supreme Court headed by Chief Justice Rose Bird. The GOP has a less clearly definable litany of constituency groups than the Democrats, but it is the party of white California along with perhaps a majority of the state's Asians and a sizable fraction of the Hispanic middle class. Like the Democrats, the Republicans lack a dominant intellectual cadre to help shape the party's thought and direction.

Many of the state's newspapers lean toward the Republicans in their political endorsements. The powerful and increasingly liberal *Los Angeles Times,* however, usually stays neutral on statewide races. Republican voting strength is in the state's suburban and rural districts, particularly in Southern California, aside from the city of Los Angeles.

Unlike the Democratic party, which has produced a range of dominant personalities in the past three decades, the Republicans have produced only one, Ronald Reagan. His 1960s antitax and antigovernment stands have set the tone for state politics for twenty years. Lesser Republican figures such as Governor George Deukmejian and Governor Pete Wilson operated in Reagan's shadow. Deukmejian, who had shown a stronger will and proved more adept at outmaneuvering his legislative opponents than Reagan, lacked Reagan's star quality and the former President's ability to dominate and set the political agenda. The inability to gain control of the state legislature for all but two of the past thirty years has contributed to the Republicans' lack of dominant legislative personalities. Additionally, failing to control any of the state's big-city mayoral jobs, the Republicans have been weak in developing a corps of well-known, second-tier politicians ready to move into statewide elective politics.

Since Reagan became governor in 1966, the Republicans have been associated with the tax reduction movement. More recently, local Republicans are becoming active in slow-growth activities, particularly in the GOP heartland of Orange County. Republicans are also closely identified with the issues of cultural conservatism, although fundamentalist religious groups do not appear to be as strong in California as they are in the South. More than the Democrats, the contemporary California Republican party is caught between its promise of no new taxes and its desire to provide costly but badly needed mass transit, highways, waste disposal, and prison and school construction priorities.

## POLITICAL PARTIES

Political parties in California have traditionally been relatively weak. Punitive reforms enacted by Hiram Johnson and his Progressives early in the twentieth century made all local and judicial offices nonpartisan and imposed the primary on the parties as the sole means of nomination for partisan office. The pre–World War I Progressives and their contemporary antiparty offspring also legislated limits on the parties. The state legislature told the parties how they must organize themselves, when and where they had to meet, what dues they could charge, and when they had to fire their state chair. By law, county and state party organizations were essentially kept separate. The state party organizations (unwieldy masses of more than one thousand members) were essentially appointed by and controlled by Democratic and Republican members of the state legislature. In addition, a limited amount of patronage, other than legislative staff, restricted the ability of the parties to build up a cadre of professional party and precinct workers.

The only party organizations worth speaking of have traditionally been the Republican and Democratic state legislative caucuses and the personal political machines of the late Democratic congressman Phil Burton in San Francisco and Democratic congressmen Henry Waxman and Howard Berman in Los Angeles. Those organizations function as independent party units recruiting candidates for office, discouraging rivals to their chosen candidates, and often supplying huge amounts of money to the campaign organizations of their protégés. State assembly speaker Willie Brown, who controls the state assembly Democratic caucus, is currently perhaps the most important player in the legislative wing of either party's organization.

Recent limits imposed by statewide initiatives on the ability of legislative leaders to transfer funds to their chosen candidates may crimp the dominant role of the legislative caucus. But the caucus leaders and their interest group allies have been creatively exploiting loopholes in the legal limits to continue to exercise influence over legislative races. Recently enacted term limits may weaken the caucus.

In the past decade or so, the Democratic and particularly the Republican state party committees have been increasing their contribution base, their budgets, and their services to candidates. In 1990 annual budget of the State Democratic committee was $6.5 million, and the Republican budget was set at $8.2 million. Both parties have a contribution base of about 150,000 givers.

As a result of a lawsuit brought by the California Committee for Party Renewal and assorted party groups in the state, the United States Supreme Court in *Eu v. San Francisco County Democratic Central Committee* ruled that the Progressive-era regulation of the political parties in California was in violation of the First Amendment of the U.S. Constitution. Since early 1989, therefore, the California parties have been free to organize as they see fit and to endorse candidates in partisan primaries. A challenge to state limits on party endorsements in nonpartisan races was rejected on procedural grounds in 1991 by the U.S. Supreme Court in *Renne v. Geary.*

Among the consequences of the unanimous Supreme Court ruling in the *Eu* case is that the state Democratic party has begun to endorse candidates in legislative and statewide races. A second consequence is that the party organization has been endowed with new potential for political influence. Why else would a nationally known former governor like Jerry Brown seek (and gain) the post of chair of the California State Democratic party in 1989—an organization whose existence and purpose he had openly demeaned a few years earlier?

## POLITICAL PARTICIPATION IN CALIFORNIA

Californians vote for a vast array of offices and ballot propositions, both state and local, on ballots that are often long. The November 1988 statewide ballot included twenty-nine propositions, of which twenty-three were approved by the voters. The ballot issues normally relate to such matters as bonds, the environment, the construction of schools, veterans' farm and home-loan programs, care of senior citizens, property taxes (which are still adjusting to the effects of Proposition 13, passed in 1978), law and order issues, and so forth. Issues on the ballot in 1984 included the establishment of a state lottery and mandating the use of English on ballots. In the 1990 June primary, California voters approved a sweeping conservative initiative to streamline criminal trials, supported a massive $5.1 billion in new bond measures for transit and education, and defeated two Republican-sponsored reapportionment initiatives. In the 1990 general election, voters defeated Big Green, a sweeping environmental plan, and approved a proposal to limit the terms of state legislators.

California is not a highly partisan state. All of its local government and judicial offices are nonpartisan, and its political party organizations appear to be quite weak. Even when voters register as members of one party or the other, many of them hold that affiliation lightly. Although Democratic registration has long outnumbered Republican by large margins, Republicans have nonetheless secured elective office at all levels. In general, even though there are more registered Democrats than Republicans, there are fewer Democrats than before; and many of them are not dependable Democrats.

In the past, the registration of Californians eligible to vote has run from 4 percent to 5 percent lower than the national average. Currently about 67 percent of the state's eligible adults are registered to vote. Turnout of those eligible to vote varies: 59 percent in 1984, 43 percent in 1986, 54 percent in 1988, and 41 percent in 1990.

Table 2.1. Trends in Party Registration: California, 1958–1991

|      | Democrat (%) | Republican (%) | Other (%) | Democratic Advantage (%) |
|------|--------------|----------------|-----------|---------------------------|
| 1958 | 57.4 | 39.6 | 3.0 | 18 |
| 1960 | 57.5 | 39.2 | 3.3 | 18 |
| 1962 | 56.9 | 39.8 | 3.1 | 17 |
| 1964 | 57.9 | 38.9 | 3.2 | 19 |
| 1966 | 56.6 | 40.2 | 3.2 | 16 |
| 1968 | 54.5 | 40.3 | 5.2 | 14 |
| 1970 | 54.9 | 39.8 | 5.3 | 15 |
| 1972 | 56.3 | 36.9 | 6.8 | 19 |
| 1974 | 56.6 | 36.0 | 7.4 | 21 |
| 1976 | 57.3 | 36.0 | 6.7 | 21 |
| 1978 | 56.6 | 34.2 | 9.2 | 22 |
| 1980 | 53.2 | 34.7 | 12.1 | 19 |
| 1982 | 53.1 | 34.9 | 12.0 | 18 |
| 1984 | 52.1 | 36.5 | 11.4 | 16 |
| 1986 | 50.8 | 38.3 | 10.9 | 13 |
| 1988 | 50.4 | 38.6 | 11 | 12 |
| 1990 | 49.7 | 39.1 | 11.2 | 11 |
| 1991 | 49.0 | 39.3 | 11.8 | 10 |

Source: California Secretary of State, Report of Registration.

Nine out of ten California voters register as either Democrats or Republicans. Democratic registration is steadily declining and Republican registration is climbing, while the percentage of independents has been relatively stable during the 1980s. In 1978 the Democrats held an advantage of 22.4 percent, but as of October 1991, the advantage dwindled to 9.7 percent (Table 2.1). The actual Democratic advantage among registered voters is almost certainly lower. California's top pollster, Mervin Field, estimates that between 600,000 and 1,600,000 of the names on the registrars' lists are deadwood. Direct mail specialists report a high rate of mail returned because the intended recipient has moved or died. Field believes that eliminating the deadwood would bring Democratic registration to 49 percent and Republican to 41 percent, reducing the registration gap between the parties to 8 percent (Field Institute 1988).

In any case, as we have already mentioned, Californians do not always vote as they have registered, especially if they have registered as Democrats. In districts where a Republican incumbent is running for office, the Democratic vote averages 14 percent behind registration; in districts where a Democratic incumbent is running for office, the

Democratic vote simply matches registration; and in open districts, the Democratic vote averages 7 percent behind Democratic registration (Constantini 1987, unpublished). In 1986 37 percent of those registered as Democrats voted for the Republican gubernatorial candidate, George Deukmejian; 24 percent of those registered Republican voted for the Democratic candidate for lieutenant governor, Leo McCarthy (Field Institute 1986).

ELECTORAL TRENDS

California has voted Republican in all presidential elections since 1964. In 1988 only fourteen of the state's fifty-eight counties voted for the Democratic presidential candidate, Michael Dukakis. Although most major state offices routinely go to the Democrats. Republicans have done better in the governorship, which has had alternating Democratic and Republican victories since 1954 (table 2.2). The seven

Table 2.2.  Voting in California, 1948–1990
Winning Party and Percentage of Total Votes in Selected Statewide Races

|      | *Presidential* | *Gubernatorial* | *Senatorial* |
|------|----------------|-----------------|--------------|
| 1948 | D (47.6)       | —               | —            |
| 1950 | —              | R (64.8)        | R (59.2)     |
| 1952 | R (56.3)       | —               | R (87.7)     |
| 1954 | —              | R (56.8)        | R (53.2)     |
| 1956 | R (55.4)       | —               | R (54.0)     |
| 1958 | —              | D (59.7)        | D (57.0)     |
| 1960 | R (50.1)       | —               | —            |
| 1962 | —              | D (51.8)        | R (56.3)     |
| 1964 | D (59.1)       | —               | R (51.5)     |
| 1966 | —              | R (57.6)        | —            |
| 1968 | R (47.8)       | —               | D (51.8)     |
| 1970 | —              | R (52.8)        | D (53.9)     |
| 1972 | R (55.0)       | —               | —            |
| 1974 | —              | D (50.2)        | D (60.5)     |
| 1976 | R (49.7)       | —               | R (50.2)     |
| 1978 | —              | D (56.0)        | —            |
| 1980 | R (52.7)       | —               | D (56.5)     |
| 1982 | —              | R (49.3)        | R (51.5)     |
| 1984 | R (57.5)       | —               | —            |
| 1986 | —              | R (60.5)        | D (49.3)     |
| 1988 | R (51.1)       | —               | R (52.8)     |
| 1990 | —              | R (48.7)        | —            |

Source: California Secretary of State, Statement of Vote.

largest cities in the state all have Democratic mayors, but more than half of the state's nonpartisan county supervisors are registered Republicans; and a majority of the nonpartisan city council members in California's 468 cities are Republicans.

Republicans have been gaining in the state legislature recently, even in some nonpresidential years. The 1992 state assembly had forty-seven Democrats and thirty-three Republicans. The Republicans picked up three seats in 1986, winning eight of eleven open seats, of which only three were considered solidly Republican. In addition, Republican registration has increased in thirteen assembly districts where Democratic victories have been by slim margins. However, in 1988 and in 1990 the Democrats added a few seats to their majority. The margin in the State Senate remains comfortably Democratic, with twenty-four Democrats to thirteen Republicans and two independents. Overall, the Democrats' percentage of seats in the legislature has slipped from 69 percent in 1976 to 59 percent in 1992.

The California delegation to Congress is split between the parties but still favors the Democrats. One senator is Republican John Seymour, who was appointed after the 1990 election by Pete Wilson. The other, Democrat Alan Cranston, achieved his victory in 1986 by a very narrow 49 percent margin. Given his involvement in the Keating Five case and health problems, he has announced he will retire in 1992, creating an open Senate seat. After the 1990 elections, the California delegation to the U.S. House consists of twenty-six Democrats (57 percent) and nineteen Republicans (43 percent). In 1980 the Republicans were close to parity, with twenty-one seats to the Democrats' twenty-two; but this dropped in 1982, a nonpresidential year, to seventeen Republicans and twenty-eight Democrats. It is remarkable that the Republicans lost no seats in the House in 1986, a nonpresidential year, and then picked up one more seat in 1990, another nonpresidential year.

The House races remind us of an important fact of life in California, the strength of gerrymandering. Republicans have taken between 49 and 53 percent of the statewide vote in the past five Congressional elections but would have to take over 55 percent to get a majority of the seats. Gerrymandering has been a way of life in California. Congressional elections now are held under the one-sided Democratic plan prepared by late San Francisco representative Phil Burton. During the 1950s the Republicans gerrymandered just as ruthlessly, albeit less efficiently. One by-product of the highhandedness with district boundaries is a high degree of security enjoyed by incumbents, which offers security for officeholders of both parties; seats almost always change partisan identity only during open elections.

Whichever party rules the game can give itself about a three-to-two advantage in the House delegation. Hence the stakes were high in the 1990 elections, since California gained seven additional seats in Congress after the 1990 census. The hopes of the Republicans rested on their holding onto the governor's office so that they could participate in the redistricting effort and prevent a repeat of the highly partisan Democratic remapping that occurred a decade ago. Pete Wilson's win assured the GOP a role in the process, and campaign consultants estimate that the Republicans have a chance to capture as many as thirty congressional seats out of the fifty-two the state is expected to have by 1992. The Republicans also tried, but failed, to qualify several reapportionment initiatives that would take the power to reapportion away from the Democratically controlled legislature.

PARTY IDENTIFICATION

Voter self-identification has shown a pronounced trend away from the Democrats and towards the Republicans over the past three decades, particularly since 1982.

In 1985 Mervin Field found that more Californians identified themselves as Republicans than as Democrats (Field Institute news release 1309, 1985). By 1986 the trend was beginning to moderate; but Republicans still had a slight edge, with 38 percent of voters identifying themselves as Republicans, 37 percent as Democrats, 19 percent as independents, 2 percent as other, and 4 percent as having no preference. Field believes that "a significantly large portion of all voters consider themselves as independents, no matter how they are registered or with which political party they identify." When the independents are asked which party they feel closer to and these results are taken into account, however, Republicans hold a 2 percent advantage, mirroring the national trend (table 2.3). A January 1990 *New York Times* nationwide poll indicated that 45 percent of Americans identified as Democrats and 44 percent as Republicans. Among those Californians not registered to vote, the GOP also has an edge. As of 1988, 46 percent of unregistered Californians identified with the Republicans, 41 percent with the Democrats. In the past a plurality of the unregistered usually thought of themselves as Democrats. Not all of those who

Table 2.3. Trends in Party Identification: California, 1958–1989

|      | Democrat (%) | Republican (%) | Other (%) | Democratic Advantage/ Disadvantage |
|------|--------------|----------------|-----------|------------------------------------|
| 1958 | 56 | 37 | 7 | +19 |
| 1960 | 55 | 39 | 6 | +16 |
| 1962 | 58 | 40 | 2 | +18 |
| 1964 | 58 | 39 | 3 | +19 |
| 1966 | 58 | 39 | 3 | +19 |
| 1968 | 54 | 38 | 6 | +16 |
| 1970 | 53 | 35 | 12 | +18 |
| 1972 | 51 | 33 | 16 | +18 |
| 1974 | 57 | 33 | 10 | +24 |
| 1976 | 59 | 32 | 9 | +27 |
| 1978 | 53 | 32 | 15 | +21 |
| 1980 | 50 | 38 | 12 | +12 |
| 1981 | 48 | 43 | 9 | +5 |
| 1982 | 51 | 39 | 10 | +12 |
| 1983 | 50 | 40 | 10 | +10 |
| 1984 | 49 | 41 | 10 | +8 |
| 1985 | 45 | 46 | 9 | −1 |
| 1986 | 45 | 46 | 9 | −1 |
| 1987 | 45 | 45 | 10 | 0 |
| 1988 | 45 | 45 | 10 | 0 |
| 1989 | 45 | 47 | 8 | −2 |

Source: The Field Institute, "Political Demography," *California Opinion Index* 1 (January 1988); January to July 1989 Code books and phone update.

identify with the Republican and Democratic parties feel a strong commitment to their party: in both groups, nearly half of the partisans rank themselves as weak or leaning identifiers.

Over the past thirty years, a mismatch between party self-identification and actual voter registration has grown. Thirty years ago party registration usually came close to reflecting voter self-identification. By the late 1980s, however, Democratic registration was running 5 to 6 percent above self-identification while Republican registration was 7 to 8 percent below self-identification percentages.

Ideological self-identification can be as revealing as party self-identification. The 1980s saw substantial increases in the number of Californians willing to call themselves conservative, with most of the increase taken from the ranks of those who used to call themselves middle-of-the-road. As of 1987, 51 percent of all Californians said they were conservative, 14 percent middle-of-the-road, and 32 percent liberal, while 3 percent had no opinion. The comparable figures in 1970 were 42 percent, 23 percent, 26 percent, and 9 percent. Conservatism is strongly correlated with Republicanism in the state since twice as many Republicans as Democrats label themselves conservatives.

Thus by all three measures—registration, voting, and self-identification—we find a definite shift in the Republicans' favor. We turn now to the questions that must be answered before we can decide whether this shift should be called by the portentous name of realignment: Who is doing the shifting? Is it likely to endure? Who are the new Republicans?

The first question is easier to answer than the others. Table 2.4, showing party identification by various demographic categories in 1976 and again in 1987, gives us some of the answers. As that table indicates, a significant share of the Republicans' gains have been made among the young (eighteen to twenty-four): where only 23 percent of young Californians thought of themselves as Republicans in 1976 and 65 percent as Democrats, by 1987 the figures were 47 percent Republicans and only 42 percent Democrats. The twenty-five to twenty-nine age group shows an even greater realignment, from 19 percent to 43 percent Republican, the largest shift of any group. Republicans have also made impressive gains among both men and women, although Democratic identification remains much stronger among women.

Republicans have gained from 6 to 15 percentage points in all educational categories, surpassing the Democrats among those with some college or trade school and among college graduates with no graduate school. They have improved their standing among voters in all income categories, although they have majority status only among those with incomes over $50,000. Republicans have gained in all religious groups, with all major U.S. religious affiliations jumping by more than 20 percent, as well as among those with no religion. The shift is stronger in the southern part of the state (from 35 percent to 49 percent Republican) than in the northern part (from 31 percent to 40 percent). Indeed, of the large Southern California counties, only Los Angeles remains Democratic. Likewise, the shift is stronger among renters (22 percent to 41 percent) than among home owners (35 percent to 48 percent); and among those with a union-affiliated family member (20 percent to 35 percent) than among those with no such affiliation (35 percent to 48 percent).

Table 2.4.  Characteristics of Party Identifiers: California, 1976, 1987

|  | 1976 | | | | 1987 | | | |
|---|---|---|---|---|---|---|---|---|
|  | Demo-crat (%) | Repub-lican (%) | Other (%) | Demo-cratic Advan-tage (%) | Demo-crat (%) | Repub-lican (%) | Other (%) | Demo-cratic Advan-tage (%) |
| Religion |  |  |  |  |  |  |  |  |
| Protestant | 54 | 40 | 6 | +15 | 39 | 55 | 6 | −16 |
| Catholic | 69 | 23 | 7 | +46 | 51 | 39 | 10 | +12 |
| No religion | 65 | 23 | 12 | +42 | 53 | 34 | 13 | +19 |
| Other religion | 59 | 24 | 16 | +35 | NA | NA | NA | NA |
| Jewish | 87 | 10 | 3 | +77 | 74 | 20 | 6 | +54 |
| Education |  |  |  |  |  |  |  |  |
| Less than high school | 70 | 21 | 9 | +51 | 53 | 32 | 14 | +21 |
| High school graduate | 62 | 28 | 10 | +34 | 47 | 43 | 10 | +4 |
| Some college/ trade school | 59 | 35 | 6 | +26 | 42 | 48 | 9 | −6 |
| College graduate | 56 | 39 | 5 | +17 | 44 | 49 | 8 | −5 |
| Graduate school | 59 | 36 | 5 | +23 | 52 | 42 | 7 | +10 |
| Income |  |  |  |  |  |  |  |  |
| Under $10,000 | 68 | 24 | 8 | +44 | 58 | 32 | 10 | +26 |
| $10,000–19,999 | 63 | 30 | 7 | +33 | 51 | 39 | 10 | +12 |
| $20,000–29,999 | 57 | 36 | 7 | +21 | 45 | 46 | 10 | −1 |
| $30,000–39,999[a] | 49 | 45 | 6 | +4 | 45 | 46 | 9 | −1 |
| $40,000–49,999 | NA | NA | NA | NA | 44 | 49 | 6 | −5 |
| $50,000+ | NA | NA | NA | NA | 38 | 55 | 8 | −17 |
| Race |  |  |  |  |  |  |  |  |
| White | 58 | 37 | 5 | +21 | 41 | 50 | 9 | −9 |
| Hispanic | 62 | 26 | 12 | +36 | 61 | 28 | 12 | +33 |
| Asian | 45 | 41 | 14 | +4 | 39 | 48 | 13 | −9 |
| Black | 92 | 5 | 3 | +87 | 83 | 8 | 9 | +75 |
| Age |  |  |  |  |  |  |  |  |
| 18–24 | 65 | 23 | 12 | +32 | 42 | 47 | 12 | −5 |
| 25–29 | 71 | 19 | 11 | +52 | 47 | 43 | 10 | +4 |
| 30–39 | 60 | 31 | 9 | +31 | 51 | 40 | 10 | +11 |
| 40–49 | 61 | 34 | 5 | +27 | 46 | 44 | 10 | +2 |
| 50–59 | 59 | 33 | 8 | +26 | 43 | 48 | 9 | −5 |
| 60+ | 57 | 39 | 4 | +18 | 43 | 51 | 6 | −8 |
| Union affiliation |  |  |  |  |  |  |  |  |
| Union member in household | 71 | 20 | 8 | +51 | 55 | 35 | 10 | +20 |
| No member | 58 | 35 | 7 | +23 | 43 | 48 | 9 | −5 |
| Home ownership |  |  |  |  |  |  |  |  |
| Home owner | 59 | 35 | 6 | +24 | 44 | 48 | 8 | −4 |
| Renter | 68 | 22 | 4 | +46 | 49 | 41 | 11 | +8 |

Table 2.4. (continued)

| | 1976 | | | | 1987 | | | |
|---|---|---|---|---|---|---|---|---|
| | Demo-crat (%) | Repub-lican (%) | Other (%) | Demo-cratic Advan-tage (%) | Demo-crat (%) | Repub-lican (%) | Other (%) | Demo-cratic Advan-tage (%) |
| Region | | | | | | | | |
| South | 56 | 35 | 9 | +21 | 42 | 49 | 9 | −7 |
| North | 61 | 31 | 8 | +30 | 50 | 40 | 10 | 10 |
| Gender | | | | | | | | |
| Men | 60 | 32 | 8 | +28 | 41 | 49 | 10 | −8 |
| Women | 63 | 30 | 7 | +33 | 50 | 41 | 9 | +8 |

Sources: The Field Institute, assorted California Polls, 1976 and 1987.
*a* For 1976 the figures include all who earned $30,000+.

Among black and Hispanic Californians there has been only a marginal shift toward the Republicans, 3 percent and 2 percent respectively. The 7 percent shift among Asians toward the GOP is more pronounced, as is the 13 percent shift among non-Hispanic whites who make up a dominant 81 percent of the electorate. It is the shift of whites, 50 percent of whom now identify as Republicans, that is most responsible for the rightward drift of the state's electorate.

CONVERSION OR MOBILIZATION?

What are the sources of the partisan shifts in California? Is it mobilization of new citizens into the political process or conversion of the existing voters from one party to the other? Certainly, some of the shift is due to the mobilization of increasing numbers of young Republican voters into the electoral system. But the generational replacement of older Democrats by younger Republicans only partially explains the role of mobilization in the current move toward Republicanism. We have varied anecdotal evidence from around the state that new citizens, particularly Asian-Americans, are registering Republican and that Republicans are registering the majority of individuals moving into new residential housing developments, particularly in Southern California.

For example, from January 1988 to January 1990 in the rapidly growing Southern California counties of San Diego, Orange, San Bernardino, Riverside, and Ventura, the Democratic percentage of new registrants was respectively only 33 percent, 25 percent, 33 percent,

39 percent, and 29 percent. Overall, from January 1988 to January 1990, 46 percent of new registrants statewide were Republican and 41 percent Democrats.

Mobilization alone cannot, however, explain the gradual move away from the Democrats. Clearly, many Democrats are being converted to Republicanism. The conversion seems to be most pronounced among renters, males, Catholics and Protestants, whites, people who are not college graduates, and Southern Californians.


IS THIS REALIGNMENT?

If by realignment we mean simply a shift of voters that moves a party from minority to majority status in voter self-identification, then California has experienced a realignment. If we define the term more stringently as an enduring shift of voters that moves a party from minority to majority status in registration, voter self-identification, and the number of partisan elected officials, then the answer is clearly that realignment has not yet arrived. Democrats maintain a majority of registrants, and a majority in number of partisan elected officials (although they are now a minority among self-identifiers).

There are, of course, powerful counterrealigning forces operating in California similar to those John Bibby identifies in the Midwest (Bibby 1989). These counterrealigning forces are gerrymandered congressional and legislative districts and the ability of the majority Democratic congressional state legislative caucuses to recruit able candidates and supply them with ample campaign funds.

The more important question is not realignment per se, however, but its potential durability should it in fact occur. This is difficult to determine, with arguments to be made on both sides of the question. The impressive gains Republicans have made among the ranks of voters traditionally associated with the Democratic party—the young, non-Protestants, the lesser educated, renters, and union-affiliated families—suggest a possible enduring realignment. Lending further support to the idea that the realignment will endure is the lack of a rigid connection between Republican gains and the popularity of California's native son, Ronald Reagan. Republican gains did not falter with the Irangate scandals or Reagan's departure from office; on the contrary, they continued to increase (Raimundo 1986). California's elderly population is expected to grow at a higher rate than that of other age groups. By the year 2000 there are likely to be more than thirty-six million Californians, of whom nearly four million will be over sixty-five, another good sign for the Republicans if the present tendency of this group to shift to that party continues.

Other shifts predicted for California, however, give a mixed message on the issue of a permanent party realignment. The most rapidly growing group is the Asian population, whose Republican identification has also been steadily growing. As of 1987, 48 percent of Asians identified themselves as Republicans and 39 percent as Democrats. Now 9.1 percent of the total population, Asians will, if present trends continue, constitute 16 percent of all Californians by the year 2030 (Aoki 1986). This is, however, a highly diverse group. Besides the more numerous Filipinos, Chinese, and Japanese, there are significant numbers of Koreans, Vietnamese, Asian Indians, and Southeast Asians. Ideologically, the group tends toward conservatism: they are strongly anti-Communist, approve of military spending (this is especially true of the Filipinos), and believe in the death penalty. Their conservatism could bring more of them into the ranks of the Republicans. Economically and sociologically, however, the new groups are often dependent on strong social services and strong enforcement of civil rights, a characteristic that could lead them toward stronger ties with the Democrats. Even so, the characteristics of California's Asian population may change as newcomers become more assimilated. The political future of the Asian vote is a major question mark.

It is also difficult to be sure what to predict for the Hispanic vote. California's Latino population, now over seven million, is rapidly growing; and by the year 2030 Hispanics will constitute about 38 percent of the population.

This may not be good news for the Republicans, since data from a 1988 Field Poll indicates that 58 percent of all Latinos identify themselves as Democrats, and only 31 percent as Republicans. The actual California Latino vote is considerably less Democratic, however. In the 1984 and 1986 general elections, only the barest majority of Hispanics voted for the Democratic nominees for president and governor. The state's Latinos are not yet strong voters: 52 percent of them were born outside the state; one third of the adults are not U.S. citizens, and many do not intend to change that situation (Freedberg 1987). Nor do all the 1.7 million who are eligible to vote take advantage of the right. Although Latinos represented 10 percent of the state's eligible voters in 1988, they accounted for only 7 percent of the vote and had a lower registration rate than any other major population group.

The state's black population, always dependable supporters of the

Democrats, seems to be holding stable at around 7 to 8 percent of the total population and electorate. California's blacks register five to one Democratic, and no one is predicting a significant change in that ratio (Sample 1987).

Finally, it is important to remember that realignment can take place only when voters are already aligned, a condition that many would argue did not and does not exist in California. As we have seen, Californians do not currently vote as party loyalists or as party defectors. In California the parties as organizations are relatively weak and are held in greater contempt than in other parts of the nation. Many Californians think *party* means the party caucus in the state legislature; they have no notion whatsoever of a separate organization, one that might even hold elected representatives accountable. The recent United States Supreme Court *Eu* decision permitting the parties to endorse in primary elections (a right only California's parties had been denied) and to set their own internal rules gives them the opportunity to develop stronger grass roots organizations. Inasmuch as the existing parties are, in fact, still under the strong influence of legislators, there has been resistance to changing the structures or functions of either party. The Republicans so far refuse to issue any endorsements; the Democrats denied only one incumbent their endorsement in the June 1988 primary election. Until more meaningful changes are achieved, both parties remain largely invisible and unpopular, incapable of attracting the kind of voter loyalty commonly associated with realignment.

Although there is clearly movement in that direction, it is too soon to assert a serious and enduring realignment to the Republicans. Until the parties grow stronger, it is not safe to talk about alignment at all. Many Californians now vote, regardless of party, as individuals for other individuals. The party affiliations of their future choices not only are difficult to predict but may in fact matter little.

# Regime and Party Change: The Arizona Pattern

## DAVID R. BERMAN

3

THE concept "regime" refers to a mode of management or governing. Each regime reflects certain basic policy objectives and has formal and informal rules on such matters as the proper style of politics and the level and distribution of benefits (Forsythe 1977). Regimes may survive several administrations or different sets of authorities. Yet, for a variety of reasons, regimes themselves may also change. When this happens or begins to happen one should be able to detect, among other developments, fundamental alterations in the party system, in the operating of governmental institutions, and in the broad pattern of public policy.

Some changes marking the transition from one regime to another may occur in a gradual and incremental manner. However, fundamental change, particularly in the area of policy, may also take place in a dramatic fashion, very rapidly and discontinuously. In one well-known scenario, abnormal stress in the socioeconomic system leads to demands that are unresolvable through "politics as usual" and to sharp reorganizations in the coalitional bases of major parties. These critical realignments, in turn, involve broad constitutional readjustments and are intimately associated with and followed by transformations in large clusters of policy (Burnham 1970, 9–10).

The notion that fundamental change may come through the electoral process—indeed, that the historical dynamics of this country require such

changes—has long fascinated political scientists (Key 1955). In looking for partisan change or realignment, however, evidence suggests
that one must look at a succession of elections rather than simply a
major one (MacRae 1960). To that end, this chapter explores regime
and party change in the electoral politics and public policy of Arizona. It draws on several studies, interviews with some fifty past or
present Arizona political activists, and an analysis of registration and
voting data.

## FROM CONSENSUS TO CONFLICT AND REFORM

In the first part of Arizona's territorial period (1863–80) there was
considerable unity around the goals of survival and economic development, a unity sometimes achieved by the suppression of partisan
differences. But by the 1880s the political parties disagreed considerably over fundamental issues—differences caused in large part by the
impact of development. Dislocations led to the creation of third parties; to a policy adjustment by the Democratic party, which came to
dominate state politics; and to debates about fundamental reforms
that continued into statehood in 1912 and lasted, though with diminishing intensity, through the 1920s.

Initially, the territory had about an equal number of Democrats and
Republicans. Democrats, many of whom had migrated to Arizona
from southern states, were particularly numerous in the southern
part of the territory. Most of the settlers in the northern part and most
of the federal officials sent into Arizona were northern, Yankee,
Republicans.

From 1863 to the mid-1870s leaders of the two partisan groups
agreed to ignore their differences in the interests of survival and territorial development. They formed a nonpartisan clique called the federal ring that controlled territorial affairs. Holding the ring together
was a consensus on the need for unity in overcoming hostile Indians,
acquiring various forms of aid from the national government, and attracting private capital to develop the territory's mineral resources.
Conflict reflected regional disputes (for example, over the location of
the capital and various government institutions) and factional in-
fighting among groups devoted to different political leaders. Legislators distributed various projects such as roads, bridges, prisons,
and educational facilities around the territory through a log-rolling
process.

Political parties began to organize as the territory started to develop. Party members serving in the legislature spearheaded the drive for state-wide Democratic and Republican organizations. But Democrats, sensing that they had the votes to dominate state politics, were the first to organize into a statewide party. Republicans soon followed suit, and by 1880 both parties were officially nominating candidates for territorial delegate to Congress and seats in the territorial legislature. Democrats usually came out on top in those contests (Kelly 1926).

During the 1880s and early 1890s both major parties stood for statehood, the somewhat radical cause of free coinage of silver, and continued economic development. The dominant elements in both local parties were slow, however, to respond to problems growing out of the territory's economic development. Their sluggishness allowed third parties, the Populists and Socialists, to assume leadership in agitating for reform. Working for similar goals during the first decade of the twentieth century was a labor movement that was particularly strong in mining areas. But the progressive wing of the Democratic party under the leadership of George W. P. Hunt effectively co-opted the third-party effort by adopting most of the labor program. The progressive-labor Democrats came to power for a brief period from 1910 to 1916, writing the first state constitution and enacting a variety of reforms in the first few years of statehood.

The GOP's strength declined in the later stages of the territorial period because of migration factors (a new influx of Democratic Southerners) and because of the party's identification with carpetbag rule (most of the appointed territorial officials were Yankee Republicans). The GOP continued to decline after 1910 because Democrats successfully portrayed it as the enemy of the new and popular progressive constitution.

As the nation neared World War I, Arizonans were less supportive of reform. The influx of relatively affluent and conservative families from the Midwest tempered enthusiasm for change. The addition of female voters to the electorate, via a constitutional amendment in 1912, also had a conservative impact on the electorate. Women supported the GOP more than any other party. While they favored prohibition, they did not favor other political-economic reforms. Hunt, meanwhile, not only faced new voters less disposed to favor his policies but lost the support of many of those who had voted for him. A hostile press depicted him as a radical who was overly sympathetic to the demands of a special segment of society comprised of foreign-born industrial miners.

Table 3.1. Changes in the Two-Party Composite and
Presidential Vote: Arizona

| | Composite[a] % Dem | Change in % Dem | Pres Vote % Dem | Change in % Dem |
|---|---|---|---|---|
| 1911–12 | 54.5 | — | 77.0 | — |
| 1914 | 70.9 | +16.4 | | |
| 1916 | 59.1 | −11.8 | 61.8 | −15.2 |
| 1918 | 59.1 | | | |
| 1920 | 48.9 | −10.2 | 44.3 | −17.5 |
| 1922 | 60.4 | +11.5 | | |
| 1924 | 63.4 | +3.0 | 46.2 | +1.9 |
| 1926 | 60.7 | −.2.7 | | |
| 1928 | 56.2 | −4.5 | 42.3 | −3.9 |
| 1930 | 58.7 | +2.5 | | |
| 1932 | 69.2 | +10.5 | 68.7 | +26.4 |
| 1934 | 70.1 | +.9 | | |
| 1936 | 75.1 | +5.0 | 72.4 | +3.7 |
| 1938 | 78.5 | +3.4 | | |
| 1940 | 73.6 | −4.9 | 63.8 | −8.6 |
| 1942 | 76.8 | +3.2 | | |
| 1944 | 71.8 | −5.0 | 58.7 | −5.1 |
| 1946 | 65.2 | −6.6 | | |
| 1948 | 64.4 | −.8 | 55.1 | −3.6 |
| 1950 | 62.3 | −2.1 | | |
| 1952 | 51.8 | −10.5 | 41.6 | −13.5 |
| 1954 | 52.7 | +.9 | | |
| 1956 | 58.3 | +5.6 | 38.9 | −2.7 |
| 1958 | 51.1 | −7.2 | | |
| 1960 | 47.2 | −.3.9 | 44.4 | +5.5 |
| 1962 | 49.3 | +2.1 | | |
| 1964 | 51.7 | +2.4 | 47.7 | +3.3 |
| 1966 | 45.3 | −6.4 | | |
| 1968 | 45.1 | −.2 | 38.9 | −8.8 |
| 1970 | 46.0 | +.9 | | |
| 1972 | 48.3 | +2.3 | 33.0 | −5.9 |
| 1974 | 50.0 | +1.7 | | |
| 1976 | 51.2 | +1.2 | 41.3 | +8.3 |
| 1978 | 47.2 | −4.0 | | |
| 1980 | 45.0 | −2.2 | 31.8 | −9.5 |
| 1982 | 51.6 | +6.6 | | |
| 1984 | 47.6 | −4.0 | 32.9 | +1.1 |
| 1986 | 45.6 | −2.0 | | |
| 1988 | 46.4 | +.8 | 39.2 | +6.3 |

[a]Calculated as the Democratic percentage of the two-party vote in contested elections for governor, attorney general, secretary of state, state treasurer, mine inspector, U.S. senator, U.S. house of representatives and, after 1972 when state officials elected statewide began to serve four-year terms, contests for seats on the state corporation commission. Source for elections up to 1960: Mason, 1961. Information on other elections taken from official state reports.

Arizona electoral politics from 1912 to 1920 was highly volatile. We find rapid swings of large numbers of voters to and from reform-minded third parties. We also find a large surge of support for the Democratic party from 1912 to 1914 (the composite, nonpresidential, Democratic vote increased more than 16 percent) and relatively large dips in support for the Democratic party from 1914 to 1916 and from 1918 to 1920. Duiring the 1920s the mood of the Arizona electorate, as in much of the rest of the country, moved rapidly toward the Republicans, especially at the presidential level. Arizona voted Republican in the national elections of 1920, 1924, and 1928. Republican candidates for governor won in 1920 and 1928. In 1920 the Republican tide was so strong that the GOP captured the Senate and came within a single member of matching the Democrats in the House. Except for the 1920 election, however, the Democratic party was clearly the majority party in Arizona throughout the 1920s in voting appeal in nonpresidential elections (table 3.1). Democrats also led by a two-to-one margin in party registration during this period (table 3.2).

The progressive element in the Arizona electorate did not altogether disappear in the 1920s. For example, some 23 percent of those Arizonans who voted in the 1924 presidential contest favored Progressive party presidential candidate Robert La Follette. The major parties who controlled Arizona offices during the 1920s, however, shunned experimentation, at least at a level anywhere compatible with the Hunt years. Democrats focused their attention after the war on protecting Arizona's interest in the Colorado River. They complained that the proposal to develop that resource—hatched and supported by national and local Republicans—would transfer control over one of Arizona's vital resources to California and deprive Arizonans of their heritage. Democrats in the 1920s and early 1930s enjoyed considerable success by claiming that they had saved the Colorado from a Republican conspiracy (Parsons 1950).

## CRISIS, ONE-PARTY POLITICS, AND THE ECONOMIC INTERESTS

From the framing of the Arizona constitution in 1910 through the end of World War II, the Democratic party usually dominated Arizona politics (table 3.1). During this period, however, the party underwent considerable change. It began as a party of reform, which had to compete for that distinction with several reform-minded third parties. By the 1930s it was virtually without competition of any kind and rela-

Table 3.2.  Trends in Party Registration: Arizona, 1924–1988

| | Total Registration | Republican (%) | Democrat (%) | Other (%) |
|---|---|---|---|---|
| 1924 | 98,691 | 32 | 66 | 3 |
| 1926 | 105,704 | 32 | 68 | 1 |
| 1928 | 119,528 | 33 | 65 | 2 |
| 1930 | 133,145 | 32 | 66 | 2 |
| 1932 | 152,393 | 22 | 77 | 1 |
| 1934[a] | 146,345 | 12 | 88 | ND[b] |
| 1936[a] | 165,650 | 14 | 86 | ND |
| 1938[a] | 179,840 | 12 | 88 | ND |
| 1940 | 180,347 | 12 | 88 | 1 |
| 1946 | 197,808 | 16 | 82 | 2 |
| 1948 | 240,998 | 18 | 80 | 2 |
| 1950 | 279,533 | 18 | 81 | 1 |
| 1952 | 329,770 | 25 | 73 | 2 |
| 1954 | 307,545 | 29 | 70 | 1 |
| 1956 | 367,705 | 30 | 68 | 2 |
| 1958 | 391,590 | 30 | 68 | 2 |
| 1960 | 417,129 | 32 | 66 | 2 |
| 1962 | 483,613 | 34 | 64 | 2 |
| 1964 | 584,284 | 35 | 63 | 2 |
| 1966 | 577,671 | 37 | 61 | 2 |
| 1968 | 614,718 | 41 | 56 | 3 |
| 1970 | 618,411 | 43 | 54 | 3 |
| 1972 | 861,812 | 42 | 53 | 5 |
| 1974 | 890,794 | 42 | 52 | 6 |
| 1976 | 979,654 | 41 | 52 | 7 |
| 1978 | 969,430 | 42 | 51 | 7 |
| 1980 | 1,120,681 | 44 | 51 | 7 |
| 1982 | 1,142,159 | 46 | 47 | 7 |
| 1984 | 1,461,128 | 44 | 45 | 10 |
| 1986 | 1,596,079 | 45 | 43 | 12 |
| 1988 | 1,797,716 | 46 | 43 | 11 |

Source: official state reports.
[a] Total for two major parties.
[b] ND = not determined.

tively uninterested in reform other than what was necessary for economic recovery. After recovery, the party continued to control the state as part of a conservative regime that was responsive to the dominant economic interests.

The severe 1930s depression and the popularity of Franklin Roosevelt and his New Deal dramatically altered the party system and general policy orientation of Arizona politics. Furthering the upsurge in support for the Democratic party in Arizona was the movement into the state of Democrats from the South. Southern migration increased in the 1920s because the emergence of cotton farming in Arizona attracted many people from that part of the country. A decade later, Arizona became home for Southerners hard hit by the depression who migrated westward in search of employment.

Democrats steadily grew in strength from 1928 through 1938 (tables 3.1 and 3.2). During that period, their share of the composite vote rose from 56.2 percent to 78.5 percent. About half of the 22 percent gain came between 1930 and 1932. As Democrats took over the state in the 1930s, Republicans went into hiding. Republican voter registration declined steadily from a high of thirty-nine thousand in 1928 to a low of around eighteen thousand in 1934. Republicans would have to wait until 1948 before once again reaching the figure of thirty-nine thousand. The percentage drop from 1928 to 1940 was from 33 to 12 (table 3.2). In the 1930s and 1940s, the GOP virtually disappeared from the state legislature and other elected positions. From 1933 to 1951 the GOP did not have any representation in the Senate. In the same period, Republican representation reached a high of only eleven of seventy-two seats in the House. The Republican state organization allowed many legislative elections to go uncontested.

Roosevelt ran well in Arizona in the realigning 1932 election. In 1932 and the subsequent three presidential elections, however, Roosevelt's percent of the vote was less than that of the Democratic percent of the composite vote. The same disparity between the Democratic presidential and composite vote was apparent in 1948 (and, indeed, into the contemporary era). Apparently, local Democrats in the 1930s and 1940s were drawing strength from factors other than, or in addition to, national trends.

One analyst, writing in 1940, concluded that the Democrats since the 1930s had made a clean sweep with new voters—both those who had entered the state and those who had come of voting age within the state—and had won over the support of Hispanic voters (Waltz 1940). In regard to migration, Democrats benefited not only because of the arrival of more Southern Democrats but because many of the newcomers with Republican backgrounds "apparently have been opportunists and have not hesitated to become Democratic electors, if they voted at all" (Waltz 1940, 287).

Other former Republicans may have felt becoming a Democrat was the only way they could get involved. The closed primary system in effect at the time (and still in effect) required those who wished to vote in the Democratic primary to register as Democrats. It was next to impossible for a non-Democrat to win any partisan contest. The primary of the Democratic party, thus, was the only election that mattered. Registrars sometimes felt it was their duty to advise those who considered registering any other way than Democratic that it would be somewhat foolish to do so.

During the period of Democratic domination, those who participated in the Democratic primary usually had several choices among candidates for major offices. The primary functioned quite frequently to frustrate the ambitions of incumbent governors who were seeking renomination. Party divisions sometimes reflected ideological splits or policy differences. More commonly, however, primaries involved contests among rival groups for the spoils of office. The promise of some type of reward—for example, a job or a government contract—provided the incentive for involvement.

Political leaders, on the other hand, expected those who secured government appointments to work in the next campaign and to make voluntary contributions amounting to a certain percentage of their salary to help build up a campaign chest. Factions or intraparty divisions based on personalities, political philosophy, regional allegiances, or ties to different interest groups showed up not only in primary voting but in state legislative politics.

The depression had a devastating effect on both the mining and farming sectors of the economy. State and local revenues dwindled because of the closing of mines and because of declines in property values. While revenues were down, officials faced increased demands to help the growing number of unemployed. State and local officials attempted to cut back where they could and to find new means of financing essential services. The depression stimulated greater social consciousness on the part of Arizona officials. As conditions worsened, however, they found little alternative but to turn over the major tasks of providing relief to the federal government (Valentine 1968).

Over the 1930s, 1940s, and into the 1950s the federal government became more important, not only as a source of support for social programs, but for the broad program of economic development. Highway construction, for example, prospered because of funds made available as an antidepression measure and later under federal highway acts. By the late 1930s the state, anxious for federal aid to finance water projects, acknowledged the authority of the federal government to allocate water from the Colorado. In 1944 under the leadership of Governor Sidney Osborn, the state finally abandoned its policy of trying to obstruct development of the Colorado River. Arizona's water policy from the late 1940s on centered on securing federal funds to bring water from the Colorado River into the central portion of the state.

Arizona's external relations from the thirties centered on relations with the federal government. The day-to-day operation of the state's political system during the 1930–50 period, however, was highly responsive to dominant economic interest groups, especially the three Cs of copper, cattle, and cotton. Of these, copper was the most influential (Bykrit 1982). Mining corporations extended themselves in politics with such autocratic control that Arizona became, in the eyes of one observer, "the most corporation-ruled state in the union" (Gunther 1947).

The mining companies and their allies in rural areas, the large farmers and ranchers, placed emphasis on avoiding increased taxation on their properties. As one state senator from a mining area remembers, the mine, farming and ranching interests "weren't about to stand for somebody raising their taxes foolishly." Their influence produced "the most conservative legislators we ever had" (Hardt 1985). The approach of conservative Democrats to their legislative duties was "to keep new legislation to a minimum, hold down appropriations, and adjourn" (Rice 1964, 69–70).

The influence of organized labor, historically a major counterbalance to corporate influence in the state, declined during the era of one-party politics. The low point for labor came in 1946 when the voters adopted a right-to-work law that banned union membership as a condition of employment. Mining, farming, and ranching interests—long interested in lower labor costs or in keeping them low—led the union-busting activity. Organized labor, on the decline, began to move to an essentially defensive position in state politics, hoping in the 1950s to hang on to what gains it had made. Matters did not get any better for labor in the new regime, which finally took hold in the 1960s.

## GROWTH, TWO-PARTY COMPETITION, AND MODERNIZATION

Writing in the early 1960s, journalist James Cooper concluded that Arizona, still a young state, remained "at a fairly primitive level of political and social development" (Cooper 1964, 40). Yet, as Cooper noted, signs of political change resulting from population and economic growth had already taken place. Much of the growth occurred in the Phoenix area where newcomers found employment as skilled technicians with newly established electronics, aerospace, and related industries. Another component of the new group of migrants were senior citizens attracted to retirement communities in the Phoenix area. Across the state, population and economic changes were to lead to a decline in the political significance of long-established economic groups, especially those representing the mining and farming sectors. Population growth also brought increased demands for governmental services.

Politically, the main beneficiary of the changes was the Republican party. Signs of partisan change and the emergence of a two-party system began to appear in voter registration statistics in the post-war period (table 3.2). From 1940 to 1952, the Republican percent of the state two-party registration moved from 12 to 25. By the mid-1970s, around 40 percent of the voters registered Republican. Looking at the composite vote, one finds a steady growth in Republican strength in the period between 1942 and 1952. Over this period Republicans increased their percentage of the two-party vote from around 23 percent to 48 percent. Nearly half of the gain came in the 1952 general election. In 1960, for the first time since 1920, Republicans had more than half of the composite vote.

What factors account for the emergence of the GOP in the post–World War II period? Certainly among the facilitating influences were national trends in favor of the GOP in the 1950s. In both 1952 and 1956 the presidential vote for Eisenhower far exceeded that for other Republican candidates. Eisenhower gave the local Republicans a quick start. Republican presidential candidates after Eisenhower also tended to do better than the composite Republican vote and help the ticket. In accounting for GOP success, one must also credit the active efforts of the Pulliam Press in Phoenix to create a two-party system, the organizational skills of the local Republicans and the attractiveness of GOP candidates such as Barry Goldwater (Berman 1985).

Also often cited as an important underlying development that helped make change possible was the steady migration into the state of large numbers of people from Republican strongholds in the East and Midwest in the years following World War II. The significance of that new group of voters was apparent to Democratic politicians in the early 1950s.

By the early 1960s, survey researchers advised established Democratic politicians that they had cause to worry about the influx of newcomers. A 1961 research report based on a statewide poll prepared for Senator Carl Hayden, for example, concluded that while native born Arizonans (some 23 percent of the voting population) had not greatly altered their attitude toward the Democratic party, the new citizens, particularly those from conservative, small-town sections of the Middle West, had dramatically shifted the electorate toward the Republican party. Thus, while over half of the native Arizonans had voted for John Kennedy in 1960, only about one third of the newcomers did likewise (Kraft 1961).

While migration was important for the increased GOP strength, the party also benefited to some extent from the conversion or partial conversion of Arizona Democrats. In 1952 Democrats like U.S. Senate majority leader Ernest McFarland lost to Barry Goldwater even though registered Democrats outnumbered registered Republicans by 73 percent to 25 percent at election time. In 1960 the margin had narrowed, but the Democrats still had a better than two-to-one lead in registration. Democratic party candidates lost the votes of a large number of registered Democrats. Many may have been newcomers who were unfamiliar with longtime Democratic leaders like McFarland and, thus, more willing to look at other candidates. Others may have been resurfacing Republicans. Growing GOP strength because of migration may have encouraged the hidden Republicans who had long resided in Arizona to abandon a party they had joined only because they had no other choice.

The conversion of one-time deeply committed Democrats is a bit more difficult to explain. A series of interviews with Arizona political activists indicates that some, perhaps many, longtime Arizona Democrats changed aliegiances simply because they became more conservative as they became more affluent. As their incomes improved and memories of the depression faded, they no longer found that the national Democratic party represented their values or interests. On the other hand, one might also contend that, at least to some extent, it was the Democratic party that changed. Certainly, changes in the national Democratic party in the immediate post-war period toward a more active concern with civil rights alienated those Democrats who had been lifelong conservatives on social issues.

Relatively liberal, reform-minded Democrats, many of whom were relative newcomers, began to gain influence within the state party as workers and candidates in the 1950s. Conservative Democrats not only found their state party less agreeable but the message of the emerging Republican party more attractive. The state GOP actively courted the conservative Democrats. The effort, however, was only partially successful. The heart of the GOP, after all, was in the big cities, not in the rural areas where a good many of the conservative Democrats resided. Moreover, though the GOP stood for many conservative causes it, like the liberal Democratic wing, stood for growth and reforms that might well result in more taxes on the farms, ranches, and mines. The GOP, like the liberal Democrats, also threatened to destroy a regime centered in a malapportioned legislature operated by and for the out-county conservative Democrats. Faced with changes prompted in large part by migration patterns, many conservative Democrats chose to remain registered Democrats—to retain a foothold in the party and influence politics in their counties—but regularly voted for Republican candidates, especially those running for statewide office. Some considered themselves Goldwater Democrats. Others, critical of that behavior, looked upon those voters as Pinto Democrats, after the horse of two colors.

During the fifties and sixties, three rather distinct ideological/ partisan groups emerged in Arizona. In one group were the rising Republicans, aided by the Pulliam Press and the growth of an urban population in Maricopa County (Phoenix). Liberal, labor-reform Democrats, also largely urban but disproportionately strong in Pima County (Tucson) where there was considerable fear over the political influence of Maricopa County, constituted a second group. The Pinto Democrats, conservative and most noticeable in the smaller mining, farming, and ranching counties, formed the third group.

On the policy level, it was clear that the state's largest newspaper and its most visible Republican spokespeople like Barry Goldwater did not like labor unions, New Deal spending programs, people seen to be soft on communism, federal aid for education, and, as a general principle, the idea of a federal government that would do more than defend the country. The dominant element in the GOP stood for free enterprise, state's rights, and, for Arizona, doing what it could to stimulate growth (even if it involved taking federal funds) and to implement the tenets of "good government." In the latter respect many of its leaders, like Barry Goldwater, had been active in the movement that attacked vice and corruption in Phoenix and had given that city a council-manager form of government. More generally, the Republican party as it emerged in the 1950s reflected the goals and aspirations of large utilities, banks, law firms, and general business interests headquartered in Phoenix. The GOP in the early 1950s depicted itself as the party of modernization and reform—in combating a tired, old

Democratic regime that had governed the state "so long and so badly." One cause going for the GOP was the campaign against organized labor initiated by the conservative Democrats in the 1940s. Right to work was an issue throughout the fifties and even into the sixties, as organized labor twice failed to secure its repeal. Labor demanded to know where candidates stood on the issue. Right to work divided the Democratic party for a generation. Republicans, on the other hand, adopted right to work as a slogan and used it effectively in their campaign against liberal, labor-Democrats (Berman 1987).

Republicans and liberal Democrats in the 1950s and 1960s were at odds over basic social programs and regulatory issues. Both groups, however, placed considerable importance on the goal of economic growth and diversification. They also emphasized the need to modernize Arizona government so it could undertake the responsibilities placed upon it. Modernization, in particular, required shifting some important functions, such as tax assessment and school financing, from the county to the state level. In addition, modernization also required a streamlining of state government and the improvement of the ability of the governor to manage the state's affairs. Conservative rural Democrats opposed those reforms. They saw growth leading to more taxes for miners, farmers, and ranchers. Modernization also threatened their control at the county level and through the legislature in state politics.

GOP success in the post–World War II era first came at a few top-of-the-ticket offices. Up until 1966, malapportionment made it impossible for the GOP to control the legislature. The major problem was in the senate where each county had equal representation regardless of population. Theoretically, about 13 percent of the voters could elect a majority of the members of the upper house. The apportionment plan discriminated against heavily populated and heavily Republican Maricopa County.

The first statewide Republican breakthrough came in 1950 with the election of Howard Pyle as governor. The Democrats, however, won just about every other contest that year. Two years later, voters reelected Pyle. Also coming to office with the aid of the Eisenhower vote were Republicans Barry Goldwater in the U.S. Senate and John Rhodes in the House of Representatives. Others emerging as GOP leaders in the late 1950s and early 1960s were Paul Fannin, elected governor in 1958, 1960, 1962, and later serving in the U.S. Senate, and Jack Williams, elected governor in 1966, 1968, and 1970. Between 1966 and 1972 Republicans captured all but one of the six congressional seats. Representative Morris Udall, Democrat from Tucson, was the exception.

A significant turnaround for the GOP in the state legislature came in the 1952 elections which sent thirty Republicans to the house and eleven to the senate. The block of thirty votes and splits in the Democratic party put house Republicans in a strong bargaining position. From 1952 and into the 1960s, conservative Democrats and Republicans entered into coalitions to organize the house. Contests over the speaker position during the era found the majority Democratic party divided between liberal and conservative candidates. Republicans, acting in unity, would support the candidate put forth by the conservative Democrats. In exchange, once the conservative Democrat became speaker he would give Republican legislators choice committee positions. The conservative Democrats, also called Pintos, were from the lightly populated mining, farming, and ranching counties. They considered themselves to be Jeffersonian Democrats. They had closer ideological ties to the Republicans than to the urban, labor-oriented, liberal Democrats.

The year 1966 provided a watershed in Arizona politics. Running on the basis of a court-ordered reapportionment plan, the Republicans in 1966, for the first time in the state's history, captured both the state house and senate. With thirty-three of the sixty house seats, the GOP no longer needed to enter coalitions with Pinto Democrats. In the senate the decline of the small county conservative Democrats was even more startling, as the urban Republicans captured a majority of the thirty seats.

The Pinto Democrats were the first casualties of the new political era. Their control of the state legislature came to an end with reapportionment in 1966. Their loss was a loss for much of old Arizona and a conservative regime tied to mining and farming interests.

THE NEW REGIME

Long-term registration and voting changes have clearly benefited the Republican party in Arizona. Republican registration has steadily increased since World War II. In February 1985 registered Republicans, for the first time in the state's history, outnumbered Democrats. Republicans have maintained the lead since 1985. Democratic registration as a percent of total registration has steadily declined since 1940. As figure 3.1 illustrates, the percent of registered Democrats has

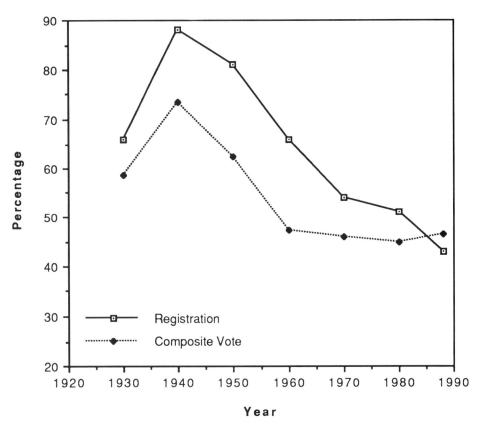

3.1 Arizona: Democratic registration and composite vote for Democratic candidates, 1930–1988

fallen to the point where, in 1988, it trailed the percent of the composite vote for Democratic candidates.

The shift to the GOP is also evident in figures involving presidential elections and the composite party vote for other elections. Arizona has voted for the Republican candidate in every election since 1952. Before that time not only was the state usually Democratic but, compared to other states, far above average in its support for Democratic presidential candidates. Since 1948 the state has been well above the average in its support for Republican presidential candidates (figure 3.2).

While the gap has not always been large, since 1960 the Republican party in Arizona has consistently done better in presidential elections

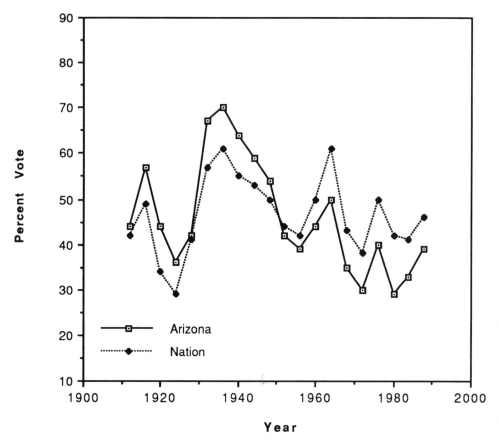

3.2  Arizona presidential votes: Vote for Democratic candidate in Arizona and the nation,
1912–1988

than it has in nonpresidential contests. Democrats can take much
greater comfort in their performance in nonpresidential elections (figure 3.3). Even this performance, however, is not all that encouraging.
Since 1960 the composite vote for the GOP has been larger than that
for the Democrats in eleven of the thirteen election years.

    Republican domination of state politics was particularly evident
from the mid-1960s to the early 1970s. Democrats enjoyed something
of a comeback from 1968 to 1976, picking up small gains in the party's
composite vote. A rejuvenated state Democratic committee redoubled
its efforts in raising funds, getting out the vote, and targeting legislative seats. That effort, aided by the Watergate scandal, increased activity in the Democratic-oriented Hispanic community (whose activ-

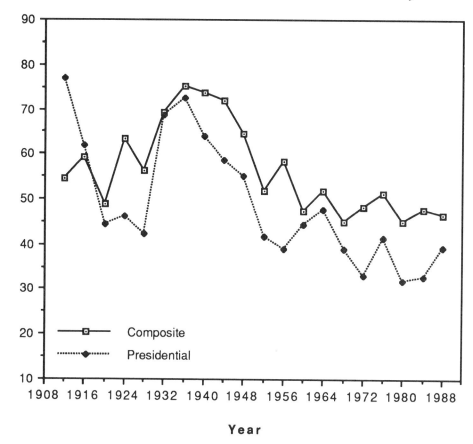

3.3 Arizona votes: Presidential and composite vote, 1912–1988

ity both influenced and was influenced by the election of a Hispanic, Raul Castro, as governor in 1974), and the emergence of strong candidates such as Bruce Babbitt, Dennis DeConcini, and Rose Mofford, brought some success. In 1974 the party won five of the seven statewide offices up for election. As table 3.1 indicates, however, most of the gains in the composite vote during the 1970s and 1980s vanished in later elections.

Democrats have done best in recent years with moderate-to-conservative candidates for top-of-the-ticket offices. They have controlled the office of governor since 1974, except for the abbreviated term of Evan Mecham (1987–88). They have not, however, done well in regard to seats in the U.S. House of Representatives or in the state legislature. The GOP has maintained control over the legislature since 1966 with the exception of 1975–76 and 1977–78, when Democrats managed to capture the senate. This problem, in part, reflects Republican control over redistricting and reapportionment. Though legislators have far less discretion than in the era before "one person one vote," the Republican majority has been able to skillfully disperse GOP voting strength to maximize the number of districts party candidates can win.

During much of the 1980s and into the 1990s, Arizona had a Democratic governor and a legislature controlled, though narrowly, by the Republicans. The situation encouraged Democratic governors to rely on their veto powers. Bruce Babbitt set an all-time state record with 114 vetoes during his career (1979–86). The GOP's margin in the senate was not large enough to override the vetos. Democrats in the legislature usually held together behind Babbitt. Use of the veto and threatened use of the veto gave the Democratic governor and Democratic legislators considerable bargaining power with Republicans in the legislature.

The Republican party in Arizona has several advantages over the Democratic party. One is that newcomers to the state still tend to be Republicans. Another advantage is that Republicans are far more likely than Democrats to vote. A third GOP asset is that many registered Democrats have been more than willing to support Republican candidates because they share a conservative outlook. The GOP in Arizona, as in much of the country, also appears to have done well recently among those entering the electorate for the first time.

Local Republicans also benefit from the image of their national party in Arizona. Many Arizonans, on the other hand, appear to view the national Democratic party as too far to the left. Given this perception, some Democratic leaders have, at times, found it wise to distance themselves from the national party. As former Democratic governor Bruce Babbitt remembers, "Whenever the chairman of the Democratic National Committee came to town, I made it a point to be in the bottom of the Grand Canyon and to leave behind a telegram welcoming him to Arizona" (Babbitt 1989).

One major problem for the GOP in recent years is finding candidates who can convert the party's edge in registered and likely voters into victories in statewide contests. John McCain, U.S. senator, has been the major exception in this regard. The party also has had severe internal divisions. Predictably, as the ranks of the GOP have swelled, it has become more heterogeneous; and party officials have found it difficult to hold the various elements together.

Chief among the Republican trouble spots has been intraparty squabbling between the moderate and conservative or ultraconservative factions. The right wing of the party has many religious fundamentalists who are intense on issues like abortion. They also have been negative on an issue of considerable importance in Arizona in recent years, a paid state holiday for Martin Luther King. The group's conservatism often contrasts with the essentially libertarian viewpoint of the Goldwater conservatives. They have also conflicted with GOP moderates who see a greater need to increase spending or to raise tax revenues. The New Right now controls much of the formal party structure and has a significant influence in the state legislature. Most prominent on the right has been Evan Mecham, longtime foe of the Republican establishment, who became governor in 1986 with 40 percent of the vote in a three-way contest. In 1988, a legislature controlled by members of his own party impeached Mecham and removed him from office. That action negated a scheduled recall election.

While Republicans continue to enjoy an edge over Democrats, one does find some evidence of dealignment from both parties. Neither party has had a majority of the registered voters since 1980. Since 1984, more than 10 percent of the registered voters have declared themselves independents or members of a third party. Voters are not hesitant about splitting their vote between Republican and Democratic candidates, though, as indicated above, this is nothing new in Arizona elections. Arizona also has historically had low rates of voting turnout. The state has usually been below the national average in the percent of voting-age population participating in presidential elections. As on the national level, that percent has declined in recent years—from around 55 percent in the 1960s to around 45 percent in the 1980s.

Particularly prominent among the nonvoters are native Americans and Hispanics. According to figures supplied by the National Association of Latino Elected and Appointed Officials, Hispanics in Arizona, with some 17 percent of the population, cast about 9 percent of the ballots. The state, in 1928, denied the ballot to Indians because they were persons under guardianship. Courts reversed the policy in 1948, but that action has not brought about a large influx of voters (Intertribal 1986). Black Americans, another low-voting group, constitute only about 3 percent of the population. Increased participation of Hispanics, Indians, and blacks would presumably work to the advantage of Democrats.

The new regime has been one of competitive parties, severe intraparty disputes, and often highly divisive issues. In many respects the parties have reversed their positions from the 1950s. Democrats in the 1980s, like Republicans in the 1950s, won statewide offices they should have lost based on party registration and turnout figures and were complaining about malapportionment. Republicans in the 1980s, like Democrats in the 1950s, were caught up in intraparty disputes that threatened their cohesion.

On policy matters, however, state government in the present two-party regime, whether under Democratic, Republican, or mixed control, has largely focused on the task of encouraging economic development. To those in power this requires making transportation improvements, protecting property rights, keeping taxes low, imposing only minimal regulations on business, and doing what can be done to keep labor costs down. Lawmakers have given social welfare a relatively low priority. Arizona joins much of the Mountain West in being particularly conservative on social-economic issues.

While the state is perhaps less conservative than it was under the old one-party regime, it still is conservative. Compared to the previous regime, interest group politics is more sophisticated. Corruption, however, is still a problem. This was illustrated in the Az Scam scandal in 1991. In that sting operation, several state legislators were indicted for accepting bribes in exchange for support of legalized gambling legislation.

CONCLUSION

Arizona's political history contains considerable discontinuity as one finds, over the years, shifts in the influence of specific groups, party support, the amount of party competition, basic political orientations, and public policy. But do the shifts constitute realignment?

National trends and developments have influenced partisan and regime changes in Arizona. Changes caused by local economic developments, the efforts of party organizations and individual candidates, and the inward movement of people from other parts of the United States have also influenced state elections and policy outcomes. Changes evolving from the state's economic development in the 1880s were a leading factor in the emergence of a competitive multi-party system and Arizona's progressive period. Behind the transition into a one-party system were a severe economic crisis, migration into the state, and the conversion of voters. Migration and conversion also help account for the emergence of a competitive two-party system since World War II. Both of the above transitions featured elections, in 1932 and 1952, in which there was considerable electoral change. Since 1952 change toward the GOP has been more gradual.

Up to the 1950s, dislocations that led to regime changes did not bring a shift in control from one major party to another. Rather, they prompted a change in the broad policy directions taken by the Democratic party, which, because of its flexibility, could retain its majority position. In the first of these eras, the Populist-Progressive period, dislocations growing out of economic development and out of the threat posed by third-party gains helped bring about the conversion of the Democratic party from a defender of corporate interests to the leading force for progressive reform. As the electorate, tiring of reform, began to change in the 1920s, so too did the Democratic party, and the articulation of the unfinished progressive agenda once again fell to third parties. In the 1930s the dominant Democratic party became the party of recovery, and in the 1940s, once recovery had set in, it became the means through which a conservative regime governed the state. Indeed, the only true realignment in terms of party control has occurred in Arizona in the post–World War II period, which brought a steady drift toward the Republican party and the installation of a new regime.

# Stability and Change in Colorado Politics

## JOHN P. McIVER AND WALTER J. STONE

4

THROUGHOUT most of the recent past, Colorado has been able to sustain extraordinary growth and economic prosperity far outstripping national averages. Since the end of World War II, the population of Colorado has grown at a pace substantially above average. Population growth has been fueled by economic prosperity as people have moved to Colorado to fill new jobs in a state offering natural beauty and an active life-style. But the opportunity and optimism that generated so much change in post-war Colorado has dimmed somewhat. Since 1985 the growth rate in new jobs has fallen below national averages. In recent years Coloradans have faced rates of unemployment higher than in many other states. During 1986 and 1987, Colorado experienced a net loss in its population through out-migration for the first time in almost three decades. Despite the strength of its tourist industry, Colorado languished in an economic trough brought on by the decline of the international oil market.

In this chapter we examine the recent history of Colorado for evidence of political change commensurate with the economic and social changes noted above. Evidence is mounting that realigning political change has taken place in the Intermountain West (Galderisi et al. 1987). In many re-

We would like to thank Thad Tecza, Julie Norton, and Paul Stecina for their assistance in collecting the data on Colorado elections and Bob Drake of Talmey-Drake Research and Strategy for recent NewsCenter 4/*Denver Post* polls. None of those individuals or organizations is responsible for the conclusions reported here.

spects the social and economic change in the region has been most prominent in Colorado, and it seems reasonable to expect evidence of significant political change as well.

## DEMOGRAPHIC CHANGE

Several changes are especially striking in Colorado since World War II. From 1950 to 1980 the population of the state more than doubled (from 1.3 million to 2.9 million) in sharp contrast to the nation, which grew less than half as quickly. Spurring the population growth was significant in-migration stimulated by economic opportunity. People follow jobs and Colorado employment grew at approximately twice the national average from 1950 to 1980, while Colorado unemployment rates have been consistently lower than U.S. unemployment rates.

Education is a second area of significant demographic change in Colorado. High school graduates have increased by almost 100 percent since mid-century. In 1950 only one-third of the state's adult population could claim to be high school graduates. Thirty years later, two-thirds of the adults had graduated from high school. By 1985 almost three-fourths of Coloradans were high school graduates and one-fifth were college graduates (up from 6 percent in 1950). The age structure of the state has remained relatively stable in the face of an aging U.S. population. Racial shifts have occurred, but most of the state remains a white society. According to the 1980 census, 89 percent of the state's residents are white. The number of blacks in the state has increased fivefold since 1950, but they still remain a very small minority group (3.5 percent). The growth of the Hispanic population in Colorado is more difficult to document due to the ever-changing official definition of that group by the U.S. Bureau of the Census. In 1980, almost 12 percent of Coloradans were classified as Spanish origin or Spanish surname. Nonetheless, it appears that significant changes have occurred in both the size and political involvement of Spanish-speaking Coloradans (Markusen 1987).

Geographic clustering of the population plays a significant role in state politics. Most of the population resides in a corridor defined by the north-south interstate highway I-25 immediately east of the Front Range, or eastern edge, of the Rocky Mountains. Very sparse populations reside on the plains of the eastern third of the state, in the mountain communities, and in the small towns of the "Western Slope". As a consequence, Colorado politicians with an eye on cultivating a statewide constituency may play to the urban audience in the Front Range corridor, while many state legislators are a good deal more attuned to the hinterland. Geographic clustering also has affected the political power of the relatively small Hispanic community. Their political clout is enhanced in metropolitan communities and several agricultural counties in south-central Colorado.

Perhaps because of the social and economic changes Colorado has experienced, the state remains politically competitive. It is a state that has regularly supported Republican presidential candidates while electing such liberals as Senators Gary Hart and Tim Wirth, and Governors Dick Lamm and Roy Romer. Since 1962, the state senate has been controlled by the Republicans, while the GOP's majority in the house has been lost only twice since 1962.

The partisan ambivalence in the state's voting patterns is complemented by the widespread use of the ballot to decide public policy questions. The initiative and referendum remain a component of the mainstream political process in Colorado. The diversity of voter preferences is reflected in the range of positions voters have taken on liberal and conservative issues over the past twenty years. Since 1968 Colorado voters have permitted a variety of state and privately operated gaming operations, supported student loan programs, raised taxes for the arts and parks, opposed nuclear weapons testing, and passed a state ERA. During the same period, they installed a death penalty in the aftermath of the Supreme Court's 1972 decision in *Furman v. Georgia*, refused to restrict construction of nuclear power plants, denied busing plans to encourage racial integration of local schools, supported bail restrictions for arrestees, defeated state funding of abortions for indigents, turned back plans to create a consumer protection agency, and instituted English as the official language of the state. The views of the state's electorate on environmental issues remains bifurcated: voters turned down two bottle recycling plans yet refused to support a plan to hold the 1976 Winter Olympics in Colorado because of its potential impact on the mountain environment.

We turn now to a more detailed account of political change in Colorado in search of the sources of the state's response to the complex changes in its recent history.

## PARTY IDENTIFICATION

Information on party identification over the past thirty-five years in Colorado is not available. While the political parties have occasionally commissioned polls of the state electorate, their interests have not always included academic concerns about party identification. Most partisan polls in Colorado conducted over the past sixteen years question citizens about their registration rather than self-identification. Consequently, one strategy we have used to measure the partisanship of Coloradans is aggregating Colorado respondents to fifty-five CBS/*New York Times* national polls conducted from 1976 to 1985. The data were drawn from a larger forty-eight-state data set (Wright, Erikson, and McIver, 1985) in which a total of 1,415 Coloradans were interviewed over that ten-year period.

According to our CBS/NYT estimates, the two political parties evenly split Colorado voters willing to identify a partisan preference. In the five-year period preceding the election of Ronald Reagan, 30.5 percent of Coloradans identified with the Democratic party while 29.8 percent indicated their preference for the Republican party. In the five-year period following Reagan's election (1981–85), the CBS/NYT estimate of the distribution of partisan identifiers shifted only marginally: 29.2 percent replied "Democratic" when asked which party they were affiliated with while 30.9 percent replied "Republican."

Privately commissioned polls in recent years confirm the picture of a competitive state in which the parties evenly split those voters willing to commit to a partisan position. Polls conducted between 1985 and 1989 by Talmey-Drake Research and Strategy of Boulder show a consistent Republican advantage statewide during 1985 and 1986, a slight lead in 1987 and a virtual tie between the parties during 1988 (figure 4.1). Indeed, during a good deal of 1988, Democratic identifiers outnumbered Republicans, a possible result of much greater media attention to Democratic races prior to a last-minute media blitz from the Bush campaign during the final days of the presidential race. Following George Bush's decisive victory over Michael Dukakis, the Republican party again emerged as the majority party in Colorado—but the honeymoon appears to be short-lived. At the end of 1989, the Democrats and Republicans stood in a virtual dead heat for the hearts of state voters.

So far, the state level data show the 1980s to be a period of competitiveness in the party affiliations of Coloradans. There is some fluctuation, to be sure, and hints of Republican ascendancy. But the available data on the partisanship of the Colorado electorate generally presents the image of a stable, competitive, bipartisan state over the past decade.

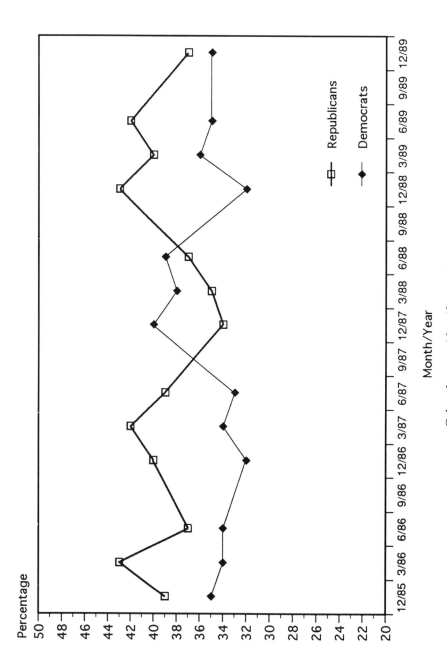

Percentage

Republicans

Democrats

Month/Year

4.1 Colorado party identifiers, 1985–1990

## PARTY IDENTIFICATION AND THE YOUNG REPUBLICAN

Recent work on the attractiveness of the Reagan administration has emphasized the mobilization and/or conversion of the youngest members of the electorate. Examining national changes during the 1980s, Norpoth (1987) concludes that younger cohorts in the electorate now profess "a marked loyalty" toward the Republican party. Similar findings have been reported in several state-level studies of shifts in aggregate partisan affiliation. Beck (1982) found that the impact of the 1980 Reagan election in Florida was most pronounced among the eighteen- to twenty-nine-year-old age group. Dyer, Vedlitz, and Hill (1988) also note that 40 percent of young Texans report supporting the GOP in contrast to less than 30 percent support from any other age group of Texas voters.

It certainly is possible that the aggregate patterns of stability we have thus far observed in Colorado mask change among the young comparable to what has been found elsewhere. Table 4.1, based as it is on fragments of information from various surveys, cannot speak with absolute authority on the question. But differences in partisan support across age groups found elsewhere are not obvious within the Colorado electorate.

Clearly, pollsters have not presented a very consistent picture of the age structure of partisanship during the early years of the Reagan presidency. Yet one common pattern is consistent with expectations: eighteen- to twenty-four-year-old voters prefer the Republican party

Table 4.1. Party Identification by Age: Colorado, 1976–1985

|  | Age | | | | | |
|---|---|---|---|---|---|---|
|  | 18–24 (%) | 25–34 (%) | 35–54 (%) | 55–64 (%) | 65+ (%) | N |
| Pre-November 1980 polls | | | | | | |
| CBS/NYT 1976–80 | −2 | +6 | −1 | −7 | −5 | 213[a] |
| Post-November 1980 polls | | | | | | |
| Marketing Opinion Research 1981 | Even | +6 | −8 | +5 | −3 | 795 |
| Marketing Opinion Research 1982 | −20 | −8 | −10 | −3 | +13 | 597 |
| DMI Research 1983–84 | −6 | +11 | −3 | −17 | −2 | 319 |
| CBS/NYT 1981–85 | −7 | +2 | +4 | +7 | −20 | 825 |

Note: Cell entries are the difference between the percentage of Democratic identifiers and Republican identifiers. Positive numbers indicate a Democratic party advantage and negative numbers show a Republican party advantage.

[a] Only about 40 percent of the pre-1980 CBS/NYT respondents were asked their age in years in a way that permitted recoding into the five age categories used by MOR and DMI.

(by 6 to 17 percent) to the Democratic party when compared with twenty-five- to thirty-four-year-old voters. However, only one poll shows the youngest cohort of voters as the group most supportive of the Republican party. Others find that groups over thirty-five are more supportive of the GOP.

## IDEOLOGICAL MAKEUP OF COLORADO PARTIES

Underlying many realignment theories is the notion that issues define political cleavages that separate parties and their members. Political ideologies summarize preferences over sets of political issues. Contemporary discussions of the Reagan Revolution have suggested that the Republican and Democratic parties have become more ideologically pure—as much as any centrist party can become pure and remain competitive. To what extent do party memberships in Colorado reflect the philosophical redefinition of the national parties? In table 4.2 we consider the ideological self-identification of Republicans, independents, and Democrats before and after 1980.

The table shows little evidence of major change in the ideological composition of Colorado's political parties from the late 1970s to the early 1980s. The Republican party is slightly more conservative, although changes of 3 percent are not significant given sample sizes. The Democratic party, while not more liberal, has lost some of its conservative members. As a consequence, the relationship (gamma) between partisanship and ideology grows from .30 to .38, a modest increase and a shift hardly worthy of the characterizations realignment or revolution. The balance of power in Colorado remains with its independent voters. And, as the table shows, those voters display no

Table 4.2. Ideology of Party Identifiers: Colorado, 1976–1985

| 1976–1980 | Liberal (%) | Moderate (%) | Conservative (%) | N |
|---|---|---|---|---|
| Democrat | 33 | 44 | 24 | 156 |
| Independent | 27 | 48 | 25 | 187 |
| Republican | 12 | 44 | 44 | 154 |
| 1981–1985 | Liberal (%) | Moderate (%) | Conservative (%) | N |
| Democrat | 33 | 52 | 15 | 193 |
| Independent | 22 | 55 | 22 | 283 |
| Republican | 14 | 38 | 47 | 217 |

leanings toward either philosophic extreme: a majority of independents identify themselves as moderate or middle of the road and the rest split evenly between liberal and conservative camps.

## LONGER-TERM TRENDS IN PARTISANSHIP

The identification of realignments has frustrated researchers who rely on microlevel theories about personal attachments to political parties. The major historical shifts in partisan politics in this country have taken place outside the scrutiny of the television camera and the survey researcher. Consequently, researchers have come to rely on indirect indicators of partisan change during other political periods. That has meant shifting focus from party identification to overt behaviors that have been measured for longer periods. Here we consider two such behavioral indicators of partisan attachments: registration and voting. Those measures enable us to embrace a much longer time frame in our analysis than is possible with the limited data we have on party identification. And, the potential for realignment surrounding the 1980 election notwithstanding, there is reason to believe significant realignment occurred in the Mountain West well before the Reagan Revolution.

Stone (1987) found evidence of a realignment in the mountain states in the 1960s. The region changed from a clear Democratic plurality in party identification and a consistent pattern of supporting the Democrats in its voting behavior, to a balance between the parties that favors the Republican party on election days. The sources of the realignment are not altogether clear, but the change in the Intermountain West is at least as dramatic as that found in the South during the same period (Stone 1987; Miller 1987; Wattenberg 1987). The question is whether we can find evidence in Colorado that is consistent with the broader pattern of realignment in the region.

### PARTY REGISTRATION

Party registration data provide the closest thing available to the concept of party identification. Colorado is one of twenty-six states that register voters into political parties. While party registration has existed in the state for many years, statewide records have been compiled by the Colorado secretary of state only since 1966. Consequently, we are limited in this measure to the period since 1966. Nonetheless, the data suggest the pattern of change that we could expect if Colorado has marched in step with the realigning change experienced through-

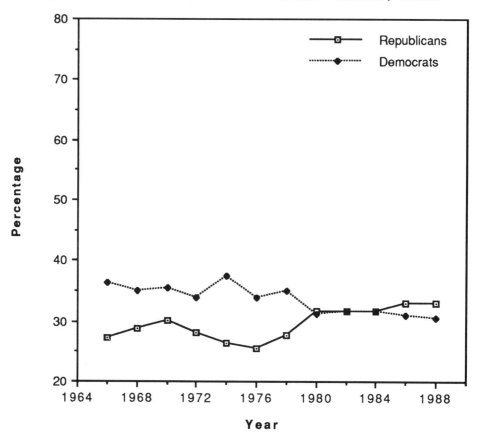

4.2 Colorado party registration, 1966–1988

out the Mountain West. In particular, figure 4.2 shows the residue in the 1960s and 1970s of a Democratic majority from the early post-war period.

The figure shows the voter registration percentages by party preceding each biennial election since 1966. From 1966 to 1978, the Democratic party clearly retained a greater degree of support among Coloradans than the Republicans. Registration for the Democrats outstripped the Republicans by an average of 7.5 percent during the period. Significant change occurred in 1980. From the perspective offered by the longer time span, 1980 may have nudged the Republican party a step closer to the dominance they enjoy in other mountain states. A 4 percent swing of registered voters from the Democratic to the Republican party equalized the parties in the electorate. For three elections (1980, 1982, 1984), voter registration percentages of the two parties remained within 0.4 percent. Then in 1986 another shift to the Republican party appears such that the Democrats are now two-to-three percentage points behind in registered voters. Overall, the picture of partisan change in figure 4.2 is consistent with the notion that Colorado participated in regional secular realignment.

INTRASTATE VARIATIONS

We do have one series of registered voters that extends further back in time: party registration totals for the city/county of Denver from 1952 to 1968 (Martin and Gomez 1972). Those data, combined with recent records compiled by the state elections commission, yield figure 4.3, a history of party registration in Denver from 1952 to 1988. These data paint a picture of change in Colorado's largest city that is very different from the statewide shifts we observed above. Major shifts in the distribution of registered voters in Denver appear to have taken place between 1952 and 1964. During that period, the Democratic party moved from a position of marginal advantage to one in which it outnumbers the Republican party by almost two to one. This shift is not at the expense of the Republican party, however, which has continued to retain about 25 percent of the electorate. Rather, the extensive changes observed appear as the result of the rush of unaffiliated voters to the Democrats. In sharp contrast to the state shifts in party registration, little change occurs in Denver during the 1980s. Perhaps half the statewide shift toward the Republican party is seen in 1980 (2 percent), while no GOP gains are recorded in 1986 and 1988.

The strength of the Democratic party in Colorado's largest city may well mask changes occurring throughout the rest of the state. During the past several decades, Denver's ability to dominate state politics through strength of numbers has fallen precipitously. From 1966 to 1988, the percentage of voters residing in Denver declined from 28 percent of the state electorate to 15.6 percent. Consequently the three-to-one Democratic advantage in Denver plays a smaller and smaller role statewide. Indeed, Denver plays a smaller role even within the Denver metropolitan area. During this period, Greater Denver (Adams, Arapahoe, Denver, Douglas, and Jefferson counties) has retained about 50 percent of the Colorado electorate. Nonetheless, Denver, once a majority, now makes up less than one-third of the metropolitan area.

If we reconstruct the partisan registration of Coloradans outside

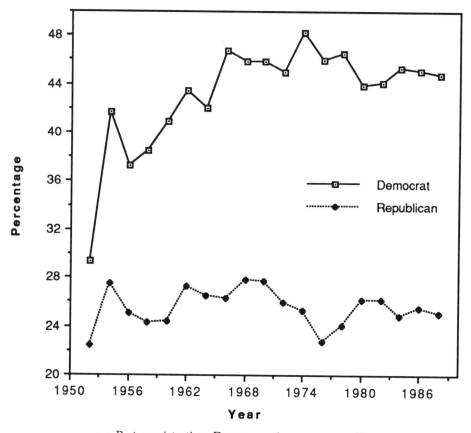

4.3 Party registration: Denver partisans, 1954–1988

the city of Denver during the past twenty-two years (see figure 4.4), it becomes clear that the Democratic edge in party registration in the rest of the state was less pronounced during the 1960s and 1970s than it originally appeared to be when we considered the state as a whole. Nonetheless, Democrats retained a real plurality over the Republicans throughout this fifteen-year period. The election of Ronald Reagan in 1980 appears as a critical election for Colorado Republicans outside of Denver. The 1980 party registration percentages appear almost as mirror images of 1978. The Republicans gained more than 4 percent of the Colorado electorate by October 1980 while Democratic registration figures fell by 3.5 percent, resulting in a Republican plurality for the first time in the series. The 1980 Republican registration advantage increased during the 1980s to a 6.5 percent lead over the Demo-

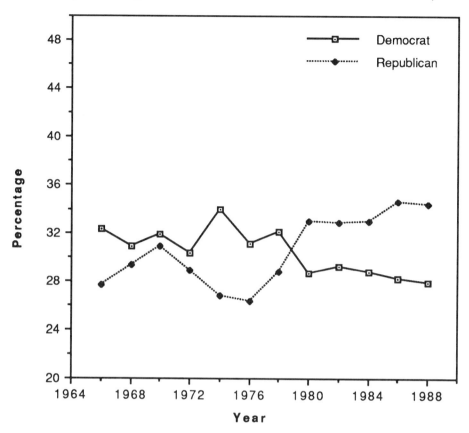

4.4 Party registration: Colorado minus Denver County, 1966–1988

crats. While retaining control over Denver, the Democratic party has lost its dominant position in many other areas of Colorado.

## TRENDS IN COLORADO'S VOTING BEHAVIOR

### TRENDS IN STATEWIDE CAMPAIGNS

The partisan divisions in Colorado, whether reflected in party identification or in party registration, would be of little consequence if they failed to affect the voting behavior of the state's electorate. Figure 4.5 shows Colorado's voting record for statewide candidates of the major political parties over the past four decades. The only clear pattern of party support has been the previously noted tendency of Colorado to vote for Republican presidential candidates: only Lyndon

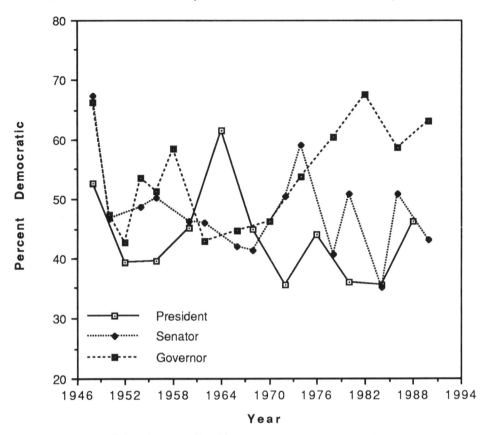

4.5 Colorado votes: President, senator, governor, 1948–1990

Johnson has broken a long string of Republican victories from Eisenhower in 1952 to Bush in 1988. Yet this "one-party state" looks sus-
piciously competitive when one examines the record of Colorado
voting for U.S. senator and governor. Since 1946, Democrats have
beaten Republican candidates sixteen times for one of those offices.
Fourteen times the Republican candidate has emerged victorious.

Some differences between senate and gubernatorial races do exist,
but both illustrate the competitiveness of Colorado state politics. Incumbency appears to offer little advantage for U.S. Senators: only half
of the incumbents running for reelection in post-World War II Colorado have been reelected, with neither party's incumbents generating
any decided advantage. Only Bill Armstrong, Peter Dominick, and
Gary Hart were able to run successfully for a second term (and no

Colorado senator has successfully run for a third term). In contrast, Colorado governors have been able to retain their offices if they so desired: only Steven McNichols (after his second term) was turned out of office by the voters. Seven other governors have won reelection, with John Love and Richard Lamm winning three terms each. The competitiveness of the parties is shown by races without incumbents. With one exception, whenever a sitting governor has failed to run for reelection, the opposition has succeeded in capturing the state house. The exception is current governor Roy Romer, who apparently has been able to ride the coattails of his former boss, Dick Lamm, allowing the Democrats to retain control of the governorship through the 1980s and into the 1990s despite shifts by the electorate toward the Republican party.

SUBSTATE RACES

Whereas the most visible statewide races show a pattern of competition throughout the post-war period, the voting patterns for substate races—U.S. House of Representatives and the Colorado house and senate—are a bit more consistent with the pattern of secular realignment in the region. In the ten U.S. House elections before 1968, the average Democratic vote was 53 percent, whereas from 1968 onward the average Democratic vote was below 50 percent. In the years following 1966, the Democrats won a majority of those voting in House elections once in the Democratic banner year of 1974 and achieved a bare majority (51 percent) in 1990. Prior to 1968, the Democrats won majorities in half of the elections.

The statewide vote divisions do not translate into a clear pattern in the partisan division of the Colorado delegation, but they do reflect the shift toward the Republicans in the underlying partisanship of the electorate. For most of the decade, the state delegation of six representatives has been evenly split between the parties. During the 1970s, the five-person Colorado delegation regularly split three to two for the Democrats. Thus, while the Republican party has made significant strides in terms of party registration in the past decade and has won the support of a greater percentage of the electorate statewide, the changes have not consistently altered the partisan division of the state's delegation to Washington, which as of 1990 stands at three to three.

The pattern of partisanship in the state legislative seats in Colorado also reflects a general decline in Democratic fortunes (see figure 4.7).

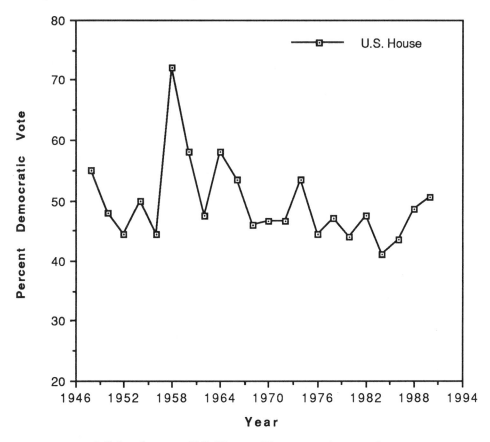

4.6 Colorado votes: U.S. House of Representatives, 1948–1990

The Democrats by no means dominated the legislature in the 1950s and early 1960s, but at least they were able to win control of the house in four of the seven elections between 1954 and 1966 and controlled the senate three of the seven sessions. From 1968 on, however, Democrats won the house but once and the senate not at all. The house series is more volatile, but the trend in both house and senate seats in Colorado is plainly consistent with the secular realignment thesis. Other than a temporary recovery brought about by voter reaction to Watergate, the number of seats held by Democratic state legislators has been declining for three decades. From dominance of both chambers of the state legislature in 1958, the Colorado Democratic party has seen its status dwindle to the point of being unable to defend the veto power of Democratic governors.

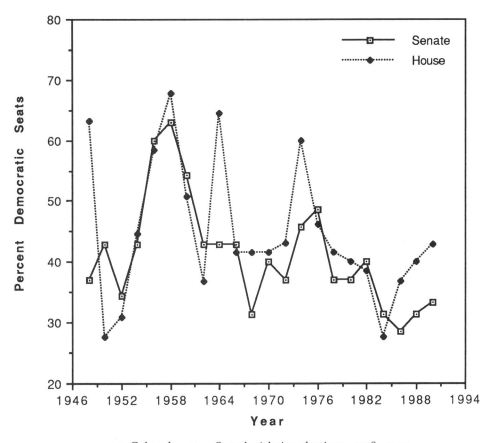

4.7 Colorado votes: State legislative elections, 1948–1990

CONCLUSIONS

Our results are broadly consistent with the thesis that Colorado participated in a regional realignment from the Democratic to the Republican party. Colorado partisan changes, however, have not been explosive but rather might be characterized as a slow drift toward the GOP over the past thirty years. Unfortunately, limitations on the kinds of data available force us to paint a picture clouded by uncertainty rather than permitting us to sketch in bold relief.

The most limited aspect of our analysis is our inability to glimpse very far back in time with the party identification series. Nonetheless, we do have data bracketing the 1980 election of Ronald Reagan, and we found no short-run gains for the Republicans in the party loyalties of Coloradans. The party identification data show the state to be competitive, with no significant change surrounding the potentially critical 1980 election.

Party registration data are not equivalent to party identification indicators from mass surveys, but the series on Colorado does have the merit of extending back into the 1960s. Two features of this series are notable: the Democrats held the edge in registration in Colorado through the 1960s and 1970s; and in these data there is a hint of significant change surrounding the 1980 election. The earlier period of Democratic advantage appears to be consistent with research on the region showing a realignment from a Democratic majority to a period of Republican dominance. That the Democrats enjoyed this edge well into the 1970s is not strictly consistent with work on change in party identification in the West that occurred in the early 1960s (Stone 1987). However, Jewell and Olson (1988) show that change in party registration tends to lag behind changes in behavior and loyalties. The registration data show change around 1980 as the Republicans emerged with a slight edge, especially outside Denver.

Voting data since the post-war years showed the most volatile changes. That is not surprising, especially for such visible offices as the U.S. president, Senate, and gubernatorial contests. In those races, Colorado has shown considerable fluctuation due, in all probability, to candidate factors. Evidence on the U.S. House of Representatives voting, and especially on the results of state legislative elections, is more congenial to the thesis of a long-term secular realignment (Key 1959) in favor of the Republicans. Indeed, the results, coupled with those on party registration, give us considerable confidence in concluding that Colorado participated in the regional realignment discussed above. Both are fair—if less than ideal—indicators of aggregate distributions of party loyalty. Party registration is a behavioral expression of such loyalty, and voting for state legislative offices usually is relatively insensitive to candidate and issue factors. Without substantial information about the particular race, most voters rely on their long-term partisan predispositions.

What of 1980? Was 1980 a critical election in Colorado? We think not because neither the party identification date nor the voting data show a dramatic shift. The registration data indicate a small but still impressive gain by the Republicans, but we see 1980 as a culmination of the longer term trend in favor of the GOP. Ronald Reagan was popular in Colorado as elsewhere, and then President Jimmy Carter was unpopular in the Rocky Mountain states. The Reagan Revolution may be credited with finally pushing many Coloradans to change their registration to reflect not only their voting preferences at the presidential level, but their voting behavior in many lower offices as well. In changing their party registration, Coloradans were merely capping several decades of change they and their fellow citizens throughout the Mountain West had quietly pursued. It is high time we took notice.

# Party Realignment in Texas

JEANIE R. STANLEY

5

ALTHOUGH Texans like to think of themselves and their state as unique, recent partisan trends in the Lone Star State are similar to those observed in the rest of the nation. Increasing numbers of Texans are identified as independents and vote for members of both parties on the basis of short-term candidate or issue factors. Most Texans do not think political parties are very important. Weakening of partisan ties among the electorate, however, has been accompanied by a strengthening of party organizations and party influence in government. The trends are similar to those observed nationally (Sorauf and Beck 1988).

Realignment, dealignment, and alignment in party identification have combined to produce a partisan scenario that did not exist in Texas ten years ago. The Democratic party continues to dominate Texas government as it has since Reconstruction. Republicans, however, have reached parity with Democrats and independents in terms of party identification and are increasingly competitive in elections at all levels. Both major political party organizations have been strengthened in recent years; and partisanship, perhaps for the first time, is evident in the daily operations of all three branches of state government.

The partisan trends in Texas cannot be explained or predicted by any simple formula. To a degree, they reflect the national and state context in which political activities take place. The historical experience of Texans, the institutional structure of state government, as well as certain demographic and economic developments within the state and nation, combine to affect the political attitudes and behavior of the electorate and the political elites. Although both Democratic and Republican party leaders make optimistic predictions about their future success, more objective observers see a continuation of the current partisan flux with the relative success of the parties depending on short-term candidate, elite, and issue factors. To ascertain which factors are likely to have a significant impact, we must examine the context in which Texas politics operates.

## POLITICAL CONTEXT

Daniel Elazar characterized the dominant Texas political culture as traditionalistic and individualistic (1972). According to that culture, the primary function of government is to maintain the traditional social and economic system with minimal government activity. Although citizens accept their governance by political and economic elites, most Texans distrust politics, political parties, and politicians. The lengthy Texas constitution, written in 1876 by conservative Democrats in reaction to what they perceived as a corrupt, wasteful, and liberal Republican administration under Reconstruction, is highly restrictive. It details what government cannot do, creates a myriad of checks and balances, makes many positions that are appointed in other states elected offices in Texas, and forces government officials to take numerous decisions to the public in the form of constitutional amendments. In 1987 alone, Texans voted on twenty-five amendments.

All three branches of Texas government are structured to restrict initiative and limit activity. Texas has a plural executive with nine statewide executives elected independently of the governor, whose formal powers are ranked as forty-sixth among the fifty states (Beyle 1983). In addition to the statewide elected officials, there are more than two hundred elected and appointed positions on boards and commissions that are largely exempt from gubernatorial direction. Although the governor appoints most of the board members, the chief executive cannot direct their activities. Instead, the legislature provides administrative oversight through programmatic and budgetary legislation. Legislative power, however, is severely curtailed by limiting legislators to biennial sessions of only 140 days, keeping salaries at a below-cost minimum, requiring pay-as-you-go appropriations, and giving the governor strong veto powers and the exclusive right to call and dictate the agenda of special sessions. Finally, the power of the judicial branch is constrained by the election of all judges as well as detailed prescriptions contained in the constitution.

Limited government is not the only principle defining Texas government. Reflecting their frontier heritage, Texans stress independence, the importance of land and other material property, and a philosophy of Social Darwinism (Kramer and Newell 1987). Under that philosophy, people are expected to "make it on their own" and receive respect if they succeed or disdain if they fail. The sense of independence and self-sufficiency reinforces support for limited government and explains the minimal social services provided by the state. In 1987, for example, Texas ranked third in population, but forty-ninth in state-level per capita spending for public welfare and total government expenditures (U.S. Bureau of the Census, series GF-87-3).

Experience as a part of the Old South and the Confederacy is evident in a negative affect toward the federal government, the long-standing control of government by conservative Democrats, and the frequent political tension between the dominant white and minority black and Hispanic populations. The political implications of the ethnic patterns are numerous. Although Hispanics and blacks fought with whites in the Texas War for Independence, both minorities largely were excluded from economic and political power until the state was forced to abandon discriminatory laws as a result of federal legislation or court rulings. Attitudes toward ethnic groups, economics, and state policy are closely intertwined in the political experience of most Texans. It has been the conservative ideology of white Texans, however, that has dictated state policy.

According to 1988 U.S. Census figures, approximately one-third of the total population of the state is either black (11.2 percent) or Hispanic (21.1 percent). Legal and illegal immigration from Mexico, Central America, and Asia, as well as the higher birthrate among Hispanic-American citizens, are expected to increase the proportion of minority ethnic groups within the state population. Although the Dallas and Houston metropolitan areas have large numbers of both blacks and Hispanics, the remaining blacks are concentrated in the eastern portion of the state, with Hispanics living in southwest or central Texas. Black and Hispanic Texans are far more likely than whites to be poor and less educated. According to the 1980 census, the median family income in Texas was 98.5 percent of the national level. For white families, however, the median income was $22,427, compared to $13,293 for Hispanics and $13,042 for blacks. Black and

Hispanic families were five times as likely to fall below the poverty line as whites (Anderson, Murray, and Farley 1989).

Similar ethnic disparities exist with regard to education. School dropout rates are much higher for black and Hispanic students than they are for whites. The educational attainment of Hispanics is particularly low, with one in four Hispanic Texans having completed less than five years of school. The lower educated, the poor, and, therefore, blacks and Hispanics, make up a disproportionate number of those who are unemployed, involved in crime, or seeking social assistance from the state. It is no surprise to find ethnic polarization on a wide variety of political issues.

The major issue in Texas politics today is the economic condition of the state. After more than a decade of economic prosperity and population growth, the dramatic drop in oil prices in the early 1980s forced the state to address difficult questions of economic diversification and associated changes in education, taxation, and social services. The state has been challenged in the courts with regard to the adequacy and equity of major state programs, but there has been no consensus on the finance of recommended improvements.

Texas is the third largest state in the nation, with an estimated population of 16,841,000 as of July 1, 1988 (U.S. Bureau of the Census, *Current Population Reports*). That represents a 24.7 percent increase above the 1978 population, compared with a 10.7 percent increase for the United States as a whole during the same period. Much of the growth is a result of in-migration, which has contributed to a nationalization of Texas politics. The in-migration was accompanied by urbanization and suburbanization. More than 80 percent of the state's population now resides in the 26 standard metropolitan statistical areas, with more than 40 percent concentrated in the Dallas–Ft. Worth or Houston–Galveston areas (Anderson, Murray, and Farley 1989). Most of the rapid population growth and movement occurred during a period of economic boom in the state when oil prices rose in the 1970s. Migration declined with the fall in oil prices in 1982.

The devastating impact of lower oil prices revealed the dependence of the state's prosperity on a few natural resources and its vulnerability to an unstable world market. While the private sector suffered through bankruptcies, plant closings, bank failures, and unemployment, the state government struggled with dilemmas resulting from an outdated tax structure, declining revenue, court-ordered improvements in major programs, and strategies to diversify its economy.

It is within that cultural, institutional, demographical, and eco-

nomic context that Texas politics operates. Changes in the nonpolitical spheres of the state have coincided with changes in the partisan
views of its citizens.

## TRENDS IN PARTISAN IDENTIFICATION

Although the political culture of Texas has been characterized as
different from that of the Deep South, current trends in partisan identification are similar to those in the rest of the South (Elazar 1972; Key
1949). A gradual shift from Democratic one-party dominance to increased numbers of independents and Republicans has occurred (Petrocik 1987). As mentioned previously, the trends appear to reflect a
mixture of dealignment, realignment, and alignment. Realignment
and dealignment have resulted from the conversion of white males,
the immigration of Republicans and independents from other states,
and the attraction of new young voters to the Republican party or to
an identification as independent.

Figure 5.1 illustrates the Democratic dominance of the earlier period as well as the recent near parity between Democratic, Republican, and independent identifiers. Although Democrats outnumber
Republicans, more independents lean Republican than lean Democratic (Tedin 1987a). With the inclusion of leaners, Democrats outnumber Republicans, but the electorate as a whole (and independents
in particular) view the GOP far more favorably than they do the
Democrats (Tedin 1987b). Such ratings suggest that independents are
more likely to vote Republican than Democratic and that Democrats
are less loyal to their party than Republicans; similar trends have been
observed nationally (Sorauf and Beck 1988). Only the popularity of
Lloyd Bentsen in 1988 and the unpopularity of Clayton Williams
among women in 1990 reversed those trends.

Republican gains among independents as well as among newcomers and new voters were critical to Republican victories in 1984
and 1986. In 1984, the composition of the Republican coalition was 22
percent newcomrs (ten years or less in Texas); 25 percent new voters
(under 30 years of age); 28 percent switchers (23 percent former
Democrats; 5 percent former independents); and 25 percent loyal
Republicans.

A 1986 survey indicates that Republicans benefited most from
changes or conversions in party identification (table 5.1). In spite of
the economic downturn in the state, Republicans have maintained
their advantage among newcomers (migration), but their margin

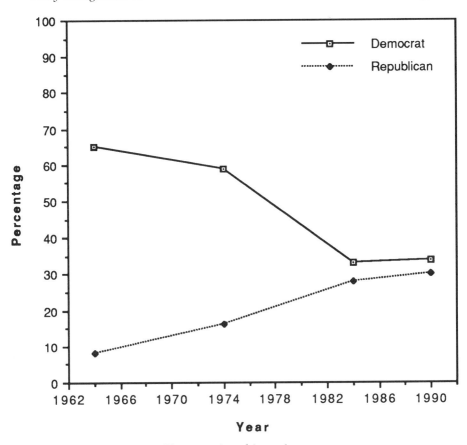

5.1 Texas partisanship, 1964–1990

among younger voters (generativity) has varied considerably from year to year.

The 1990 elections were characterized by high levels of ticket splitting among all categories of voters. Republicans attracted Democrats and independents in the U.S. Senate, treasurer, and commissioner of agriculture races; but Democrats successfully appealed to independents and Republicans in the gubernatorial and other statewide executive positions. Independents favored Democrat Ann Richards over Republican gubernatorial candidate Clayton Williams, but straight-ticket voting reached an all time low.

The 1988 and 1990 elections indicate a continuation of previous ethnic patterns in partisan identification and voting (table 5.2). Blacks and Hispanics are significantly more likely to support Democrats than

Table 5.1. Party Switchers and Their Original Party Preferences: Texas, 1986

|  | Yes (%) | No (%) |
|---|---|---|
| Democrats: Were you ever a Republican? | 9 | 91 |
| Independents: Were you ever a Republican? | 7 | 93 |
| Independents: Were you ever a Democrat? | 30 | 70 |
| Republicans: Were you ever a Democrat? | 43 | 57 |

Source: University of Houston Public Affairs Research Center Survey, April 1986.

Table 5.2. Trends in Party Identification: Texas, 1985–1990

|  | 1985 | | | 1988 | | | 1990 | | |
|---|---|---|---|---|---|---|---|---|---|
|  | Rep (%) | Ind (%) | Dem (%) | Rep (%) | Ind (%) | Dem (%) | Rep (%) | Ind (%) | Dem (%) |
| Residency |  |  |  |  |  |  |  |  |  |
| Ten years or less | 41 | 35 | 24 | 40 | 38 | 23 | 38 | 30 | 23 |
| More than ten years | 34 | 35 | 32 | 26 | 39 | 31 | 33 | 31 | 31 |
| Natives | 28 | 32 | 40 | 27 | 29 | 39 | 29 | 34 | 32 |
| Age |  |  |  |  |  |  |  |  |  |
| 18–29 | 44 | 27 | 29 | 33 | 35 | 30 | 40 | 31 | 22 |
| 30–45 | 26 | 39 | 35 | 34 | 30 | 29 | 34 | 33 | 27 |
| 45–61 | 26 | 40 | 34 | 21 | 37 | 38 | 30 | 31 | 35 |
| 62+ | 28 | 23 | 49 | 21 | 30 | 43 | 17 | 28 | 50 |
| Race |  |  |  |  |  |  |  |  |  |
| White | 31 | 37 | 27 | 34 | 34 | 29 | 36 | 33 | 26 |
| Black | 4 | 33 | 57 | 7 | 30 | 57 | 8 | 24 | 65 |
| Hispanic | 11 | 33 | 39 | 14 | 34 | 44 | 18 | 25 | 45 |

Source: The Texas Poll, 1985–90.

Republicans. The opposite is true of whites, particularly with respect to presidential elections. The Texas Poll (October 1988) reported that blacks favored Michael Dukakis 70 percent to 20 percent and Hispanics supported him by 63 to 27 percent. In contrast, whites picked the Republican ticket by 64 percent to 28 percent. According to 1990 CBS exit polls, 89 percent of the black voters preferred Ann Richards over Clayton Williams; and the Hispanic vote for Richards ranged from 67 to 77 percent. In contrast, only 41 percent of the white voters preferred Richards.

Some higher income Hispanics have moved from Democratic to independent or Republican identification, but ethnic patterns have remained fairly consistent. Hispanics were particularly attracted to the 1990 Democratic ticket by the opportunity to elect the first Hispanic statewide executive, Attorney General Dan Morales, who received more than 90 percent of the Hispanic vote. Ironically, blacks were given a choice between two black candidates for a statewide court position in 1990. They were the first black candidates for statewide office to receive either party's nomination since Reconstruction. Democrat Morris Overstreet won the race with the support of more than 90 percent of black voters.

Since 1980, men have been more likely than women to identify with the Republican party and support Republican candidates for statewide and presidential office. Women are more likely to support the Democratic party and candidates. The most dramatic gap (11 and 20 percent) occurred in the 1982 and 1990 gubernatorial votes, but a fairly consistent 6 percent difference in partisan support has been observed in most elections (see table 5.4, p. 000). As women comprise as much as 53 percent of recent electorates, the gap has tended to draw attention to the women's vote.

The 1990 elections, with a female Democratic gubernatorial candidate facing a macho cowboy Republican, revealed marked gender patterns. Although there have not been significant gender differences on most aspects of the abortion issue, the greater attention this issue received during the 1990 campaign, as well as other gender-specific campaign rhetoric used by both candidates, appeared to heighten gender differences in candidate preference. Republican and independent women opted for the Democratic "choice" candidate and were uncomfortable with a Republican candidate who joked that women faced with inevitable rape should "lie back and enjoy it." Richards received the support of more than 61 percent of women voters, including 21 percent of those identifying themselves as Republicans.

## ELECTORAL TRENDS

Although Lamis (1984) and others describe Texas politics as "the least Southern" of the former Confederate states, the southern pattern of one-party Democratic dominance prevailed in Texas with gradual Republican gains only after the 1950s. The first partisan breakthrough came in presidential voting (table 5.3). Beginning with the 1952 election, Texas has mirrored national presidential voting patterns (Ippolito 1986). In recent years, Texas has voted slightly more Republican than the national average.

Table 5.3. Presidential Voting: Nationwide and Texas, 1952–1988

| | Republican Percentage of Total Vote | | Differential |
| | National | Texas | National − Texas |
|---|---|---|---|
| 1952 | 55.1 | 53.1 | −2.0 |
| 1956 | 57.4 | 55.3 | −2.1 |
| 1960 | 49.5 | 48.5 | −1.1 |
| 1964 | 38.5 | 36.5 | −2.0 |
| 1968 | 43.4 | 39.9 | −3.5 |
| 1972 | 60.7 | 66.2 | +5.5 |
| 1976 | 48.4 | 48.0 | −0.4 |
| 1980 | 50.7 | 55.3 | +4.6 |
| 1984 | 59.1 | 63.6 | +4.5 |
| 1988 | 54.0 | 56.0 | +2.0 |

Sources: Dennis Ippolito, "Texas," in R. C. Steed, L. W. Moreland, and T. A. Baker, *The 1984 Presidential Election in the South: Patterns of Southern Party Politics.* (New York: Praeger, 1986), 162; Office of the Texas Secretary of State.

Below the presidential level, Republican gains have been mixed, in spite of substantial presidential coattails in 1980 and 1984. Republicans won their first statewide office since Reconstruction when John Tower was elected to the U.S. Senate in 1961. Upon retirement, Tower was succeeded by Democrat-turned-Republican Phil Gramm, who won his second term in 1990 with 62 percent of the vote. The other U.S. Senate seat remains firmly in the Democratic camp with incumbent Lloyd Bentsen, who received 59 percent of the vote in 1988.

The first Republican governor in a century was elected in 1978. Until that time, running as a Republican for a statewide office was similar to running as a third-party candidate in other states (Tedin 1987b). After a defeat by Democrat Mark White in 1982, Republican Bill Clements was reelected as governor in 1986. Clements was followed by Democrat Ann Richards in 1991.

Republicans gained six of their other ten statewide positions since Reconstruction initially through vacancies filled by gubernatorial appointment. All but two of the openings have been on the supreme court or court of criminal appeals. The remaining two appointments were on the railroad commission. The appointees, however, have not always been successful in winning reelections. In 1991, Republicans held four of the nine supreme court judgeships, including that of chief justice, but Republicans lost their places on the court of criminal appeals and railroad commission. Although Republican hopes of winning the gubernatorial race in 1990 were dashed, the election of Republicans as treasurer and commissioner of agriculture marks another breakthrough for the GOP in statewide contests. The remaining statewide executive and judicial positions are held by Democrats.

Although Republicans have yet to gain control of state government, many observers see the 1988 and 1990 elections as evidence of GOP progress. Given the parity in partisan identification and the greater positive attitude among independents toward the Republican party, strong Republican candidates could do well in future elections. The Republican base vote (the lowest percentage of votes received by Republican statewide candidates) during years in which the Republican ticket was admittedly weak indicates a potential for Republican success. In 1984 the low water mark was 49 percent, in 1988 it fell to 41 percent and in 1990 it was 31 percent. A major problem for Republicans has been the shortage of credible candidates (Tedin 1987b).

Similar candidate recruitment problems have blocked Republican gains in the U.S. House and state legislative delegations. Republicans secured their first state legislative seat in 1950 and U.S. House seat in 1954. The GOP made substantial gains in the 1980s, moving from a ratio of five to twenty-two in the 1982 congressional delegation to a ten to seventeen ratio in 1984 (figure 5.2). Republicans lost two seats in 1988 and maintained the same eight to nineteen ratio after the 1990 elections.

A critical milestone in the Texas legislature was reached when Republicans could produce a one-third vote in the house to block key votes (Figure 5.2). Republican gains in the senate are not as notable, but the gain of two seats in 1988 and the maintenance of incumbents in 1990 is a positive sign for the GOP.

Republicans considered their maintenance of the congressional and senate ratios and an increase of one house seat during the 1986 nonpresidential year a victory, but the GOP was disappointed with the meager gain of only one state house seat in 1988 and a loss of two seats in 1990. Their failure to achieve majority status before redistricting in 1991 may preclude Republican control of the state legislature and congressional delegation during the next decade. Republicans similarly had hoped for greater wins at the local level.

The GOP initially began winning local offices in counties surrounding Dallas and Houston, the Panhandle, and a few oil-based counties in east and west Texas. Presidential coattails, for example, swept almost the entire Houston- and Dallas-area Democratic judiciary slates from office in 1980 and 1984. In 1990, Republicans held 102 of the 127 elected offices in Dallas County. In 1979, there were only four Republican judges in Dallas County; in 1987, all but two of the fifty-six

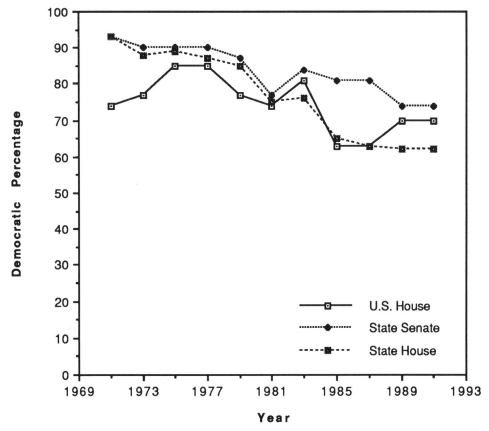

5.2 Texas: Percent Democratic representation in the U.S. House, state senate, and state house seats, 1971–1991

benches were held by Republicans as well as the county judgeship, the district attorney, and the sheriff positions. In Harris County (Houston), over half of the local officials elected on a partisan ballot are now Republican. The GOP picked up 127 local offices in 1986, surpassing other states in net electoral gains (South Carolina was second with forty-one). Republican party leaders boast of their steady growth in local strength: 270 local offices in 1982, 377 in 1984, 504 in 1986, 608 in 1988, and 725 in 1990. The 1990 elections gave Republicans sixty-six additional local positions.

Democrats are quick to stress that GOP gains are marginal at the local level. Indeed, if one excludes district judgeships, Republicans hold less than 10 percent of more than five thousand local offices and

Table 5.4. Votes Cast in Primary and General Elections: Texas, 1970–1990

|  | Office | Primaries | | General Elections | |
|---|---|---|---|---|---|
|  |  | Democratic | Republican | Democratic | Republican |
| 1970 | Governor | 1,011,300 | 109,021 | 1,232,506 | 1,073,831 |
| 1974 | Governor | 1,521,306 | 69,101 | 1,016,334 | 514,725 |
| 1978 | Governor | 1,812,896 | 158,403 | 1,166,919 | 1,183,828 |
| 1980 | President[a] | 1,377,354 | 526,769 | 1,881,147 | 2,510,705 |
| 1982 | Governor | 1,318,663 | 265,851 | 1,697,870 | 1,465,937 |
| 1984 | President[a] | 1,463,447 | 336,814 | 1,949,276 | 3,433,428 |
| 1986 | Governor | 1,093,887 | 545,745 | 1,578,025 | 1,806,944 |
| 1988 | President | 1,767,045 | 1,018,147 | 2,347,684 | 3,034,004 |
| 1990 | Governor | 1,466,869 | 852,121 | 1,924,458 | 1,824,785 |

Sources: R. Kraemer and C. Newell, *Texas Politics*, 1987; *The Texas Almanac*; Office of the Secretary of State; *Texas State Directory* (St. Paul, MN: West Publishers).

[a]If presidential primary is not held, the greatest total vote cast for any primary is listed.

have a majority of the county commissioners courts in only twenty-one of 254 counties. Most counties have no local Republican office-holders. Although many voters in the Democratically controlled counties are Presidential Republicans, they continue to vote for local Democrats who face little or no Republican competition. The weakness of GOP grass-roots organization and candidate recruitment at the local level results in a shortage of credible candidates at higher levels and keeps the GOP in minority status.

More promising signs for Republicans come from an examination of trends in primary participation (table 5.4). In 1950 almost three times as many people voted in the Democratic primary as voted in the November election. Isolated from national politics, Texas settled their general elections in their primaries until the late 1970s (Tedin 1987b). Republicans held no primary before 1960 and had few competitive races to attract voters until the 1980s.

The 1988 and 1990 primaries were the most competitive to date. With the addition of 534 new Republican voting precincts (for a total of 5,687 compared to approximately 7,000 Democratic precincts) and the influx of Robertson supporters, the Republicans dramatically increased participation in 1988. Democratic-dominated local elections brought independents back to the Democratic primaries in 1990, but Republicans attracted more voters than in previous nonpresidential election years.

The increase in Republican primary participation is partially a result of effective party organization and the greater political activity exhibited by Republicans than Democrats. The Texas Republican Party was ranked as moderately strong by one national study of activities during 1975–80; the Texas Democratic state party organization was classified as moderately weak (Cotter et al. 1984). Respondents in a 1989 Texas Poll suggest that Republicans and their party are more active than independents, Democrats, and the Texas Democratic party.

In six of nine areas of personal political participation, Texas Democrats and Republicans appeared to be nearly identical: voting in local elections, attending political meetings, displaying bumper stickers for candidates, working for candidates, working to solve community problems, and joining groups designed specifically to solve community problems. Republicans, however, were more likely than Democrats to report they had written a letter to a local politician during the past five years, contacted a school administrator, or given money to a political candidate.

Although Democratic fund-raising efforts have improved in recent years, Republicans outperform the Democrats with, among other projects, a year round in-house small donor phone bank and a 1 percent credit card subscriber program. Funding by the state party and the independent Associated Republicans of Texas (which usually concentrates on legislative and local races but assisted in some statewide executive and judicial races in 1988 and 1990) has been hurt by the economic misfortunes of large contributors, but statewide party support has been buttressed by the national party and other Republican political action committees.

An area in which Republicans are not competitive with Democrats, however, is that of grass roots organization. The Texas Federation of Republican Women, claiming more than 180 local clubs with a membership of ten thousand, is generally considered the grass roots organization of the party. Approximately forty male Republican groups and ten to twenty male and female groups supplement the federation's work, but the Young Republican organization has declined since 1986. Republicans must expand local organizations for increased campaign effectiveness as well as candidate recruitment.

In addition to enhancing their grass roots organization, the Texas GOP has welcomed a more heterogeneous constituency. With inclusiveness, however, has come a divisiveness unusual for the party. Some Republicans privately speak of two Republican parties: the oldline, moderate, national, or country-club Republicans and the right wing, populist, fundamentalist, or Robertson Republicans. The moderates have been able to mollify enough of the fundamentalist delegates at recent state conventions to retain control over the state and national party offices, but the platform has been used to appease the more conservative delegates. One observer suggested the state party mainstream had moved a "quantum leap to the right" but still had not satisfied all of the "true believers."

Other dissension has resulted from efforts to appeal to minority ethnic groups. Demographics suggest that Republicans must increase their support among Hispanics and blacks to become the majority party in the state. The minority share of the 1988 vote in Texas was estimated at 22 percent, up from the 18 percent reported in 1984; the potential minority vote, however, exceeds 33 percent. Although two blacks were elected to the State Republican Executive Committee in 1988 (the first since Reconstruction) and a black Republican received the nomination for a statewide court seat in 1990, there is little evidence of increased black support for the GOP. The party has fared better with Hispanics, particularly those of higher income. Hispanic support, however, has been hurt by the Republican party's endorsement of the English Only amendment. Although Republican gubernatorial candidate Clayton Williams spent significant amounts of time and money to woo the Spanish-speaking vote in 1990, he received less than 20 percent of the Hispanic vote. The Democratic ticket, with popular Hispanic Dan Morales winning the attorney general's position, continued as the party of choice for Texas Hispanics.

Both Democratic and Republican party organizations have been frustrated by continuing nonpartisan campaigning on the part of certain government officials, consultants, and political action committees. In the legislature, that trend benefits incumbents. State legislative sessions and campaigns are becoming increasingly partisan and strident, but many incumbents still accept the unwritten commandment, "Thou shalt not mess with another member's reelection." When State Republican chairman George Strake traveled with several GOP lawmakers into Democratic legislators' hometowns in 1988, both Democratic and Republican incumbents called it bad form. During the campaign, Democratic speaker Gib Lewis appeared at a fish fry for a Republican incumbent targeted by House Democrats. Similarly, several Republican officials attended 1990 campaign events for Lewis. Although other officeholders are more discreet in their bipartisan campaigning, nonpartisan politics is the heritage of this formerly one-party state. Texans have been accustomed to basing their politics on issues or individual characteristics rather than party. That tradition makes these factors critical to the political future of the state.

## LEADERSHIP AND ISSUES

Texas is in a period of political as well as nonpolitical transition. As mentioned previously, the state is in the process of diversifying its economy from its previous natural resource base. The revenue shortfall in a state already funding services at minimal levels has produced a series of fiscal crises when funds were insufficient to fund court-mandated programs.

Republican legislative candidates frequently label Democrats as tax-and-spend liberals. Democrats are accused of being in the pockets of the trial lawyers and supporting unreasonable insurance, malpractice, and worker's compensation claims. Democrats counter the Republican attack with the observation that Republican governor Clements and several Republican senators have supported tax increases as the only responsible way to maintain the essential services provided by a lean state government. Republicans are accused of wanting to close down educational institutions or increase the burden on local property tax payers. Democrats claim to be pragmatic leaders making tough decisions during economically difficult times. Democratic claims are made easier by the conservative leadership in the state senate by William Hobby (succeeded in 1991 by another conservative Democrat, Bob Bullock) and in the house by Gib Lewis. Few would call Hobby, Bullock, Lewis, or Bentsen liberal. Although there are liberal Democratic members of the Texas legislature and the congressional delegation, they tend to reside in minority districts where Republicans have little chance of winning. Democrats in other districts tend to be moderate or conservative.

Most races in 1988 and 1990 were not determined on a strictly partisan basis. The large number of split-ticket voters and independents suggest that the trend will continue. A candidate's record, campaign organization, and issue agenda may be more important than his or her partisan ties. Although the two major parties have strengthened their organization and campaign activity, the weakening of partisan identification within the electorate, as well as the history of nonpartisan government, lessens the impact of partisan changes on electoral outcomes.

Similarly, only marginal policy changes can be directly attributed to partisan changes. Texas government has been dominated by conservative Democrats who, for the most part, have policy goals that are compatible with those of Republicans. Neither party has presented a unified policy agenda in recent years. Leadership in both parties is constrained by the current economic difficulties in the state and federal court mandates with regard to educational funding, prison reform, and mental health services. Unlike policy changes, however, the operational style of government has begun to reflect the increased partisan competition.

For years, conservative Democrats and Republicans have worked amicably in state government in a largely bipartisan manner. Democratic legislative leaders have given Republicans key committee assignments, including committee chair positions; and partisan loyalty often has not been a primary criterion for executive appointments. As increasing numbers of Democrats have been threatened or defeated by Republican opposition, however, both executive and legislative branches have adopted more partisan behavior. Governor White (1982–86) was careful to apply a partisan litmus test to prospective appointees and rewarded key Democratic constituencies. White appointed more women and minorities during his first year of office than his Democratic or Republican predecessors had appointed in four year terms (Stanley 1986). Republican governor Clements, after criticism for his first-term (1978–82) Democratic appointments, carefully filled most of his second-term (1986–90) positions with known Republicans. In 1991 Ann Richards emphasized a pledge to appoint minorities and women in proportion to their representation in the population, but her appointments are expected to be predominantly Democratic.

In addition to his partisan appointive powers, Clements affected state policy along partisan lines through his legislative veto. Because of the weak administrative powers given Texas governors, the appointive and veto powers are the primary ways in which partisan electoral changes are reflected in state policy. The impact of partisan changes on legislation is more difficult to measure.

As the number of Republicans in the Texas house approaches the crucial potential of a one-third voting block, members of both parties increased their partisan rhetoric and behavior. House Democrats formed a party caucus in 1981 with thirty-seven members. The speaker and most conservative Democrats initially refused to join. By 1989 all Democratic house members were participating in the caucus, which meets regularly, addresses a variety of legislative issues, and provides campaign assistance. Republicans have met for weekly breakfasts for several years but did not formally organize until 1989 for fear of jeopardizing bipartisan committee chair appointments. Although the 1988 elections did not focus on state issues and resulted in few partisan changes in the executive or legislature, state politics became more partisan in 1989 and 1990 as legislators, executives, and activists anticipated the 1990 elections and 1991 redistricting.

CONCLUSION AND PROJECTIONS

Texas has experienced dramatic changes with regard to partisan trends in politics. In contrast to a century of one-party Democratic dominance and no-party state government, Texans currently are divided almost equally in their identification as Democrats, Republicans, and independents. While this shift in voter identification constitutes a realignment, the political significance of this change remains unclear. Although the GOP receives more positive ratings from the voters than the Democrats, the positive affect has not been translated into proportional electoral victories at the state and local levels. Republican success is constrained by their limited candidate pool and the tendency of Texans to disregard party identification in making their voting choice. The large number of independents and ticket splitters portend the likely importance of short-term forces of candidates and issues in future elections. Although Republicans are expected to increase their percentage of state and local offices, Democratic dominance of the critical redistricting process in 1991 improved the Democrats' chances to maintain control of the congressional delegation and state legislature.

The impact of changes in partisan identification in the electorate on government policy outcomes is weakened by the philosophical similarities between conservative Democratic leaders and Republicans, the nonpartisan manner in which most legislative and executive business is conducted, and the fiscal and institutional constraints on government action. State, local, and legislative party organizations are growing stronger, however, and the 1991 redistricting battles are expected to heighten partisan activity in government. There is some indication that increased party competition has been associated with more distinct partisan policy differences. Such distinctiveness should increase the impact of party on voter choice and governmental policy.

# Alabama: The Unsettled Electorate

## PATRICK R. COTTER

6

CHANGE is a constant feature of politics. Yet since mid-century, Alabama has experienced more than the normal amount of change. The composition of its electorate has shifted, old issues have declined and new ones emerged, and the leader who dominated the state's politics for more than two decades has retired. As a result of these changes, and the new situations they have produced in the state, political alignments in Alabama presently are quite unstable.

NO LONGER SOLIDLY DEMOCRATIC

Change and uncertainty have not always so markedly characterized Alabama's electoral politics. Throughout the first half of this century, Alabama was a member in good standing of the Solid South (Key 1949). That meant that every four years, for election after election, Alabama religiously supported the presidential nominee of the Democratic party. Just as faithfully, Alabama sent only Democrats to represent its interests in Congress. Devotion to the Democratic party was, if possible, even stronger at the state and local level. With few exceptions, the Democratic primary was the critical contest in selecting local and state officeholders.

Soon after the end of World War II, the foundations of the Solid South began to dissolve. In particular, wartime experiences gave additional

The assistance of James Stovall on this project is greatly appreciated.

energy and determination to the civil rights movement. Also, the migration of blacks, both before and during the war, from the South to the urban centers of the East and Midwest caused the national Democratic party (which was concerned about its support in those electorally rich areas) to become increasingly sensitive to the interests of black voters. Additionally, the Cold War strengthened the national government's commitment to protecting the rights of black citizens (see Bartley and Graham 1976; Black and Black 1987; Lamis 1984; and Grantham 1988. For discussions of Alabama's politics during this period see Barnard 1974 and Hamilton 1987.)

By loosening traditional bonds, introducing new issues, and increasing the number of potential supporters for political change, population changes also contributed to the end of the Solid South in Alabama and elsewhere in the region. For example, between 1940 and 1990 Alabama evolved from a predominantly rural to a predominantly urban state, with more than two-thirds of its population now living in urban areas. Additionally, the state's middle class grew. Median years of education increased from 7.1 in 1940 to more than 11 in 1980. Similarly, between 1955 and 1980 per capita family income (in terms of 1967 dollars) increased from $1,473 to $3,011. Finally, Alabama's population, which increased overall by about one million citizens, changed from being about 65 percent white in 1940 to about 74 percent white in 1990, primarily due to the out-migration of blacks.

As a result of the post-war Second Reconstruction and the accompanying population shifts, the politics of Alabama and the entire South underwent many changes. Among the more significant of the changes in Alabama were (1) an increase in the number of black voters, (2) a reduction in the visibility and importance of race as a political issue, and (3) a decline in the fortunes of the Democratic party and the development of an increasingly competitive Republican party.

In 1940 less than 1 percent of Alabama's black citizens were registered to vote. By 1960 that figure had grown to only about 14 percent. The 1965 passage of the Voting Rights Act (the struggle for which was largely fought in Alabama) dramatically changed the racial makeup of the Alabama electorate. As a result, by 1970 voter registration among blacks had increased to 64 percent (Garrow 1978). Today black voters make up between one-fifth and one-fourth of the state's electorate.

V. O. Key (1949) argued that in the days of the Solid South, race was the central issue around which Southern, and Alabama, politics revolved. This is no longer the case today. Openly segregationist candidates have disappeared from the political landscape (Black 1976) and race is rarely mentioned directly in political campaigns. In part this silence is the result of a high degree of consensus among citizens on the basic principle of racial equality (Black and Black 1987). For example, a 1987 survey of Alabama citizens found that about two-thirds of the public (including a majority of white citizens) do not think that "blacks are getting too demanding in their push for equal rights."

The lack of open discussion about race and the resultingly greater emphasis given to issues such as taxation and quality of government does not mean, however, that race has totally disappeared as an issue in Alabama's politics. In some electoral contests, race indirectly emerges as an issue through discussions of related topics, such as crime or the use of standardized tests. Similarly, race sometimes appears as an issue during debates over racially related symbols such as the influence of special interests or the displaying of the Confederate flag. The inconsistent and often oblique appearance of race as an issue has led to considerable uncertainty concerning the importance of racial attitudes in contemporary Southern politics (Stanley 1985).

The Democratic stranglehold on the state's politics was initially loosened by the short-lived emergence of the Dixiecrat party in 1948. The potential for GOP growth in the state became evident in the 1952 election when Dwight Eisenhower received an astonishingly high, for the time, 35 percent of Alabama's presidential vote (compared to 18 percent for Dewey in 1944). Further gains were achieved by Eisenhower in 1956 (40 percent) and Nixon in 1960 (42 percent).

The first GOP presidential victories in Alabama came in 1964 when Goldwater, with his conservative stance on civil rights and other issues, swept the state with 70 percent of the vote (Democrat Lyndon Johnson did not even appear on the state's ballot). Republican prospects were put on hold in 1968 when favorite son George Wallace carried the state. Since 1972 Republican presidential candidates have carried the state in each election except 1976. In 1984 Ronald Reagan won 60 percent of the vote in Alabama. George Bush received the same percentage in 1988.

Republican growth has also occurred at the congressional level. In the 1962 U.S. Senate race, Jim Martin nearly defeated veteran New Dealer Lister Hill (Burnham 1964; Hamilton 1987). It was the 1964 Goldwater landslide, however, that gave the GOP its first congressional victories in Alabama. In that year, Republican candidates won

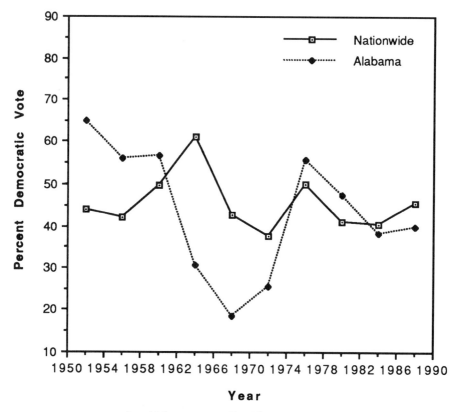

6.1 Alabama votes: President, 1952–1988

five of the state's eight House seats. Republicans have continued to hold two to three of the state's more urban congressional seats since then (figure 2).

In 1980 the Republican party won its first U.S. Senate seat in the state. In that contest Jeremiah Denton, a Vietnam War hero, narrowly defeated Jim Folsom, Jr., the son of a former governor. Folsom had earlier defeated incumbent Donald Stewart in the Democratic primary election. Stewart had only been in the Senate for two years, having won a special election in 1978 following the death of Senator Jim Allen.

Republican congressional prospects suffered a setback in 1986 when Denton lost his seat to Democratic congressman Richard Shelby. Denton's alleged inattention to the state's interests and willingness to cut Social Security benefits were the major issues of the campaign (Cotter and Stovall 1987).

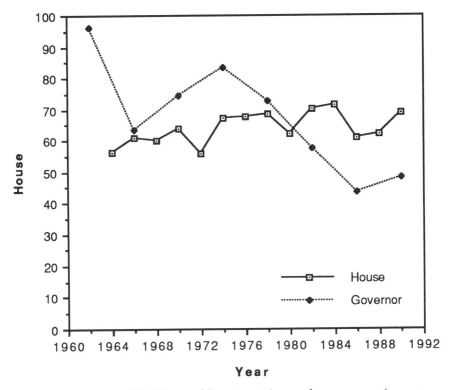

6.2 Alabama votes: U.S. House of Representatives and governor, 1962–1990

Republican gains have occurred at a slower pace in Alabama's state- and local-level politics. One factor accounting for slower growth is the durability of George Wallace (Carlson 1981). Wallace was first elected governor of Alabama in 1962. In all his campaigns, Wallace presented himself as a champion of the little man and as an opponent of the big interests. In 1962 Wallace also campaigned as a strong supporter of racial segregation, a candidate willing "to stand in the schoolhouse door" to prevent federally mandated integration of schools. In later contests, when blacks began to vote in greater numbers and the issue of legal segregation was largely settled, Wallace ceased directly talking about the issue of race and instead campaigned against all forms of federal intrusion. Constitutionally barred from seeking reelection in 1966, Wallace had his wife, Lurleen, elected. When Mrs. Wallace died in 1968, her husband was left without an official power base in the state. In 1970, however, Wallace regained the governorship following an exceptionally hard-fought campaign. He was reelected in

1974, after the adoption of a constitutional amendment permitting an officeholder to serve two consecutive terms as governor. In 1982, Wallace overcame tough primary and general election opponents to win another term as governor.

Wallace's political ambitions were not confined to Alabama. He successfully competed in several presidential primaries in 1964. In the 1968 presidential election, Wallace ran as a candidate of the American Independent party. In that year's election, he won five southern states but failed to cause a deadlock in the Electoral College. Four years later Wallace sought the Democratic presidential nomination. He won primary elections in several states, but his bid was ended when he was shot and his legs paralyzed in an assassination attempt. Wallace ran for the presidency again in 1976. However, a changing national political scene, his health, and the presence of fellow southerner Jimmy Carter soon resulted in his withdrawal from the contest.

From his first successful gubernatorial election to the mid-1980s Wallace had a strong, if not dominating, influence over Alabama politics. That, plus a career that spanned the upheavals of the Second Reconstruction, meant that traditional issues and coalitions were kept alive longer in Alabama than in other southern states. As a result, Republican efforts within the state were often frustrated (Bass and DeVries 1976; Lamis 1984).

It is important to note, however, that while Wallace slowed the pace of political change within Alabama, he did not stop it. Indeed Wallace's long career is largely the product of his ability to adapt to new political realities. That capacity is most clearly illustrated by the 54 percent of the black vote the former segregationist received in the 1982 gubernatorial runoff election. In that year's general election, an estimated 81 percent of the state's black voters supported Wallace (Cotter and Kline 1987).

GOP prospects in state politics improved with Wallace's retirement in 1986. His decision not to seek reelection removed from the political scene one of the few unifying elements within the state's Democratic party. As a result, the battle for the Democratic gubernatorial nomination was especially deep and divisive. Ultimately, a protracted dispute over the outcome of the party's runoff election (involving whether the winning candidate had illegally encouraged the participation of Republican primary voters in the Democratic runoff) led to the election of Alabama's first Republican governor, Guy Hunt, in more than a century (Cotter and Stovall 1987).

Both parties claimed success in the 1990 election. In the governor's

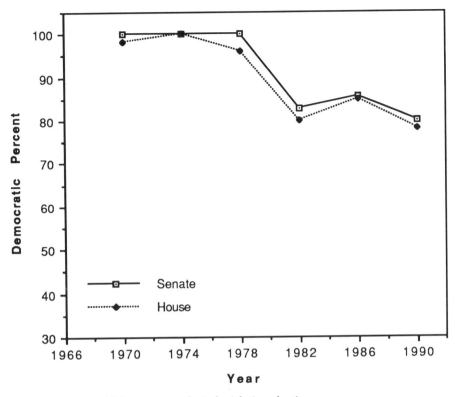

6.3  Alabama votes: State legislative elections, 1970–1990

race, Hunt defeated Alabama Education Association director Paul Hubbert by a narrow 52 to 48 percent margin. The other statewide races, however, were easily won by Democrats. Unlike previous years, Democrats maintained their overwhelming majority in the state legislature (figure 6.3).

## PARTY IDENTIFICATION IN ALABAMA

The data used to examine the party identifications of Alabamians come from two sources. The first is a series of public affairs surveys conducted by the University of Alabama between the fall of 1981 and the fall of 1987. The second is from several surveys conducted by Southern Opinion Research. In each of the surveys examined, the party identifications of Alabamians are measured by a question that asked respondents, "When it comes to national politics do you think of yourself as a Republican, a Democrat, an independent or what?"

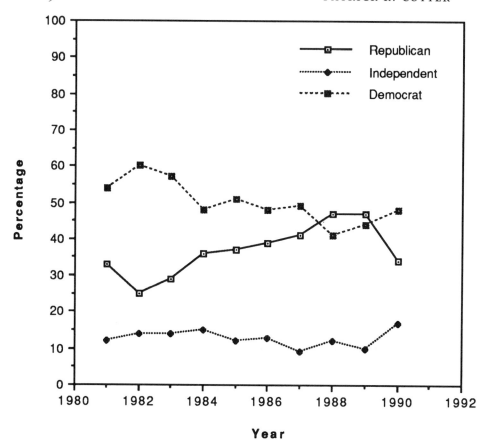

6.4 Alabama party identification, 1981–1990

The standard follow-up questions constructed a seven-point measure of party identification.

Figure 6.4 shows that considerable change occurred in the distribution of party identification among Alabamians during the 1981–90 period. In the spring of 1981, Democrats outnumbered Republicans by a 51 percent to 34 percent margin. A year later, the Democrats outpaced Republicans by 64 percent to 26 percent. By the fall of 1982, only about 24 percent of the state's citizens said they were Republicans. The number of Republicans grew and the number of Democrats declined during the next two years so that by fall 1984 Democrats outnumbered Republicans by a relatively small 46 to 40 percent margin. The margin widened, narrowed, and then widened again during the next two to three years. As a result, in 1987 about 39 percent of Alabamians said that they were Republicans and about 51 percent identified themselves as Democrats. Studies in 1988 found about equal numbers of Democrats and Republicans. However, the Republican lead in party identification vanished in the 1990 study. That survey, like those conducted prior to 1988, found more Democratic (48 percent) than Republican (34 percent) party identifiers in Alabama.

DEALIGNMENT OR REALIGNMENT?

After examining both the outcome of recent elections and the party identification data presented in figure 6.4, it is easy to conclude that Alabama is in a period of political change. Whether the change takes the form of a dealignment, a realignment, or some other situation is less certain.

With regard to the possibility of a dealignment, the shifting balance of Democrats and Republicans indicates that many Alabamians are only weakly tied to either political party. This suggests that the state is experiencing a political dealignment. Other evidence, however, points to a different conclusion.

Specifically, one indicator of a dealignment is the presence and growth of a substantial number of independents. Figure 6.4 shows relatively few pure independents among Alabama citizens. Additionally, the number of independents (between 9 and 14 percent of the respondents) has varied little during the 1981–90 period.

A dealignment is also indicated if citizens fail to use their party identifications in making political evaluations. Strong relationships, however, are found between Alabamians' party identifications and other political indicators. In particular, each of the surveys examined (with the exception of the 1989 and 1990 studies) contained a question asking respondents to evaluate Ronald Reagan's performance as president. The correlations (r) between those evaluations and party identification range between .46 and .62. The average of the correlations is .54. Similar relationships (average $r = .70$) are found in the three 1988 preelection studies between party identification and presidential preference. Overall the findings indicate that Alabama is not experiencing a political dealignment.

If not a dealignment, then do the changes found in the distribution of party identification mean that Alabama has experienced a realignment? Realignments, both critical and secular, involve durable and not temporary shifts in partisanship. Because the distribution of party identification has fluctuated so much during the 1980s, it is not at all certain that the recent growth in the number of Republican identifiers is permanent. Thus, whether Alabama is experiencing a realignment is also unclear.

One way to investigate the permanence of recent changes in partisanship, and thus the occurrence of a realignment, is to examine the sources of the shifts in party identification. In particular the investigation can examine whether the shifts in party identification are related to relatively permanent characteristics, such as social status and generation, or to more temporary, short-term phenomena such as the influence of political leaders.

SOURCES OF CHANGE

*Race.* Before identifying the specific sources of partisan change, it is first necessary to determine what type of citizen has experienced the greatest change in party identification. Previous studies have found large differences in the party identifications of blacks and whites (Stanley 1988). Researchers have also found that in recent years whites have experienced more change in their party identification than have blacks (Beck 1977; Wolfinger and Arseneau 1978). The same patterns are found in Alabama.

Specifically, as table 6.1 shows, black Alabamians overwhelmingly and consistently identify themselves as Democrats. In each of the surveys examined, with the exception of the November 1988 preelection study, more than 70 percent, and typically more than 80 percent, of black respondents are Democrats. Even in the November 1988 study, about two-thirds of black Alabamians called themselves Democrats.

White Alabamians are more evenly divided and less stable in their party allegiances. In particular, Democrats outnumbered Republicans in the spring of 1981 by a narrow 44 to 40 percent margin. A year later, 57 percent of white Alabamians identified themselves as Democrats compared to 33 percent who said that they were Republicans. The number of Republicans reached its lowest point (29 percent) in fall 1982. In each of the 1988–89 surveys, a majority of white Alabamians claimed some identification with the GOP. Conversely, in the 1988–89 surveys only about one in three whites identified themselves as Democrats. In the 1990 study, a small plurality of whites identified with the GOP.

Overall, the results presented in table 6.1 show that throughout the period examined blacks have remained loyal Democrats, while the party identifications of whites have fluctuated. Consequently, in

Table 6.1. Trends in Party Identification among Blacks and Whites: Alabama, 1981–1990

| | Strong Repub- lican (%) | Weak Repub- lican (%) | Indepen- dent Re- publican (%) | Indepen- dent (%) | Indepen- dent Democrat (%) | Weak Demo- crat (%) | Strong Democrat (%) |
|---|---|---|---|---|---|---|---|
| *Black Alabamians* | | | | | | | |
| Spring 1981 | 2 | 2 | 4 | 9 | 8 | 22 | 52 |
| Fall 1981 | 6 | 6 | 7 | 1 | 10 | 21 | 48 |
| Spring 1982 | 3 | 4 | 2 | 8 | 6 | 24 | 52 |
| Fall 1982 | 0 | 2 | 1 | 9 | 5 | 22 | 61 |
| Spring 1983 | 2 | 2 | 0 | 6 | 10 | 32 | 46 |
| Fall 1983 | 3 | 1 | 3 | 7 | 3 | 26 | 57 |
| Spring 1984 | 2 | 4 | 2 | 9 | 6 | 26 | 51 |
| Fall 1984 | 5 | 2 | 1 | 7 | 3 | 21 | 61 |
| Spring 1985 | 2 | 4 | 2 | 5 | 12 | 25 | 51 |
| Fall 1985 | 6 | 4 | 3 | 3 | 12 | 22 | 50 |
| Spring 1986 | 3 | 3 | 0 | 9 | 10 | 18 | 57 |
| Fall 1986 | 7 | 3 | 1 | 4 | 8 | 22 | 55 |
| Spring 1987 | 3 | 5 | 3 | 2 | 5 | 25 | 57 |
| Fall 1987 | 0 | 5 | 5 | 4 | 10 | 14 | 63 |
| Aug. 1988 | 1 | 2 | 4 | 5 | 9 | 21 | 58 |
| Sept. 1988 | 8 | 6 | 5 | 4 | 9 | 20 | 48 |
| Nov. 1988 | 10 | 12 | 7 | 6 | 8 | 16 | 40 |
| Dec. 1988 | 6 | 4 | 1 | 9 | 4 | 25 | 52 |
| July 1989 | 4 | 2 | 6 | 6 | 6 | 48 | 28 |
| July 1990 | 4 | 5 | 0 | 7 | 4 | 23 | 57 |
| *White Alabamians* | | | | | | | |
| Spring 1981 | 14 | 16 | 10 | 16 | 11 | 17 | 16 |
| Fall 1981 | 12 | 13 | 11 | 10 | 11 | 23 | 20 |
| Spring 1982 | 8 | 15 | 10 | 11 | 12 | 25 | 20 |
| Fall 1982 | 7 | 12 | 10 | 20 | 9 | 21 | 21 |
| Spring 1983 | 10 | 11 | 12 | 16 | 11 | 20 | 20 |
| Fall 1983 | 9 | 14 | 12 | 16 | 12 | 22 | 17 |
| Spring 1984 | 11 | 14 | 12 | 19 | 10 | 20 | 14 |
| Fall 1984 | 19 | 16 | 13 | 15 | 3 | 17 | 17 |
| Spring 1985 | 16 | 16 | 12 | 12 | 10 | 18 | 16 |
| Fall 1985 | 14 | 17 | 11 | 14 | 9 | 18 | 16 |
| Spring 1986 | 16 | 14 | 14 | 14 | 7 | 18 | 17 |
| Fall 1986 | 16 | 15 | 15 | 15 | 10 | 13 | 16 |
| Spring 1987 | 19 | 14 | 15 | 11 | 6 | 19 | 15 |
| Fall 1987 | 14 | 17 | 14 | 10 | 8 | 21 | 15 |
| Aug. 1988 | 15 | 14 | 22 | 16 | 7 | 17 | 10 |
| Sept. 1988 | 17 | 15 | 20 | 11 | 10 | 15 | 12 |
| Nov. 1988 | 24 | 17 | 18 | 9 | 7 | 12 | 13 |
| Dec. 1988 | 21 | 17 | 15 | 17 | 7 | 11 | 12 |
| July 1989 | 22 | 21 | 11 | 11 | 9 | 15 | 11 |
| July 1990 | 10 | 19 | 13 | 20 | 9 | 17 | 14 |

Source: University of Alabama/Southern Opinion Research.
Note: Missing data deleted.

seeking to identify the specific sources of the changing distribution of party identification in Alabama, this study will limit its attention to white citizens.

*Social status.* A changing relationship between partisanship and social status is one possible source of the shifts in the distribution of party identification (Converse 1966; Gatlin 1975; Wolfinger and Arenseau 1978). Specifically, changes in the distribution of party identification may occur as middle- and upper-class southerners abandon (through conversion or generational replacement) the region's traditional party and identify instead with the GOP.

Such a scenario does not seem to have occurred in Alabama. Instead, social status (as measured by education, the only measure of status available in each of the surveys) is only mildly related to party identification among white Alabamians (the average of the correlations (*r*) is .18). Nor has the relationship between status and party identification gotten stronger over time. Indeed, the largest differences between the party identifications of more- and less-educated citizens are found in the 1982–83 period (average *r* = .23). The smallest differences exist in the 1986–89 (average *r* = .16) period.

Overall, the results indicate that social status is not a characteristic that is very important in determining the partisan identities of white Alabamians. Higher status white Alabamians are only slightly more likely to identify themselves as Republicans than are lower status whites. Thus, changes in the distribution of party identification in Alabama cannot be attributed to an electorate increasingly (or decreasingly) polarized on the basis of social status.

*Generational replacement.* Several studies trace shifts in the number of Democrats and Republicans to differences in the party identification of younger and older citizens (Beck 1977; Stanley 1988). Generational variations are believed to reflect the differences in the political context that individuals encountered while they were forming their party identifications.

The 1964 presidential election is often described as a watershed event in the breakup of the Solid South. In examining generational differences, therefore, younger citizens are those who have entered the electorate since 1960; and older southerners are those who were at least 21 years old in 1960 (Stanley 1988; Wolfinger and Arseneau 1978).

In Alabama younger citizens are somewhat more Republican and somewhat less Democratic than are older citizens. Indeed, since 1984 Republicans have outnumbered Democrats among younger whites.

Only in the 1988–89 surveys have Republicans edged out (by a maximum of 10 percent) Democrats among older whites. However, as was the case with social status, the differences in party identification between young and old Alabamians are relatively slight (average correlation = .14). The strength of that relationship has also changed little over time. Thus, age, like social status, is not a characteristic that distinguishes Alabamians politically. Nor is it a characteristic that helps account for the changing distribution of party identification in the state.

*Elites.* Clubb, Flanigan, and Zingale (1980) have suggested that the presence or absence of effective political leadership will determine whether a particular event or crisis will lead to a realignment. Consistent with that notion is the finding that evaluations of political leaders can affect an individual's party identification (see Franklin and Jackson 1983).

The most visible and perhaps most controversial political leader in the 1980s was Ronald Reagan. As already noted, party identification is strongly related to evaluations of Reagan. Among white Alabamians the average correlation ($r$) between party affiliation and Reagan's job performance rating is .48.

As Figure 6.5 shows, there is a close positive relationship between the number of white Alabamians identifying themselves as Republicans and the number of white citizens saying that Reagan did a good or excellent job as president (the correlation ($r$) between number of Republicans and positive rating of Reagan is .73). During the 1981–88 period, as Reagan's support increased, so did the number of Republican identifiers. Conversely, when Reagan's performance ratings declined, so did the number of Republicans. Thus, during this period whatever forces influenced evaluations of Reagan also influenced citizens' willingness to identify themselves as Republicans. What was good for Ronald Reagan was good for the Alabama Republican party.

Closer examination of figure 6.5 shows that the parallel movements of Reagan's evaluation and the number of Republicans diminished beginning in the fall of 1986. Specifically, eliminating the data from the fall 1986 through the fall 1988 surveys raises the correlation between evaluations of Reagan and number of Republicans from .73 to .85. As he became a lame duck, evaluations of Reagan and the party identifications of white Alabama citizens became increasingly independent of one another.

A number of factors influence the way in which citizens evaluate a

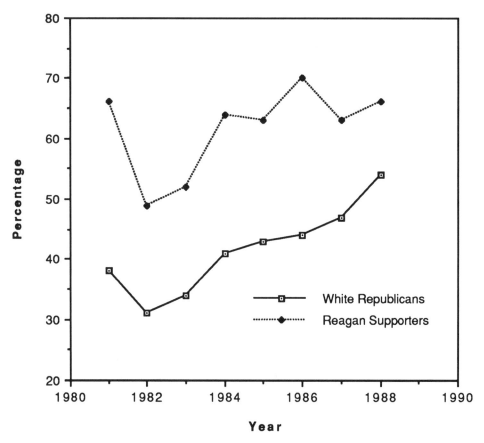

6.5 Alabama: Whites' evaluation of Reagan and party identification

president (Mueller 1973). Undoubtedly a complex set of relationships exists between those factors, evaluations of Ronald Reagan, and the party identification of white Alabamians. Identification of those relationships is beyond the scope of this research effort.

It is the case, however, that the results presented in figure 6.5 show that the distribution of party identification in Alabama is responsive to current, or short-term, forces present in the political environment. The forces influencing citizens' reactions to President Reagan (and perhaps feelings about Reagan himself) had a strong influence on the distribution of party identification through 1986. Since then the Reagan factor has diminished. Whether feelings about George Bush or some other factor replaces it is not immediately obvious.

CONCLUSION

The changes that Alabama experienced during the 1980s do not completely fulfill the requirements for a political dealignment. The number of independents has remained small. Additionally, the analysis shows that Alabamians use their party identifications in making political judgments.

Despite the recent growth in Republican strength, it is not certain that Alabama has undergone, or is experiencing, a realignment. The fluctuations in party identification and the fact that the shifts appear to be related to short-term forces, rather than characteristics such as social status or age, suggest that change will continue to characterize Alabama politics. Consequently, it is premature to conclude that Alabama has experienced a realignment.

What, then, can we conclude about the current state of Alabama politics? Clearly, Alabama has moved into a more competitive era. Just as clearly, Alabamians have changed their party identifications. Such identifications, however, are quite sensitive to citizens' evaluations of contemporary political events and leaders. Such a situation is neither a realignment nor a dealignment. Rather it is an electorate in a state of flux.

Perhaps it is not surprising that political alignments in Alabama are so unsettled. Having two parties compete in elections is a relatively new phenomenon for Alabama, particularly at the level of state and local elections. As the remnants of George Wallace's influence diminish, and as more Republican candidates contest elections (Wolfinger and Arseneau 1978), more stable political alignments may develop within the state.

For now, however, political alignments in Alabama are unsettled. Rather than experiencing political maturity, Alabama is in a state of political adolescence. As is the case with most adolescents, Alabama finds itself in a situation in which old familiar patterns and ways of doing things no longer apply; current conditions and identities change on a frequent basis; and the future, and the factors that will determine its course, are far from certain.

# Florida: A Polity in Transition

## SUZANNE L. PARKER

7

DURING the 1980s, meaningful Republican competition returned to Florida politics for the first time in more than one hundred years. This change marked the culmination of a decade of growth in Republican identifiers. To understand the meaning and ramifications of the change, this chapter examines both the nature of Florida politics and the forces that have promoted the growth of Republicanism in the state. The purpose is to shed light on the durability of the changes and to consider whether they represent a realignment of the Florida electorate.

## THE POLITICAL CONTEXT

The study of politics in Florida is a study of fragmentation. Since Reconstruction, the major forces driving politics in Florida have promoted a very fluid and atomized political system. Among the conditions promoting this state of affairs are the geographic characteristics of the state and a large, diverse, nonnative population. This section examines the major forces defining the political context in Florida—geographic characteristics, social and population trends, and economic conditions. These aspects of Florida define the parameters within which government operates and politicians compete for political office.

### GEOGRAPHIC CHARACTERISTICS

Florida is a huge state, and the long distances between population centers have contributed to the fragmentation of politics. As V. O. Key noted in his 1949 book on southern politics, "From

Miami to Pensacola, as the crow flies, is about the same distance as from Atlanta to Washington, from Indianapolis to Lincoln, Nebraska, or from San Francisco to Portland, Oregon" (p. 83). The distances between the political cultures of the northern Panhandle and those in central and southeastern Florida are almost as large as the physical distance. In the early 1900s when Florida had the smallest population in the South, most of southern Florida was only sparsely populated. As a result of the long distances and the poor communication, few ties grew up between the major population centers. Hence, most of the major population areas have developed their own political cultures in isolation from the other areas of the state. This in turn has promoted localism in Florida politics.

Unlike many of its southern neighbors, much of Florida's population (84 percent) is centered in urban areas (Dye 1989). It is the most urbanized southern state, ranking eighth in urbanization nationally. Similar to other areas in the South, the growth of Republicanism in the state has centered in the urban areas. The large size of the state and diversity of the population centers present a formidable challenge to candidates for statewide office. Florida has seven major media markets that they must cover.

DEMOGRAPHIC TRENDS

Another important influence on Florida politics is demographics— the nature, size, and change in Florida's population. As one of the faster growing states in the nation, the population has increased from 2.7 million in 1950 to 9.7 million in 1980. During that period new residents arrived at a rate of 893 per day. In fact, Florida's growth rate has exceeded the national average in every decade since the beginning of the twentieth century.

A consequence of a large nonnative population (75 percent of Floridians) is that a large proportion of the citizens have only weak ties to the political community and participate less in politics (Squire, Wolfinger, and Glass 1987). In addition, residents come from many different parts of the country and not just from other southern states, which adds diversity to the state's population. However, the migratory patterns followed by the new residents exacerbate political fragmentation because immigrants from different areas of the United States tend to settle in distinct areas of Florida.

For instance, southern migrants tend to settle in the northern part of the state; and as a result, the politics there tend to resemble those of states such as Georgia and Alabama in their conservatism and Democratic dominance. In contrast, migrants from the Midwest tend to settle in central Florida and on the gulf coast. That has been the area of greatest Republican strength, reflecting in part the strength of the Republican party in the Midwest. Finally, the southeastern section of the state has attracted migrants from the northeastern seaboard, such as New York and New Jersey. Those residents have tended to favor liberal Democratic policies and candidates. Mingling with the migrants to southeastern Florida are the Cubans who fled Cuba in the 1950s and in 1980. That group tends to be far more conservative and Republican than their neighbors from the eastern seaboard.

Another consequence of the influx of new residents is that race has played a much smaller role in Florida's politics than in neighboring states. As in other southern states, blacks migrated out of Florida in the 1940s and 1950s; at the same time a steady stream of predominantly white citizens flowed into Florida from other states. The result was that the percentage of blacks in Florida fell from 21.8 percent in the 1950 census to 13.8 percent in 1980. Thus, despite blacks' strong loyalty to the Democratic party in Florida, their voting strength has a much smaller impact than in many other southern states; and the dispersion of the black population in rural, sparsely populated nothern counties has further diluted their impact on state politics.

A final important demographic characteristic of Florida is its large elderly population. Florida has long been the destination of retirees because of its warm climate, low tax rate, and relatively inexpensive standard of living. Twenty-six percent of Florida's population is sixty-five or older, compared to 11 percent nationally. That segment of the population tends to be conservative on issues of taxation and represents an active, influential portion of the electorate.

ECONOMIC CONDITIONS

Economically, the state has been transformed in the last eighty years from a predominantly rural and agricultural economy to an urbanized and economically diversified state. Unlike its southern neighbors, Florida never developed a cotton economy; and today its agricultural products are fruits, vegetables, cattle, and dairy products. Tourism contributes greatly to the Florida economy as do service and high-tech industries. Its manufacturing base is quite small, ranking forty-third nationally (Dye 1989). Florida benefited from the movement of business to the Sun Belt states during the late 1970s. In the 1980s, Florida's economy performed at a rate that exceeded the national economy.

Since the early 1900s, the emphasis has been on growth and on attracting businesses in order to diversify the economy. The weather and the low tax rate have made Florida attractive and have contributed to growth. With the exception of southeastern Florida, the state has a low union membership, which makes it attractive to many businesses. The major sources of revenue for state and local governments are the sales tax, the property tax, and the gasoline tax. Prohibitions against a state income tax are written into the state constitution. As a result, Florida is a low service state that ranks thirty-eighth in primary and secondary educational funding, forty-ninth in funding for higher education, and forty-eighth in welfare spending (Dye 1989). The inadequate tax base poses continuing problems, especially meeting needs created by the burgeoning population.

## GOVERNMENT STRUCTURE, POLITICAL PARTIES, AND ELECTIONS

The peculiar structure of state government, the domination of the political scene by the Democratic party since 1876, and the lack of important persistent issues have also contributed to a fragmentation of politics in Florida.

### GOVERNMENTAL STRUCTURE

Florida's governor is elected every four years in off-year elections and is limited to two terms of office. Florida differs from other states in the limitations it imposes on the power of the governor. Six cabinet members in the state are elected—the heads of the departments of legal affairs, agriculture, education, banking, state, and insurance. Since the cabinet members are beholden to the Florida public for their position, they need not necessarily follow the dictates of the governor, thus weakening his leadership power. Further, since the public may elect members of different parties for the positions, the governor of one party can serve with six cabinet members from the opposition party. (See Colburn and Scher 1980.)

Relative to the executive's power, the state legislature is quite strong in Florida. Similar to many state legislatures in the 1950s and early 1960s, the Florida legislature was badly malapportioned, with an overrepresentation of northern and rural areas of the state and an underrepresentation of urban and south Florida residents. The U.S. Supreme Court ordered redistricting in 1967 on the basis of "one man, one vote" (*Swann v. Adams*). The new system created in 1971 consisted of multi- and single-member legislative districts and even-sized populations within the districts.

One result of the change was far-reaching: it marked the demise of the "pork choppers," the northern, rural legislative members who controlled the legislature prior to reapportionment. Power shifted to members representing south Florida and urban and suburban interests, which gained seats from reapportionment; and that increased Republican membership in the legislature because those areas were traditionally more Republican. The Democratic leadership also changed, since most of the northern, rural members who had formerly controlled the legislature were Democrats. Finally, the changes resulted in the modernization of the Florida legislature, including the appointment of a legislative staff and the establishment of a sixty-day session each year. In 1982, the state's remaining multi-member districts were changed to single-member districts. Currently, there are 120 members in the Florida House of Representatives who serve two-year terms, and forty senate members who serve for four years.

POLITICAL PARTIES

Between the end of Reconstruction in 1876 and 1966, the Democratic party was the only viable party in Florida. Prior to the 1950s the Republican party was virtually nonexistent in the state. Any work that was undertaken by the party concerned presidential politics and presidential patronage; the bulk of statewide and local races went uncontested. Consequently, Democratic primaries were more important than general elections in determining who held statewide office.

Further, Florida's closed primary system allows only registered Democrats to vote in Democratic primaries. Citizens must declare a party affiliation or independent status at the time of registering to vote. Only citizens who have declared an affiliation with the party are allowed to vote in party primaries. Citizens registering as independents are not allowed to vote in any party primaries, and must wait until general elections to vote. Until recently, many Floridians who were not Democrats registered as Democrats anyway in order to participate meaningfully in elections.

Despite the Democratic dominance, Florida politics had not developed along the same lines as other Deep South states that displayed one-partyism. In fact, V. O. Key (1949) found that the post-World War II Democratic party was so weakened by a multiplicity of factions that "no partyism" was a better description of Florida politics. A political individualism persists in Florida politics to the present day; candidates from the same party rarely cooperate or coordinate their efforts to win office. Political support is built around the personalities of the individual candidates rather than on consistent policies or party platforms. Not surprisingly, issues play little role in elections.

The lack of persistent, detectable cleavages in the Florida electorate can be traced to the emphasis on individual followings. Politics organized around personalities rather than issues does not promote the growth of stable factions or cleavages that persist beyond the tenure of specific individuals. Hence, a continuous process of forming factions, dissolving factions, and re-forming new factions cycles through Florida politics promoting instability. "Anything can happen in elections, and does" (Key 1949, 82).

Although the Republicans have become more competitive since the late 1960s, which Key predicted would lessen the degree of factionalism in politics, evidence suggests his prediction may have been wrong. In spite of increased Republican competition in the late 1960s and early 1970s, Democratic factionalism persisted unabated (Echols and Ranney 1976). Further, recent evidence suggests that the Republican party displays the same multifactionalism as the Democratic party.

> Party factionalism and party switching currently threaten organizational stability. In fact, party factionalism has been a long-standing problem for both parties. Both Republican and Democratic grassroots party activists say the continuance of personal followings and related animosities from the "no party" era in Florida politics are a major cause of factional problems. Factionalism is especially threatening to present day Republicans (Bowen, Hulbary, and Kelly 1987).

This suggests that factionalism is probably the result of more than lack of competition in politics. It is linked as well to the influx of new residents who know little about state politics, the long distances between many population centers in the southern and northern parts of the state, and the conditions under which Florida politics developed.

ELECTIONS

On the presidential level, Florida has looked like a Republican state for some time. Florida's electoral votes went to Republican presidential candidates in eight of the last ten elections (1952, 1956, 1960, 1968, 1972, 1980, 1984, and 1988). As indicated by figure 7.1, the strongest Republican showings were in 1972 when Richard Nixon won 72 percent of the popular vote, 1984 when Ronald Reagan won

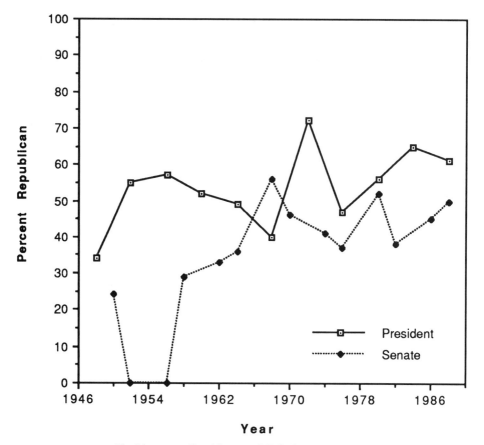

7.1 Florida votes: President and U.S. Senate, 1948–1988

65 percent, and 1988 when George Bush received his strongest support nationwide in Florida (61 percent).

Until the 1980s, however, Republican support on the presidential
level did not translate to gains on other levels. Between 1876 and
1968, no Republicans were elected to the U.S. Senate from Florida or
served as governor. On the gubernatorial level, the first Republican
elected was Claude Kirk in 1966; and on the senatorial level, Edward
Gurney was elected in 1968.

As noted earlier, the reapportionment in the late 1960s opened the
door for an influx of Republicans from urban and suburban areas in
the southern part of the state. The expanded representation is evident
in the number of seats the Republicans gained in the state legislature
(figure 7.2) in the late 1960s.

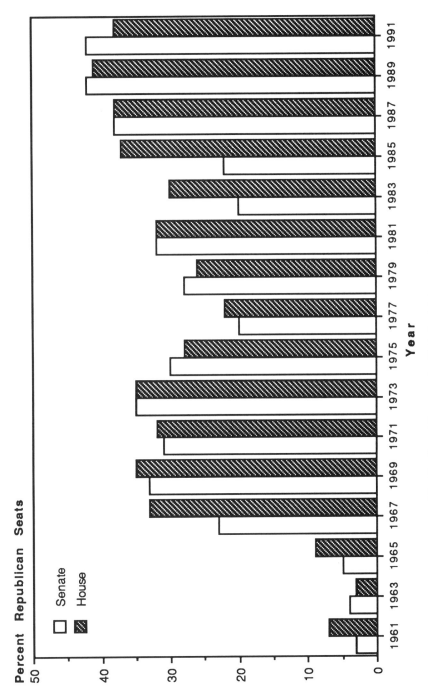

7.2 Florida Republican seats: State legislature, 1961–1991

The election of a Republican governor and U.S. senator was hailed as a new era in Florida politics, but the prediction was premature. The Republican governor, Kirk, ran into problems providing leadership to a Democratically controlled legislature and cabinet and lost his bid for reelection in 1970. After serving on the Watergate committee as a Nixon supporter, Gurney, the Republican senator, faced charges he had accepted political payoffs and was replaced in 1974 by a Democrat. Even the surge in state legislative seats began to decline in the mid-1970s. At the same time a revitalized Democratic party emerged in the 1970s, delivering the state to a Democratic presidential contender for the first time in twelve years and recapturing both senate seats and the governorship.

In contrast to the 1970s, the 1980s marked a period of more sustained gains for the Republican party at all levels. On the presidential level, the state's electoral votes went to Republicans throughout the decade: Reagan defeated Jimmy Carter in 1980 and Walter Mondale in 1984, and George Bush received his highest level of electoral support nationally in the state of Florida. On the senate level, Reagan's strong showing in 1980 helped provide a victory to the Republican senatorial candidate, Paula Hawkins. Even though Hawkins lost her seat after one term to former Democratic governor Bob Graham in 1986, the Republicans claimed another U.S. Senate seat in 1988 with the coattail victory of Connie Mack (50 percent of the vote).

The Republican party's resurgence is also reflected in the record of U.S. House seats during the decade (figure 7.3). The Republicans started the decade holding only three of Florida's U.S. House seats, and ended the decade holding a majority of Florida's nineteen seats through a process of winning open seats and party switching by former Democrats. In the 1983 session of Congress, Florida gained five new seats; and three of the five were won by Republicans. Further, a Democratic congressman switched to the Republicans, bringing the total number of Republicans to seven of nineteen. That number held steady until the 1989 session of Congress; in the 1988 election the Republicans picked up two Democratic seats. Following the election, one north Florida representative (Bill Grant) switched to the Republican party, giving the Republicans a majority of the Florida delegation. In the 1990 election, Grant lost his U.S. House seat to a Democrat; and the balance in the Florida delegation changed to ten to nine in favor of the Republicans.

On the gubernatorial level, a Republican (Bob Martinez) won the

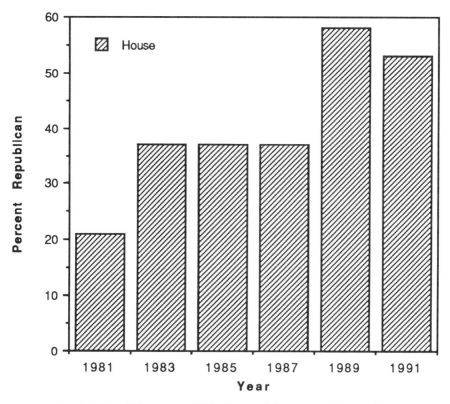

7.3 Florida Republican seats: U.S. House of Representatives, 1981–1991

governorship in 1986 for only the second time since Reconstruction. A divisive Democratic primary so badly split the Democrats that Martinez was able to win 54 percent of the vote. In 1990 Martinez tried to become the only Republican governor reelected in Florida, but he lost to former U.S. senator Lawton Chiles. Chiles garnered 57 percent of the vote in that election. In the same election, Republicans had hoped to pick up four seats in the state Senate to gain control of that body. Instead, the balance of power held in the Senate with twenty-three Democrats and seventeen Republicans. The balance in the Florida house shifted in 1990 from seventy-two Democratic members and forty-eight Republican to seventy-four Democrats and forty-six Republican. Finally, registration figures also show a similar pattern of Republican identifiers—an initial surge in the early 1970s that leveled off and then new growth throughout the 1980s (figure 7.4).

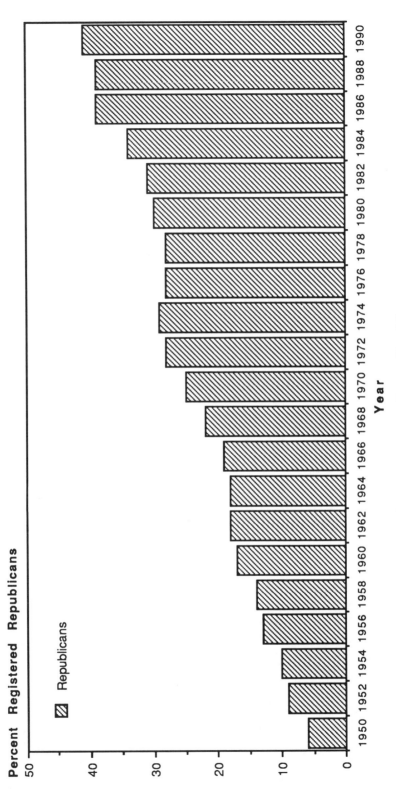

7.4 Florida party registration: Percent Republican, 1950–1990

TRENDS IN PARTY IDENTIFICATION

Given the degree to which politics in Florida is built upon personal followings, it would be foolish to consider only electoral results in assessing political change in the state. Aggregate trends in the party preferences of adult Floridians must also be examined. The data for the analysis are from cross-sectional statewide surveys conducted annually since 1980.

The fortunes of the Democratic party have declined significantly among the entire adult population (figure 7.5). The Democrats started the decade with a two to one lead over the Republicans (Republicans, 21 percent; Democrats 44 percent; and independents, 35 percent). However, by the end of the decade, the percentage of Republicans in the state had doubled and the Republicans led Democrats in identifiers by 9 percentage points (1989: Republicans, 42 percent; Democrats, 33 percent, independents, 24 percent). A second notable feature of the data is that the independent category remained relatively stable at around 30 percent of the population throughout the 1980s. The failure of the independents to commit to a party leads to volatility in elections and high levels of split-ticket voting.

The changes have been even more dramatic among the white population. In 1980, 22 percent of white Floridians identified with the Republican party. By 1989 that percentage had increased to 46 percent. The gains appear to have come in three stages—increases in 1981 and 1982 and a leveling off in 1983 and 1984, more increases in 1985 and 1986 and a leveling off in 1987 and 1988, and finally a new surge in 1989 with slight declines in 1990. In contrast to whites, blacks display little change in party identification between 1980 and 1989, and the small changes that occur are inconsistent and insufficient to produce the aggregate level changes identified in the data. Therefore, it appears that the changes are centered in the white population. The rest of the analysis focuses on that segment of the population.

Any explanation offered for changes in party identification has to take into account racial differences. A rich literature suggests the forces that might be at work. Studies of previous realignments provide theoretical explanations that might be applied to the changes occurring in Florida. For instance, given the large nonnative population, changes in party identification might result from an influx of a large number of Republicans from other areas over the last decade. The influx might disturb the balance of party identification that previously existed.

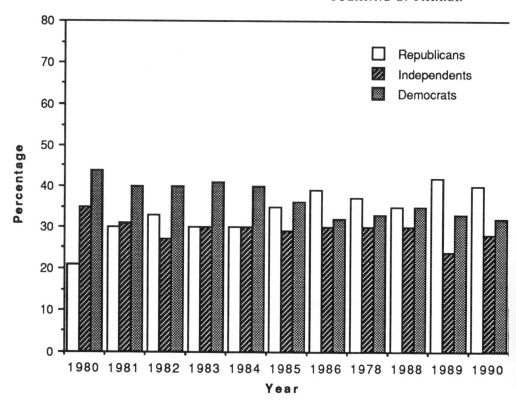

7.5 Florida party identification, 1980–1990

A second explanation is that a shift in ideological and issue preferences may have caused more Floridians to look to the Republican
party for leadership. Another alternative is that a generational change
in the Florida electorate may have caused certain age groups to give
greater support to Republicans. This sort of generational shifting has
been associated with previous realignments on the national level. A
final explanation is that the shifts have occurred throughout the electorate in response to period forces operating in the 1980s; that is, the
change itself is a manifestation of the period forces. In the latter case,
the trends could change again once the period forces weaken.

Florida has the largest nonnative population in the south and the
largest percentage of Yankees living in the south (Black and Black
1987). That certainly provides the prerequisites for an immigration explanation of changes in party loyalties in Florida. Some have found
migration to be an important determinant of political change in the
South (Wolfinger and Hagen 1985; Converse 1972), while still others

have found that immigration has had no significant impact on partisan change (Beck 1977; Petrocik 1987). An earlier analysis of the Florida data indicates that newer residents of Florida tend to express lower levels of Democratic loyalty than natives (Parker 1988a). However, the same analysis showed that substantial declines in Democratic loyalties have occurred in every group from new residents to natives, and immigration would not explain the changes among natives and long-term residents. Further, immigration does not explain the recent upturn in Republican electoral victories because new residents are far less likely to participate in politics than natives and long-term residents. Hence, it appears that although length of residence might help to explain party identification, it is not a sufficient explanation of the growth in Republican identifiers in the 1980s.

Given the explanations of the causes of recent realignments, one might expect that a durable shift in party loyalties would be accompanied by changes in the ideological positions of Floridians. That is, if the Florida public became more conservative over the last decade, then substantial numbers of voters might shift to the more conservative Republican party. There is no evidence, however, that a growing number of Floridians have identified themselves as conservatives. Compared to 1982 when 42 percent of white Floridians considered themselves to be conservatives, in 1989, 38 percent said they were conservatives. The percentage of the public identifying themselves as liberals has declined from 18 percent in 1982 to 16 percent in 1990; but the category that has registered increases has been the moderates (middle-of-the-roaders), not the conservatives. Further, the percentage of Democrats has declined in all three ideological groups, not just among conservatives (Parker 1988a).

Although Floridians may not have changed their ideological label, it is possible that they have moved to the right on issues advocated by the Republican party, particularly those advocated by Reagan and his supporters. For example, one issue emphasized both nationally and in the state by Republicans during the 1980s is the tradeoff between taxes and services. Republicans have been very successful in labeling Democrats as big taxers and big spenders. If the issues emphasized by the Republicans have served as an impetus for the change in party loyalties during the 1980s, we might expect to see support for cutting taxes to have grown over the 1980s. Instead, support for cutting state and local taxes has declined, while support for maintaining services in the state has grown over the decade.

The same is true of other national issues as well. When asked if the federal government should "see to it that every person has a job and good standard of living," or whether each person should "get ahead on his own," or if the respondent was somewhere between those two positions, support for each individual getting ahead on his own declined during the period (54 percent in 1981, 41 percent in 1987, and 39 percent in 1990). On other national issues, Floridians tend to hold more moderate or liberal opinions than national samples. For instance, statewide positions on abortion are more liberal than national opinions (Osmond and Pavalko 1987).

The findings suggest that changes have taken place in Floridians' ideological positions and specific issue positions; the noted changes, however, have not been in the anticipated direction. Rather than a movement to the right as might be suggested by realignment arguments, the Florida public has moved to more moderate positions both on the ideological spectrum and on specific issues. Equally surprising is that moderation has occurred on issues that have been emphasized by the Republicans—aid to minorities, jobs for the poor, taxes versus services, and abortion. Undoubtedly, an individual's positions on issues and the ideological spectrum do affect one's party identification; but changes in those attitudes over the decade cannot explain the growth in Republican identifiers during the 1980s.

From our understanding of party loyalties, the development of political attitudes, and studies of previous realignment periods, certain expectations have emerged concerning behavioral change among different age groups (or cohorts) within the electorate. For example, Paul Beck (1976) develops a socialization theory of partisan realignment that hypothesizes that the further a cohort is from a realignment, the weaker that group's ties to the party that emerged as the dominant party in the realignment. According to that hypothesis, young adults entering the electorate in the 1970s should show far weaker identification with the Democratic party than adults who were entering the electorate in the last realignment in the late 1920s and 1930s (the New Deal realignment).

The dynamic behind this argument is that the strongest socialization into the dominant party occurs for those who actually entered the electorate during a realignment, and each successive generation is more weakly socialized. In the case of Florida, according to this argument, members of the youngest generation would be expected to show the greatest change because they are furthest of all the generations from the last realignment, and because they have entered the electorate during a Republican resurgence. The smallest amount of

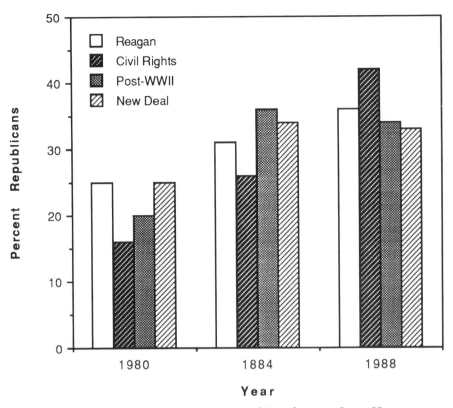

7.6 Florida Republicanism among white cohorts, 1980–1988

change would be expected in members of the New-Deal realignment generation—those who entered the electorate between 1929 and 1948.

To test whether the pattern is present in the Florida data, whites in each survey are categorized according to the year they entered the electorate; and four groups are formed—the Reagan generation (entering the electorate between 1978 and 1984), the Civil Rights generation (entering the electorate between 1965 and 1977), the post–WWII generation (entering the electorate between 1949 and 1963), and the New Deal–Realignment generation (entering between 1929 and 1948). Figure 7.6 presents the percentage of Republicans in each of the four generations in the years 1980, 1984, and 1988. The Reagan generation would be expected to show the most substantial gains in Republican identifiers, followed by the Civil Rights generation. The smallest gains should be found among the post–WWII and New Deal generations. In fact, very little change should be found at all among the New

Deal generation if a generational explanation were to explain the growth of Republican loyalties during the 1980s.

Instead, what is observed in figure 7.6 is that all four cohorts display substantial growth in the percentage of Republican identifiers. The largest increase occurred among those Floridians who entered the electorate between 1965 and 1977, and those entering between 1949 and 1964. By 1988 the cohorts display essentially the same percentage of Republican identifiers. Contrary to what might be expected by a generational explanation, the youngest age groups do not show substantially more change than the older age groups. Further, by the end of the decade, the oldest and youngest group show essentially the same percentage of Republican identifiers.

This section was designed to test several popular explanations of changes in party identification in the South on changes in the Florida population during the 1980s. Three explanations of this change were examined with the Florida data—the immigration of a large number of new residents with predominantly Republican loyalties, a shift to the conservative end of the political spectrum in the Florida population, and a generational explanation based on observations of previous realignments. While each may have had an impact, none of these factors provided a sufficient explanation of the changes that occurred in Florida.

## PRESIDENTIAL POPULARITY
## AND FLORIDIANS' PARTY LOYALTIES

The fact that the growth of Republicanism occurred among all groups in the white population suggests that some force (or forces) during the 1980s had a similar effect on most members of the white population that encouraged a move toward the Republican party.

One force that could have had that effect—and is consistent with Florida politics—is the popularity of Ronald Reagan. In a state where most politics revolves around personalities and individuals rather than parties, it might be possible for a very popular president to move major segments of the population in the direction of his party. Further, Reagan's popularity could have provided a sustained impetus to change throughout the decade because, unlike most modern presidents, Reagan's popularity in Florida was actually as high or higher at the end of his term as at the beginning of his tenure.

To test whether Reagan's popularity could have produced a change in white Floridians' party loyalties, we first note that whites gave

Reagan substantially higher evaluations during the decade than blacks. In 1981, 62 percent of the whites compared to 32 percent of the blacks rated Reagan's job performance as good or excellent. The same disparity exists between black and white evaluations in 1989—64 percent of the whites rate Reagan as excellent or good while only 35 percent of the blacks gave him those ratings. Thus it appears that Reagan's popularity could have affected the loyalties of whites while leaving black loyalties virtually untouched.

To test the impact of Reagan's popularity on party loyalty, Reagan evaluations were included in a regression analysis with other variables that could affect whites' party loyalties such as ideology, and length of residence. If Reagan's evaluations were an important determinant of changes in party loyalties, three patterns should emerge from the regression analysis: (1) presidential evaluations should have a significant impact on party choice in all (or almost all) years between 1981 and 1989; (2) the impact of Reagan's evaluations should be stronger than the other variables included in the regression equations; and (3) the impact of Reagan's evaluations should increase after 1981 just as the percentage of Republican identifiers substantially grows.

Presidential evaluations proved significant in every time period, ideology was significant in every time period except 1983, and length of residence was significant in every time period but 1990. Two other variables tested in these regressions, socioeconomic status and age, proved not to be significant in most time periods.

The findings indicate that presidential evaluations, ideology, and length of residence have had a significant impact on the partisan loyalties of Floridians during the past decade. That is, those who evaluate the president highly tend to identify with the president's party. Also, ideological conservatives tend to identify with the Republicans and liberals tend to identify with the Democrats, while moderates (middle-of-the-roaders) tend to split their loyalties between the two or claim independent status. Finally, native and long-term residents are more likely to identify with the Democratic party than newer residents.

In 1980, these three variables are equally important predictors of party identification. That is, in predicting party choice using Carter evaluations, ideology, and length of residence, each of the variables is about equally important. Thereafter, however, presidential evaluations become a much more important predictor relative to ideology and length of residence. As can be noted in figure 7.7, the beta

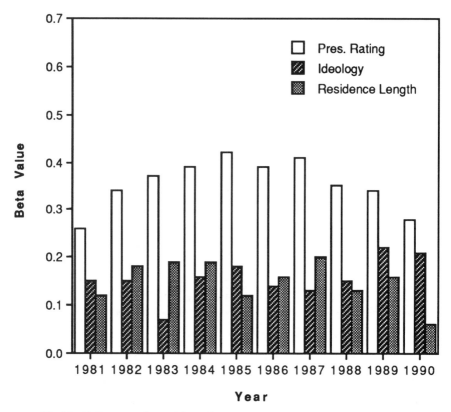

7.7 Florida: Influence of presidential rating, ideology, and years of residence on party choice among whites

weights for presidential evaluations become larger relative to those for the other two variables after Reagan assumed the presidency in 1981. This indicates that presidential evaluations become more important predictors of party choice than ideology and length of residence after 1981. This is precisely the time period in which the partisan loyalties of white Floridians were changing rapidly.

Whether the change in the importance of presidential evaluations did in fact result from an increase in their predictive power—and not from declines in the predictive power of ideology and length of residence—was tested using the unstandardized betas to provide a comparison of the same variable at different points in time. In fact, the predictive power of presidential evaluations increases from 1980 through 1985 and drops thereafter. However, the predictive power of the variable remains higher than under the Carter administration, even in 1990. Further, the magnitude of the beta for length of residence remains stable over the period, indicating no change in the predictive power of that variable. Ideology does manifest some changes over the period. During the 1983 recession, the variable is not a significant predictor of party choice. In other words, knowing whether an individual was a conservative or liberal no longer helped one to predict whether the individual would identify with the Democratic or Republican party, whereas in the earlier period knowing someone was a conservative would lead to the prediction that the individual was more likely to identify with the Republican party. The other noteworthy thing about ideology is the rise in magnitude of the variable in 1989 and 1990. This suggests that ideology may become a more important predictor of party choice since Reagan left office.

The results of the regression analysis suggest that the major force driving the changes in party identification during the 1980s among whites was the popularity of Ronald Reagan in the state. Age and class differences had no significant impact on party choice during the period; ideology and length of residence had a smaller effect relative to presidential evaluations; and the effect of these variables did not grow in the same manner as presidential evaluations. In short, there is little evidence to support the traditional realignment explanations of changes in party identification; issues and ideology do not appear to be major forces driving the changes, no major generational differences appear in the data, and Floridians do not seem to be changing parties on the basis of socioeconomic status. Instead, Floridians appear to have responded to strong period forces that favored the Republicans.

## IMPLICATIONS OF CHANGES IN PARTY IDENTIFICATION IN FLORIDA

The absence of trends associated with previous durable shifts in the party balance raises some questions about the nature of the recent changes. When attitudes underlying party identification, such as ideological preferences and party images, are not changing in the same direction as party identification, the changes may be of limited duration and meaning. This is compounded when changes in party identification are tied to short-term forces such as the popularity of particular politicians. Then the question becomes, what happens to those loyalties when the popular incumbent leaves office; do party loyalties shift again? If the Florida electorate had shifted to greater congruence with Republican issue stands, it might be expected that those attitudes would sustain Republican ties during and after the transition to new leadership. Further, the ties would extend down to nonnational candidates.

These findings suggest that rather than a strengthening of party politics in Florida, the recent changes just present more evidence of the multifactionalism and no-party politics in the state. This is supported by recent evidence showing that most Floridians are ambivalent toward the political parties. In a recent survey, 44 percent of Floridians could not mention one thing they liked about either party (Parker 1988b). In addition, many of the recent victories have come in elections marked by a high level of split-ticket voting. Thus, it may be that party identification no longer denotes a long-term, stable loyalty to a particular party and the issues positions that the party supports. Further, party identificatoin may no longer be as good a predictor of voting behavior as it once was.

Although the recent changes do not appear to mark a stable realignment of Floridians' party preferences, they have accomplished several things. Florida's election outcomes are no longer as predictable as they were during Democratic dominance. Previously, the choice of which Democrat would win might have been unpredictable; but it was always a Democrat who won. With renewed party competition, elections are even more volatile and less predictable. General elections are also more meaningful than they were before the changes in party loyalties. No longer do Democratic primaries automatically determine which candidate will win. As a result, Democrats no longer control the governmental process in the state; they are still very influential, but they no longer dictate policy. In short, Florida's political system has become more competitive than it has been in more than one hundred years. Whether it will remain that way is open to question.

# Virginia's Party System: From "Museum Piece" to Mainstream

## SCOTT KEETER

**8**

OBSERVERS of Virginia's party politics—as well as its participants—will be excused if they find the recent attention to realignment somewhat quaint. Little in Virginia's politics has conformed to the model of partisan politics in other parts of the South, much less the rest of the nation. Although one can find evidence of increased Republican identification among the public in recent years, the 1980s were actually a time of resurgence for the Democratic party in the Old Dominion, culminated by the election of Democrat L. Douglas Wilder as governor.

The past forty years in Virginia have seen a series of convulsive changes in the party landscape. Dominance of the state's politics shifted from one faction to another, influenced largely by external events but with effects peculiar to the state's unusual political makeup.

Recent events, however, suggest that the state is arriving at the end of the century with a genuine competitive two-party system in which Virginia Democrats and Republicans resemble their fellow partisans across the country.

### THE POLITICAL CONTEXT

The Old Dominion is a political scientist's dream and, perhaps, a voter's nightmare. An election takes place every year, a consequence of the decision to schedule state-level elections in odd-numbered years. The practice had certain benefits for the Byrd machine that initiated it. The electorate, already greatly restricted by tactics such as the poll tax, would be further reduced by inertia and the absence of interesting national elections being held at the same time as the state elections. Furthermore, the state's politics would be insulated from whatever was happening in national politics, guaranteeing greater autonomy for the Virginia way of doing things. Both consequences of odd-year elections have been felt. Turnout has always been low compared with other states; and although the national political winds have certainly been felt in Virginia, at least some of the trends in the state have run counter to what was happening nationally at the same time.

## CHANGE AND CONFUSION MARK VIRGINIA'S PARTY POLITICS

While nominally a Democratic state for much of the century, control of the Democratic party from roughly 1925 to 1965 was in the hands of a conservative, locally based oligarchy that had nothing to do with, or nothing in common with, the national Democratic party— the so-called Byrd machine, named after Senator Harry Bird, Sr. The *Almanac of American Politics* described it as "bankers and lawyers and landholders who worshipped their Revolutionary past and were filled with bitterness over the failure of their Lost Cause" (Barone and Ujifusa, 1987). The Byrd machine fought hard to keep the electorate small and predictable, and it prevented the development of an active state government that would promote education or economic development. It was also staunchly segregationist; and even when much of its constituency came to desire a more activist government, it continued to command their allegiance with its racial policies. Political scientist V. O. Key's classic book on Southern politics described Virginia as a "political museum piece" (Key 1949).

Virginia voters got some early practice in casting Republican votes in 1952 when they gave Dwight Eisenhower a large majority. Since then, the voters have given the state's presidential electoral votes to Republicans in evey election except 1964, even denying them to southerner Jimmy Carter in 1976.

On the home front, the rise of Republicanism was more gradual. Serious antiorganization challenges to the Byrd machine arose in 1949, and a Republican candidate for governor got 44 percent of the vote in 1953. Subsequently, other challenges came from within the organization in 1954. In the short run, the Supreme Court's 1954 decision in *Brown v. Board of Education of Topeka, Kansas* helped galvanize the organization against its opponents, as Virginia entered the era of massive resistance against desegregation.

However, events outside Virginia would eventually have their impact on the state's politics; and the Byrd machine's dominance would end. Perhaps the most significant change was the elimination of the poll tax by an amendment to the U.S. Constitution in 1965. Though only $1.50, voters were required to pay the poll tax for three years in order to be eligible to vote; and the last payment was due six months prior to the election. The barrier to the participation of the poor and less educated was exceedingly effective; an average of less than 10 percent of the state's adult population participated in Democratic primary elections from 1925 to 1945.

In addition to the poll tax, the literacy test was also eliminated; and the Supreme Court ruled that legislative districts must be apportioned according to population. All of those changes had the effect of shifting power to previously weak groups, especially blacks and urban workers. From 1961 to 1969, the Virginia electorate more than doubled. The Byrd machine was no longer able to control the outcome of the Democratic primary, nor was the Democratic nomination tantamount to election.

While the changes helped strengthen moderate and liberal forces in Virginia, which fought conservative organization officials for control of the Democratic party, other events were occurring that would strengthen the Republican party and damage the Democrats at the national level. An unpopular war in Vietnam led President Lyndon Johnson to decide not to seek reelection, and Richard Nixon effectively harnessed voter weariness with the war and resentment over rapid cultural change into a Republican victory in 1968. Until the Watergate affair interrupted Republican gains in the middle of the 1970s, the Democratic party suffered attrition among its traditional blue-collar constituency, developing an image of cultural liberalism and uncertainty on defense issues. That image was particularly unappealing to many of Virginia's old-guard rural Democrats.

The net effect of national events and political changes was to produce an extremely confused and fluid situation in Virginia party politics during the 1970s. For the most part, the Republican party benefited from the situation. The Democratic party was divided between conservative and moderate/liberal forces. Many conservative organization politicians fled the party, going directly to the Republicans or becoming independents as a way station on the road to the GOP. The Virginia Republican party, traditionally moderate in outlook, became more conservative with the influx of many hard-core Byrd machine individuals. That change emboldened Republican conservatives, who pushed the party further to the right.

During the period from 1966 to 1981, no Democrat won a U.S. Senate seat or gubernatorial election; Virginia was the only state in the nation to accomplish that feat. Harry Byrd, Jr., son of the organization's namesake, won reelection to the Senate as an independent (after being appointed following his father's death in 1966). The Democrats did not even field a candidate for governor in 1973, a race won by former organization Democratic governor Mills Godwin, now a Republican.

The 1980 elections began a new decade with a Republican performance that promised more disaster for the Democrats. In addition to giving Ronald Reagan a 53 percent majority (to 40 percent for Jimmy Carter), Virginia's voters elected nine conservative Republicans (and one conservative organization Democrat) to Congress. Viewed from Washington, Virginia was arguably among the nation's most Republican and conservative states.

However, beginning in 1981 the Democrats in Virginia fought back. In 1981 they swept the three executive-branch elections; in 1982 they recaptured three House seats, defeating two incumbents; in 1985 they again swept the executive-branch elections; and then they took another House seat in 1986. In 1988 a moderate Democrat who had won a special election for the House seat of the late Dan Daniel, a Byrd Democrat, won a full two-year term against a credible Republican opponent. And significantly, former governor Charles S. Robb won a Senate seat for the Democrats, the first since the 1960s.

The final, and perhaps most significant, achievement for the Democrats was the 1989 sweep of the executive-branch elections, including Douglas Wilder's victory to become the first elected black governor in U.S. history. In addition, to the surprise of everyone, a little-known automobile dealer from Falls Church won the lieutenant governorship against Republican state senator Eddy Dalton, widow of the popular governor John Dalton. And Attorney General Mary Sue Terry was reelected with 63 percent of the vote. With this third sweep of the statewide offices during the decade, the Democrats had coalesced into a formidable political force, and the Republicans found themselves in disarray. The only bright spot in a dismal decade for the Republicans was a gain of four seats in the House of Delegates, which gave them thirty-nine of one hundred seats—their greatest strength ever.

ECONOMIC AND DEMOGRAPHIC CHANGES IN VIRGINIA

Like other southern states, the economic base of Virginia has been changing all through the twentieth century. Agriculture has declined, certain sectors of manufacturing rose and then fell in importance, and—like most of the U.S.—the service sector became increasingly important. Particularly in the Tidewater region, the economy is dependent on the U.S. military and the variety of industries that support it. Northern Virginia is a company town, and the federal government—along with its entourage of consultants, lobbyists, and so forth—is the company.

The robust economy of northern and Tidewater Virginia lure thousands of educated, relatively young professional and technical people to the state each year. Their impact on the state's politics is examined in detail below. Of significance for this review of change in Virginia is the fact that a diverse and growing economy requires a more active state government—active in building roads, schools, and providing social services and amenities that its increasingly suburban population has come to expect. The government provided by organization politicians, even if clean and relatively competent, was not large enough or sophisticated enough to meet the demands of its citizenry.

Virginia's population is about 17 percent black, with small but steadily increasing Hispanic and Asian populations (about 1 percent each). Race remains an important factor in the state's politics, as it does all through the south. Black participation has increased to the point that moderate Democrats—even black candidates like Douglas Wilder—who attract large black majorities can almost always run competitive races. Outright race baiting in campaigns appears to be a thing of the past.

ELECTORAL TRENDS

As the review of recent political history shows, both the Democratic and Republican parties have shown strength in particular races at one time or another. The overall view is one of increasing competitiveness at all levels, except, of course, for the presidency. Republican and Democrats battle on even terms for U.S. House and Senate seats, for the governor's mansion, and increasingly for seats in the general as-

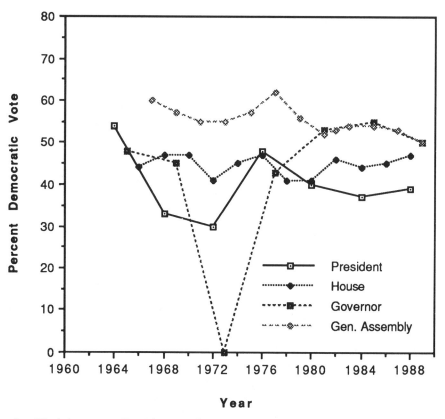

8.1 Virginia votes: President, U.S. House, governor, and general assembly, 1966–1989

sembly. Figure 8.1 shows the Democratic percentage of votes cast for the U.S. House, governor, president, and general assembly from 1966 to 1989.

In contested races for the U.S. House of Representatives, Democratic candidates have failed to receive half of the total votes cast in contested elections since the 1960s. The Democratic percentage of votes cast in contested elections reached lows of 41 percent in 1972, 1978, and 1980, but since then has been stable at 44 to 46 percent. As noted earlier, the number of U.S. House seats held by Democrats rose from only one (a conservative Byrd Democrat) in 1980 to five in 1986, where it has remained.

From 1969 to 1989, the Republican percentage of the vote for governor varied from 56 percent to 45 percent, with Republicans winning majorities from 1969–77 while losing them in the 1980s. The 1989 election for governor was decided by less than seven thousand votes out of 1.79 million cast.

Even though the Democrats continue to hold majorities in the state house and senate, Republicans have made recent gains and now have their strongest representation in the modern era. The 1987 senate elections gave Republicans ten seats (out of forty). The 1989 house elections were the most competitive ever for the Republicans, who won thirty-nine seats (out of one hundred) and received nearly 50 percent of the two-party vote in races where both a Democrat and a Republican were on the ballot.

Party performance in U.S. Senate races has been more idiosyncratic. Following victories in 1966 as the Byrd machine was disintegrating, the Democrats did not win another Senate seat until 1988, when popular former governor Charles S. Robb easily defeated Maurice Dawkins for the seat voluntarily vacated by Republican Paul Trible. Republican John Warner, first elected in 1978, claimed his third term in 1990 unopposed.

## CHANGES IN PARTY IDENTIFICATION

In terms of citizen identification with the parties, Virginia must be considered to be the least Democratic of all southern states (Wright, Erikson, and McIver 1985). However, by comparison with the rest of the South, Virginia is not especially Republican in identification. Instead, the difference is in the reluctance of its citizens to identify with any party.

Unfortunately, good survey data for tracking party identification over time does not exist in Virginia. Until the late 1970s, polling was not conducted consistently by any organization. Beginning in the late 1970s, the Media General Corporation conducted election-year polls of registered voters for its newspapers, the *Richmond Times–Dispatch* and the *Richmond News Leader*. The data provide a consistent measure of nominal partisanship for the period 1976–85. In 1985 the Survey Research Laboratory began its regular statewide survey titled the Commonwealth Poll. The analysis presented here is based principally on those two sources of data.

Figure 8.2 presents the trend of voter identification from 1976 to 1990. In this graph, no effort has been made to allocate leaners to their respective parties. Support for the Democratic party has remained relatively stable through the period, after a slight decline in the late 1970s. By contrast, Republican support increased after 1978, surging

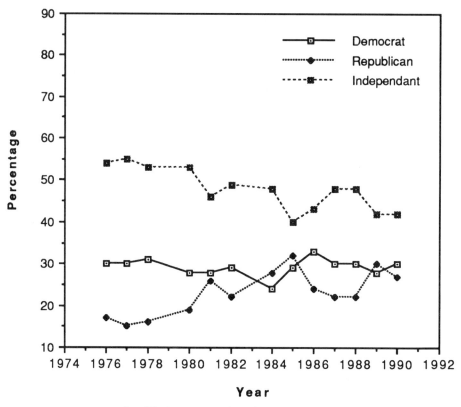

8.2 Virginia party identification, 1976–1990

with the arrival of Ronald Reagan as president. During the 1980s, the Republican party made further gains after a dip associated with the recession of 1982. Republican identification increased after the presidential elections of 1980, 1984, and 1988, with moderate declines between election years. At the beginning of the decade of the 1990s, Democratic and Republican support among Virginia citizens was nearly equal.

For purposes of examining the composition of the party groups in Virginia and looking for evidence of secular realignment in the demographics of party support, three Commonwealth Polls conducted between November 1987 and January 1989 were combined to boost the total sample size. Table 8.1 shows these data divided according to major demographic variables.

The party groups in Virginia look much like they do in most parts of the U.S. Nearly half of whites are Republican, while three-fourths

Table 8.1.   Characteristics of Party Identifiers: Virginia, 1987–1989

|  | Demo-crat (%) | Leaning Demo-crat (%) | Indepen-dent (%) | Leaning Repub-lican (%) | Repub-lican (%) |
|---|---|---|---|---|---|
| Total | 29 | 11 | 20 | 15 | 24 |
| Sex |  |  |  |  |  |
|   Male | 27 | 12 | 20 | 18 | 24 |
|   Female | 31 | 11 | 19 | 14 | 25 |
| Race |  |  |  |  |  |
|   White | 22 | 11 | 20 | 19 | 28 |
|   Black | 62 | 13 | 17 | 2 | 6 |
| Age |  |  |  |  |  |
|   18–24 | 22 | 15 | 14 | 18 | 31 |
|   25–34 | 24 | 12 | 17 | 17 | 29 |
|   35–44 | 25 | 12 | 22 | 16 | 25 |
|   45–54 | 31 | 15 | 18 | 18 | 19 |
|   55–64 | 37 | 8 | 20 | 13 | 22 |
|   65+ | 41 | 7 | 23 | 10 | 20 |
| Income |  |  |  |  |  |
|   Less than $10,000 | 42 | 10 | 22 | 6 | 20 |
|   $10,000–20,000 | 34 | 12 | 21 | 12 | 21 |
|   $20,000–30,000 | 30 | 12 | 19 | 16 | 22 |
|   $30,000–40,000 | 29 | 16 | 17 | 15 | 23 |
|   $40,000–50,000 | 19 | 7 | 19 | 23 | 33 |
|   $50,000–60,000 | 18 | 12 | 13 | 24 | 32 |
|   $60,000+ | 22 | 14 | 14 | 18 | 31 |
| Ideology |  |  |  |  |  |
|   Liberal | 47 | 16 | 14 | 10 | 13 |
|   Conservative | 21 | 10 | 17 | 21 | 31 |
|   Something else | 25 | 12 | 27 | 15 | 20 |
|   Don't think in those terms | 37 | 10 | 27 | 12 | 14 |
| Education |  |  |  |  |  |
|   Grade school | 48 | 4 | 27 | 5 | 16 |
|   Some high school | 36 | 12 | 26 | 10 | 16 |
|   High school graduate | 27 | 13 | 20 | 17 | 23 |
|   Some college, business, or tech school | 25 | 12 | 19 | 15 | 29 |
|   College graduate | 21 | 12 | 14 | 20 | 32 |
|   Post-graduate work or degree | 24 | 13 | 14 | 21 | 28 |
| Economic conditions |  |  |  |  |  |
|   Better | 25 | 12 | 19 | 18 | 26 |
|   Worse | 36 | 15 | 23 | 9 | 17 |
|   Same | 34 | 9 | 25 | 14 | 18 |
| Currently registered to vote |  |  |  |  |  |
|   Yes | 31 | 11 | 18 | 15 | 25 |
|   No | 22 | 13 | 23 | 17 | 25 |
| Length of residence |  |  |  |  |  |
|   Native Virginian | 32 | 10 | 21 | 15 | 22 |
|   More than 10 years | 25 | 10 | 18 | 18 | 29 |
|   6–10 years | 28 | 12 | 15 | 17 | 28 |
|   5 years or less | 22 | 10 | 17 | 15 | 36 |

Source: 1989 Commonwealth Poll (statewide survey of adult Virginia residents) conducted by Virginia Commonwealth University Survey Research Laboratory.

of blacks identify with the Democrats. Democratic identification is stronger among less-educated and low-income citizens and among those financially worse off or unchanged from the previous year. A very slight gender gap is evident. Nearly two-thirds of liberals identify with the Democratic party, while half of conservatives say they are Republican or leaning Republican.

### EVIDENCE OF REALIGNMENT

Realignment of citizen attachment to the parties can occur in one of two general ways: either by the conversion of citizens from one party to the other, or by the addition to the electorate of new citizens with allegiances different from those of the existing electorate. The Republican party in Virginia has benefited from both methods of realignment.

### CONVERSION

Conversion is thought to be the more difficult means of realignment, especially in the absence of a galvanizing historical event that discredits one party while giving citizens a reason to support the other. Partisan attachments, once formed, are said to be resistent to change. Even the Great Depression, which damaged the Republican party in the eyes of the public, is believed by many political scientists to have produced relatively little conversion of Republicans to Democrats. Many scholars argue that the realignment of the 1930s occurred because the depression and Roosevelt's New Deal served to bring a large number of new citizens into the electorate as Democrats—the so-called mobilization hypothesis (Andersen 1979; see Erikson and Tedin 1981 and Sundquist 1983 for dissenting views).

In Virginia, the Republican party has benefited from conversions somewhat more than the Democrats have, though movement has occurred in both directions (table 8.2). According to a 1989 Commonwealth Poll, about one-fourth of those who call themselves Republicans say that they were once Democrats. Among leaning Republicans, a third were once Democrats. Among Democrats, 17 percent say they were once Republicans; and among leaning Democrats, 19 percent were once affiliated with the GOP. Twelve percent of pure independents were once Democrats, while 4 percent were once Republicans. Among the citizenry as a whole, 14 percent previously thought of themselves as Democrats and 7 percent recalled having once considered themselves Republicans.

Table 8.2. Party Conversion and Identification: Virginia, 1989

| | *Ever thought of yourself as a (Democrat) (Republican)?* | | | *Unweighted* |
| | *Democrat (%)* | *No (%)* | *Republican (%)* | *Number of Cases* |
| --- | --- | --- | --- | --- |
| Total | 14 | 79 | 7 | 813 |
| Current party identification | | | | |
|   Democrat | — | 83 | 17 | 204 |
|   Leaning Democrat | — | 81 | 19 | 84 |
|   Independent/don't know | 12 | 84 | 4 | 139 |
|   Leaning Republican | 32 | 68 | — | 136 |
|   Republican | 23 | 77 | — | 250 |

Source: 1989 Commonwealth Poll (statewide survey of adult Virginia residents) conducted by Virginia Commonwealth University Survey Research Laboratory.

NEW VOTERS

More significant than conversion as a source of partisan change is the arrival of new voters in the Virginia electorate. On balance, the new voters have helped the Republicans more than the Democrats, but ironically the Democrats have probably benefited from the arrival of new blood, too. The new voters are of two types: those moving in from other states, and young people coming of age to vote or becoming socialized into the political process. In the short run, the most significant of the two types are the legions of citizens moving to Virginia from other states. In the long run, generational change may be more significant if a Republican majority is to be forged.

Virginia is in the midst of a rapid in-migration of citizens that rivals that of Florida, New Hampshire, or the West (*Richmond Times–Dispatch* 1988). Virginia is one of the few eastern states that will gain a U.S. House seat with reapportionment in 1992. Hundreds of people arrive daily in the state, drawn to the booming suburbs of Washington, D.C., or the Tidewater area of Norfolk, Virginia Beach, and Newport News. The newcomers are relatively young, affluent, and well educated. About half of those arriving in the last five years have a four-year college degree.

As table 8.1 shows, the newcomers are more Republican than other Virginians. Of those living in the state five years or less, 36 percent were Republicans, compared with 22 percent who said they were Democrats. By contrast, 22 percent of native Virginians said they were Republicans, compared with 32 percent Democrats. Thus, the growth in the state's population resulting from in-migration has the net effect of increasing the base of Republicans.

The full potential boost for the Republican party held by the new citizens has not yet been felt in Virginia for at least two reasons. One is that, like new arrivals anywhere, they are slow to become involved in the politics of their new home. And as a relatively young group, they are less active politically than older citizens. According to the Commonwealth Poll, nearly half of newcomers are not yet registered to vote.

The second reason is that although the newcomers are relatively affluent and presumably conservative on economic matters, their level of education and roots outside the South render them moderate-to-liberal on many social and cultural issues, and hence not necessarily in tune with Virginia's conservative Republican party. Individuals with that demographic profile are apt to support abortion rights, state lotteries, environmental protection, sex education in schools, and other policies opposed by many traditional politicians in Virginia. They also favor government spending on such things as schools, highways, and mental health, and are likely to support regulations and controls on growth that contribute to a better quality of suburban life. While such policies are not necessarily opposed by all of Virginia's Republican establishment, the agenda of the new Virginian, and his or her willingness to use government to achieve certain ends, is different in many ways from that of the Republican party that won most of the statewide elections during the 1970s.

Thus, the state's newcomers bring more Republicans to the state in name, if not yet in voting strength. When Republicans nominate moderately conservative or nonideological candidates, the newcomers will help assure victory. But the net impact of the new citizens is probably to bring greater ideological diversity to the state, a development with the potential of helping the Democratic party, too. Indeed, it is hard to imagine a black politician such as Governor Douglas Wilder winning a statewide office with an electorate composed only of native Virginians. Exit polls of voters in 1989 indicate that Wilder received approximately 40 percent of the white vote, and he fared much better in northern Virginia than in other regions of the state.

In-migration is not the only source of new voters to the system. A new cohort of Virginians turns eighteen yearly, and it is upon the youngest voters that Republicans place their greatest hopes for a realignment in partisan affiliation. Numerous surveys nationally as well as in the states have shown a surge of Republicanism among younger citizens (Norpoth 1987).

The simplest explanation for the phenomenon is Ronald Reagan. Citizens socialized to politics during the 1980s saw the Republican party embodied in a popular and strong politician who presided over a period of relative peace and prosperity. The contrast with the previous chief executive was not helpful to the Democrats, as Republicans missed no opportunity to associate Jimmy Carter with the inflation of the 1970s, as well as international problems such as the Iranian hostage affair.

Virginia was not immune to Reagan's influence on the image of the Republican party. Figure 8.2 shows the surge in Republican identification following Reagan's election in 1980, interrupted briefly by the recession of 1982, and continuing into the latter half of the decade. The surge was felt most strongly among those citizens with the weakest prior attachments to party—the young. John McGlennon's analysis of Media General polling data from 1981–85 showed that the growth of Republican identification among citizens aged eighteen to twenty-five—14 percentage points—was greater than for any other demographic group in the population (McGlennon 1988). The analysis also suggested that, on balance, the growth was largely at the expense of independent identification, as the percentage of Democrats among that age group declined only one point over the period.

Viewed in cross-section, pooled data from the Commonwealth Poll in 1987–89 show the distinctiveness of young Virginians. Figure 8.3 shows the relationship of party identification and age (also see table 8.1). The highest percentage of pure Republican identification (31 percent) is found among Virginians aged eighteen to twenty-four, with those aged twenty-five to thirty-four just behind at 29 percent. Combining leaners and pure partisans, about half of the youngest cohorts of Virginians are Republican in their political orientation. That compares with less than one-third of the oldest cohort.

Young people are notoriously fickle politically and, in addition, are less likely than older citizens to participate in politics. They are also more likely to think of themselves as liberals, and thus where certain issues are concerned, to find themselves in disagreement with the Republican party. Yet Republicans everywhere must be encouraged by the pattern of party identification among the young. Every year that passes with a Republican president in the White House and without

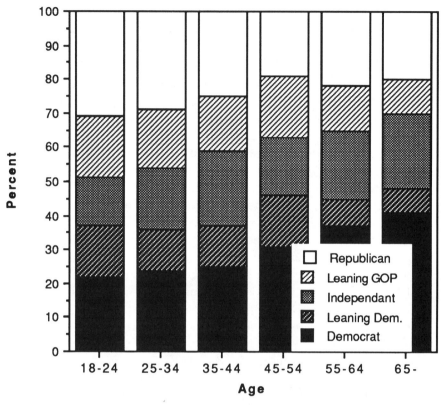

8.3 Virginia party identification by age, 1987–1989

events discrediting the Republican party helps to solidify the self-image of Republican young people. A key mechanism of secular realignment is operating smoothly in Virginia and across the nation.

### DUAL-PARTY IDENTIFICATION?

Some observers of southern politics have argued that many southerners continue to think of themselves as Democrats on the local level and Republicans in national elections. This would be a rational response of conservatives to the situation in much of the south, where the local Republican party is still weak and seldom fields reasonable alternatives to Democratic candidates. However, there is little evidence that many of Virginia's citizens carry such a dual-party identification. Respondents in a 1988 Commonwealth Poll were asked about their party affiliation in elections for federal offices and then for state offices. Nine out of ten gave the same answer for both questions. The Republican party, as expected, was a little more likely to have consistency between the levels of identification, but the differences are minor. Among state-level Democrats, 90 pecent said they were Democrats in national elections, while 96 percent of state-level Republicans identified as Republicans at the national level.

## DISCUSSION

Virginia's politics and its citizens have been in a state of realignment for more than two decades. Some of the change has mirrored trends in the nation at large or the South as a whole. But the process of change has been unlike that in most places, because Virginia had a unique political environment when it began to change.

Over the past two decades, Virginia has in most respects become more like the rest of the nation and less like the Old South. For its party system to change as the rest of the state was changing, a great deal of chaos was probably necessary. That chaos appears to be mostly, if not completely, at an end. The future of realignment in Virginia will probably be determined in much the same way as states all across the U.S.

### VIRGINIA'S CONSERVATISM: CATALYST FOR REPUBLICAN REALIGNMENT?

Numerous observers have remarked on Virginia's conservatism. Certainly its state and local officials through the Byrd era were exceedingly conservative in almost every respect. Most of its representatives to the U.S. House and Senate, Democrat and Republican alike, have been to the right of thier colleagues in both parties.

The state's conservatism, especially as manifested in election outcomes through the 1970s, suggests that Virginia should be in the vanguard of an emerging Republican majority. But a number of factors will slow and perhaps prevent such an eventuality. First, the state's Republican party organization remains weak at the grass-roots level. It is well financed and has made effective use of the new campaign technologies that are the stuff of modern politics. But if "all politics is local," the Republicans have lacked the local organization and leadership to challenge the Democrats for control of the general assembly and the important political powers that come with it—among others, the right to draw congressional district lines. The paucity of opportunities for winning entry-level offices also hurts recruitment. Promising young political talent must still figure that it's better to be a Democrat and have a chance of getting elected. That fact has consequences for the quality of the party's candidates at all levels.

Second, while the Democrats remain better organized at the local level, they have also made substantial progress in building an effective state-level organization, emulating the techniques used successfully by Republicans. They have also been fortunate in the political development of two men, former governors Charles S. Robb and Gerald Baliles. Both were very popular incumbents with political philosophies in the mainstream. Robb, son-in-law of the late president Lyndon B. Johnson, was the more conservative of the two but rewarded important parts of the Democratic coalition by appointing many blacks and women to offices in state government. Baliles continued the pattern of appointments started by Robb and championed an expansion of the state's role in education, transportation, and mental health, among other areas. Robb parlayed his popularity into a Senate seat, and many believe Baliles will seek public office again in the future.

More generally, there is ample reason to question the image of Virginia as exceptionally conservative, at least in the 1980s. Public opinion is a very slippery entity, a function both of the underlying philosophy of the citizenry and the cues of its leaders. Both the citizenry and its leaders are becoming more diverse in Virginia. New arrivals to the state bring new attitudes. New politicians (or old ones emboldened by the example of others) show the public new directions. The result is a public with attitudes not so different from the rest of the nation.

Several items asked on the statewide Commonwealth Poll over the past few years call into question the distinctiveness of the Virginia public. In July 1988, respondents were asked whether they favored "a smaller national government providing fewer services, or bigger government providing more services." The public divided evenly between the options (39 percent bigger and 37 percent smaller), almost exactly the same distribution found by CBS News and the *New York Times* when they asked an identical question of a national sample in May 1988. When asked in the fall of 1989 if they would favor "a smaller state government providing fewer services, or bigger government providing more services," a majority of Virginians chose an expanded state government (by a margin of 51 percent to 28 percent). Similarly, on questions on government health care for the indigent, support for Contra aid, protection of the environment, abortion, and other issues, Virginians were virtually indistinguishable from their fellow citizens in the nation as a whole.

Electorally, Virginians will probably continue to give Republican presidential candidates a larger share of their votes than is true nationwide. That is certainly one measure of conservatism. But Virginia's electoral conservatism is a matter of degree, as evidenced by the unpopularity of conservative evangelists Jerry Falwell and Pat Robertson, himself the son of a U.S. senator and member of the Byrd organization. Virginia's voters have also surprised its leaders in recent years, approving referenda to establish a state lottery and pari-mutuel betting. Highest levels of support for the referenda were seen in precisely those areas of the state currently undergoing rapid inmigration.

CONCLUSION

Even as the New Deal party alignment appears less and less relevant in U.S. politics, one can see evidence that the basic contours of the New Deal party system have finally arrived in Virginia. Contemporary discussions of realignment throughout much of the U.S. focus on the possible replacement of a Democratic majority. For Virginia, Republican parity—if not majority—might have been the natural state of affairs since the New Deal were it not for the historical circumstances that bound Virginia and the rest of the South to the Democratic party.

However, Republican hegemony is not the likely outcome of change in Virginia. The delayed realignment in Virginia arrives at the time that the state's public is rapidly becoming more diverse. Many of Virginia's new citizens—and many of its natives—want things from government that the Democratic party is accustomed to supporting. Splits within the Democratic party, and the continuing development of the Republican party have made it possible for Democrats to be Democrats in Virginia. As a result, the state's citizens are increasingly presented with choices in its elections—something that was usually not true in the Byrd era. A mature, competitive two-party system is in the making in Virginia. For the state's citizens, it's about time.

# Wisconsin Electoral Politics: Realignment Bypasses the Badger State

JOHN F. BIBBY

STATE politics does not function in isolation from national political forces. Partisan loyalties are often forged in the heat of presidential campaigns, and voters do tend to support the same parties in national and state elections. Even so, state political parties have been able to establish distinctive bases of electoral support (Epstein 1982, 71). Each of the states has its own peculiar history, political culture, economy, and demographic composition. The national partisan alignment, therefore, "extends in different ways to different states, making for Republican or Democratic dominance in some situations and for serious Republican-Democratic competition in others" (Epstein 1986, 124). In Wisconsin the interplay of national and state-level forces has produced an electoral alignment that shows similarities to the national pattern, but which is also unique.

Unlike the South (Lamis 1984) and Mountain West (Galderisi et al. 1987), Wisconsin has not witnessed a major electoral realignment. In spite of Republican successes nationally in the 1970s and 1980s, the state's Democrats have continued to enjoy an advantage in terms of the voters' party identification. Statewide elections have remained competitive; Democrats have held firm control of the legislature, most constitutional offices, and a majority of the U.S. House seats; incumbent members of Congress and the state legislature have achieved consistent electoral success; voters have engaged in a high level of ticket-splitting; and independence from party affiliations and interest groups has remained an admired attribute of political leaders.

## THE WISCONSIN SETTING

In spite of its reputation for progressive social legislation and the tendency of Democratic presidential candidates to run stronger within the state than they have nationally, Wisconsin has deep Republican roots. Indeed, a recent study of the impact of state political culture showed that Wisconsin has a higher level of Republican identifiers than would be predicted by the demographics of its population (Erikson, McIver, and Wright 1987, 805).

### DEMOGRAPHIC CHARACTERISTICS

Wisconsin ranks sixteenth among the states in population with 4.9 million residents, but like most midwestern states it is lagging behind the nation in its rate of population growth (Voss 1988). With an economy that relies heavily on manufacturing, a 33 percent blue-collar work force, an activist labor movement, a substantial Catholic population (many of whom have eastern and southern European backgrounds), a major metropolitan area (Milwaukee) with an expanding black and Hispanic population, and a large marginal farming area in the northwest, the state provides a strong base of voters with characteristics that encourage Democratic proclivities. There are, however, characteristics of the population that operate to hold down Democratic electoral strength. With the decline of the state's manufacturing sector, the percentage of the population affiliated with organized labor has declined since the early 1970s. Wisconsin has a minority population well below the national average. Blacks constitute only 4 percent of the population and Hispanics but 1 percent. Jews are only .7 of a percent of the population. Wisconsin is also below the national average in terms of the percentage of its population with incomes below the government's poverty line.

A particularly important feature of the state population is the extent to which its people are scattered among small and medium-sized cities rather than major metropolitan areas. Wisconsin has only two cities with populations in excess of 100,000—Milwaukee (628,000) and Madison (191,000). Both are heavily Democratic in their voting patterns. Of the nineteen cities with populations between 30,000 and 100,000, only a few consistently turn in large Democratic pluralities. In addition, there are thirty-seven municipalities in the 10,000 to 29,999 population range. Traditionally, small and medium-sized cities have been an important base of Republican electoral strength (Epstein 1958, 57–76).

## ONE-PARTY, MULTI-PARTY, AND TWO-PARTY POLITICS

Wisconsin was a bastion of Republicanism in both national and state voting from the Civil War until the 1930s. From early in the 1900s until the Great Depression, the most meaningful state elections were the Republican primaries as the stalwart (conservative) and progressive wings of the party battled for ascendancy. The moribund Democratic party's gubernatorial candidates averaged only 28.4 percent of the vote in the 1920s and won statewide elections and control of the state legislature only under unusual circumstances, such as the 1932 Roosevelt landslide.

When Republican fortunes ebbed in the early 1930s, the progressive Republicans led by Senator Robert La Follette, Jr., and his brother, former governor Philip La Follette, formed the Progressive party. The Progressives became the GOP's major competition in congressional and state elections, as Wisconsin and Minnesota became the only two states in which a third party captured control of the governorship and state legislature during the 1930s. The Democrats—an organizationally weak, ideologically conservative, and patronage-oriented party— remained a minor force in most state elections other than presidential contests.

In the post–World War II era, the force of the national political alignments was just too strong to sustain a three-party system in the state. Faced with declining electoral prospects and the likelihood of sweeping Republican electoral victories in 1946, the Progressives voted to disband and to reenter the Republican party. Although many Progressives in urban areas did not follow their leaders back into the GOP, the return of substantial numbers of Progressives helped ensure continued Republican dominance of Wisconsin electoral politics for a decade (Epstein 1958, 51–54; Sundquist 1983, 248; Dykstra and Reynolds 1978, 229–326). The demise of the Progressive party did, however, result in many rank-and-file Progressive voters shifting their allegiance to the Democrats. As a result, the Democratic share of the gubernatorial vote rose in the 1940s from 12.3 percent in 1942 to 44.1 percent in 1948.

The Republicans were challenged after the war by a new state Democratic party whose leaders espoused a liberal ideology consistent with that of the national party. The new Wisconsin Democratic party was also similar to the party nationally in terms of the sectors of the population from which it drew its support. The Democrats achieved their first major post-war statewide electoral victory with the election of William Proxmire to the Senate in a special election in 1957 and followed it with gubernatorial victories in 1958, 1960, and 1962. In 1974, the party gained control of both houses of the legislature for the first time since 1932 and has maintained firm legislative control since that time.

Wisconsin in the 1980s and early 1990s was characterized by competitive two-party politics for control of the governorship, other state constitutional offices, the state legislature, and U.S. Senate seats. In this struggle, however, the Democrats have had a distinct edge since 1970, especially in legislative elections.

THE LEGAL AND CULTURAL ENVIRONMENT FOR PARTISANSHIP

Wisconsin's election laws reflect the state's Progressive heritage and its distinctly antiparty organization bias. The legal climate is not conducive to allowing cohesive organizations to control nominations, mobilize voters, or dispense patronage. Municipal and judicial elections are nonpartisan, and the state does not have partisan voter registration. The party and candidate organizations must, therefore, rely on expensive and labor-intensive efforts to identify their supporters and get them to the polls on election day. In addition, Wisconsin uses an open primary to nominate partisan candidates, thereby severely restricting the capacity of party organizations to control nominations. With only an extremely limited number of patronage appointments available to the governor and a moral climate that has brought the state clean and honest government, little in the way of patronage or government preferments nurtures party organizations. Finally, campaign finance legislation restricts the parties' role in financing campaigns. As Leon D. Epstein observed, "Wisconsin treats parties as though they might pervert the real will of the voters" (Epstein 1958, 31).

Wisconsin election laws have strengthened the state's strongly individualistic political tradition. In commenting on the impact of the state'e fierce adherence during the 1980s to the open presidential primary in the face of sanctions by the national Democratic party, Epstein noted:

voters in Wisconsin have had no experience with a system in which they must publicly disclose their party preference in order to cast primary ballots . . . a requirement of public disclosure of party preference, as condition for primary voting, would for many Wisconsin citizens violate the secrecy of the ballot much as would a forced disclosure of party preference in the general election (1986, 230).

Evidence of Wisconsinites' weak support for parties and tendency to glorify political independence abound in both survey data and election outcomes. The research of Jack Dennis (1980, 1975) presents a portrait of an electorate with (1) lower levels of party identification than either the Gallup Poll or Center for Political Studies/Survey Research Center found in the electorate nationally, and (2) weak and diminishing support for a party role in the political process. In keeping with the state's party-weakening electoral laws and the electorate's weak level of support for party institutions, Wisconsin voters have shown a special affinity for maverick politicians who have flouted their independence and stood against the party establishment. Although different in ideology and policy orientation, the Senators Robert La Follette, Sr. and Jr.; Joseph McCarthy; and William Proxmire all exemplify the maverick tradition, as did Governor Lee Sherman Dreyfus (elected in 1978 while claiming he was a Republicrat). More recently in 1988, Milwaukee businessman Herbert Kohl won the Democratic senatorial primary and the general election while stressing that he was not a politician and that his multimillion dollar contributions to his own campaign would assure his independence in Washington. He said he would be "nobody's senator but yours!"

Although Wisconsin does not have either a legal or cultural environment that is conducive to strong party organizations, the state has developed a type of party organization that is untypical of American state parties. Because of the unusually restrictive nature of state legislation regulating the statutory party organizations, conservative Republican activists in the late 1920s created an extra-legal or voluntary party organization that quickly became the dominant Republican organization in the state (Sorauf 1954). Late in the 1940s, the Democrats developed a similar extra-legal party organization. These voluntary associations with thousands of dues-paying/card-carrying party members resemble mass membership parties (Epstein 1958, 96–97; Adamany 1969, 25), in contrast to the more common American pattern of cadre parties. Thus, ironically, in the antiparty atmosphere of Wisconsin, mass membership-type party organizations were developed that have exhibited striking traits of durability and adaptability.

In the 1980s, the Republican party in particular has been strengthened in its capacity to provide campaign assistance to candidates by the infusion of national party financial and technical resources.

## PARTY IDENTIFICATION AMONG WISCONSINITES

Since 1964 the Democrats have held a relatively consistent advantage over the Republicans in terms of partisan identifiers, though in 1984–86 the parties were at rough parity (see table 9.1). While the Republican proportion of party identifiers in Wisconsin is quite close to the party's share of the national electorate, the state has proportionately fewer Democratic identifiers than exist in the country as a whole.

Table 9.1 demonstrates that no partisan realignment has occurred in Wisconsin since the 1960s. In the 1980s, the percentages for Republican and Democratic identifiers have remained quite stable, with Republican identifiers staying within a 20 to 28 percent range and the Democrats showing a 27 to 32 percentage point spread. The gains registered by the Republicans in the South and Mountain West have not been replicated in the Badger State. Indeed, Wisconsin's electorate seems to have contributed its share of independents to the national

Table 9.1.  Trends in Party Identification: Wisconsin, 1964–1990

|      | Republican | Democrat | Independent | Other[a] |
|------|-----------|----------|-------------|----------|
| 1964 | 28[b]     | 42       | 25          | 5        |
| 1966 | 27        | 39       | 26          | 8        |
| 1970 | 28        | 31       | 29          | 12       |
| 1972 | 29        | 32       | 27          | 12       |
| 1974 | 23        | 36       | 26          | 14       |
| 1976 | 23        | 33       | 33          | 10       |
| 1980 | 20        | 31       | 39          | 10       |
| 1982 | 21        | 27       | 42          | 10       |
| 1984 | 28        | 28       | 37          | 7        |
| 1986 | 26        | 27       | 38          | 9        |
| 1988 | 25        | 32       | 32          | 11       |
| 1990 | 26        | 32       | 37          | 5        |

Sources: 1964–76 and 1984 data provided by Professor Jack Dennis, University of Wisconsin–Madison, from surveys conducted by the University of Wisconsin Survey Research Laboratory; 1980 and 1982 data derived from surveys conducted by Market Opinion Research; 1986–1990 data derived from *Milwaukee Journal* surveys.

[a]Includes no preference, don't know, and no answer.
[b]Totals may not sum to 100 due to rounding.

tendency toward dealignment. Persons identifying themselves as independents first surpassed Republican identifiers in 1970, and in 1980 they also outnumbered Democrats. The Democrats have sustained a substantially larger drop in partisan identifiers than have the Republicans, but the GOP has not seen a proportionate rise in its percentage of partisan identifiers. As it has since the 1960s, the Democratic party enters the 1990s holding an advantage over the GOP in terms of the voters' partisan orientation.

Although the Republican party is in the minority within the party-in-the-electorate, it tends to be organizationally stronger than the Democratic party. The regular party organizations (state and county committees) are a more important campaign resource for Republican candidates at all levels than is the Democratic party organization for its candidates. Democratic candidates must rely more heavily on their own personal campaign organizations and groups allied with the party such as labor unions, the Wisconsin Education Association Council, and the Farmers Union. The most important party organizations for the Democrats are the legislative campaign committees composed of incumbent state representatives and senators. Majority status in the legislature has enabled those committees to raise substantial funds from interest groups and has made it possible for them to provide significant technical and financial assistance to their party's legislative candidates. The Republican legislative campaign committees are also major participants in legislative elections.

In addition to party identification, the extent of Wisconsin voters' attachment to political parties in terms of their party loyalty on election day should be considered. Data derived from surveys taken between 1980 and 1989, in which voters were asked about how they cast their ballots in the last general election, show that Wisconsinites are prone to split their tickets. Ticket-splitters outnumbered both Republican and Democratic voters and constituted approximately 40 percent of the electorate during the 1980s. The pattern of ticket splitting is reflected in the differing partisan outcomes among presidential, senatorial, congressional, gubernatorial, and legislative elections (and will be discussed later).

PARTY COMPOSITION

The social characteristics of partisans in Wisconsin follow the expected national patterns. Table 9.2 reports the responses of voters in 1989 when asked about how they usually voted in past elections. The

Table 9.2.  Characteristics of Party Identifiers and Likely Voting Behavior: Wisconsin, 1989

| | Mostly Repub- licans (%) | A Few More Re- publicans than Demo- crats (%) | Ticket- Splitter Inde- pendents/ Vote for the Man (%) | A Few More Democrats than Repub- licans (%) | Mostly Demo- crats (%) | Don't Know/ No Answer (%) |
|---|---|---|---|---|---|---|
| **Age** | | | | | | |
| 18–24 | 30 | 24 | 9 | 8 | 22 | 7 |
| 25–29 | 41 | 20 | 9 | 13 | 16 | 1 |
| 30–34 | 23 | 22 | 4 | 16 | 33 | 1 |
| 40–44 | 28 | 23 | 12 | 16 | 22 | — |
| 45–54 | 21 | 17 | 11 | 26 | 23 | 2 |
| 55–64 | 27 | 11 | 16 | 19 | 27 | — |
| 65+ | 31 | 11 | 15 | 11 | 31 | 2 |
| **Education** | | | | | | |
| Less than high school | 22 | 6 | 21 | 14 | 35 | 1 |
| High school graduate | 28 | 16 | 12 | 17 | 25 | 3 |
| Some college | 27 | 26 | 5 | 17 | 25 | — |
| College graduate | 27 | 26 | 5 | 17 | 25 | — |
| **Race/Ethnicity** | | | | | | |
| Black | 23 | — | 3 | 17 | 57 | — |
| Hispanic | 11 | 22 | 22 | 22 | 11 | 11 |
| **Gender** | | | | | | |
| Male/employed | 26 | 22 | 12 | 16 | 23 | 1 |
| Male/unemployed | 27 | 16 | 14 | 12 | 31 | 2 |
| Female at home | 33 | 11 | 15 | 14 | 25 | 2 |
| Female/employed | 24 | 20 | 3 | 22 | 27 | 2 |
| Union household | 15 | 15 | 11 | 23 | 35 | 2 |
| Nonunion household | 33 | 20 | 10 | 14 | 21 | 2 |
| **Income** | | | | | | |
| Less than $10,000 | 26 | 9 | 22 | 11 | 29 | 3 |
| $10,000–19,999 | 22 | 15 | 12 | 17 | 29 | 3 |
| $20,000–29,999 | 27 | 19 | 7 | 21 | 25 | 1 |
| $30,000–39,999 | 24 | 20 | 10 | 19 | 26 | 1 |
| $40,000–49,999 | 29 | 17 | 6 | 21 | 26 | 1 |
| $50,000+ | 36 | 28 | 8 | 10 | 17 | 1 |
| **Religion** | | | | | | |
| Evangelical | 86 | 5 | 10 | — | — | — |
| Conservative Catholics | 30 | 21 | 9 | 18 | 21 | 1 |
| Other Catholics | 13 | 16 | 14 | 22 | 34 | 1 |
| Conservative main- stream Protestants | 40 | 26 | 8 | 10 | 15 | 2 |
| Other mainstream Protestants | 17 | 13 | 9 | 22 | 36 | 1 |
| Other/no church | 22 | 13 | 15 | 17 | 29 | 4 |

Source: 1989 survey by Tarrance and Associates.

data reveal that the following characteristics are associated with Democratic party voting: employed female, lower educational level, lower
income, black race, Catholicism, and union household. Republicanism is associated with the following characteristics: employed
male, youth, college education, middle and upper income, non-union
household, Evangelical Protestantism, conservative mainstream Protestantism, and conservative Catholicism.

The fugitive nature of survey data for the decades before the 1980s
severely complicates the task of identifying changes in the level of
support the two parties have received from various social groups over
time. It does appear, however, that Democratic support among Catholics and younger voters has declined since the 1960s, while the party's
support among middle- and upper-income Wisconsinites has increased. Over all, however, no dramatic shifts in the bases of party
support are readily identifiable since the 1970s.

Wisconsin politics has a reputation for being ideological and policy-
oriented (Fenton 1966; Adamany 1969, 23–32). Since the 1960s party
activists have been shown to have strongly liberal orientations in the
Democratic party and conservative orientations in the GOP (Adamany
1969, 30). The extent of ideological polarization among the two major
parties' identifiers is reflected in table 9.3. Liberals constitute the
largest ideological group among Democratic identifiers, while conser-

Table 9.3. Ideology of Party Identifiers: Wisconsin, 1984–1990

|  | 1984 (%) | 1986 (%) | 1990 (%) |
|---|---|---|---|
| Democrat |  |  |  |
| Liberal | 56.9[a] | 47.4 | 55.5 |
| Middle of the road | 6.9 | 11.9 | 7.0 |
| Conservative | 36.3 | 41.6 | 34.0 |
| Republican |  |  |  |
| Liberal | 21.2 | 37.1 | 23.4 |
| Middle of the road | 11.0 | 4.2 | 3.0 |
| Conservative | 67.8 | 58.6 | 73.1 |
| Independent |  |  |  |
| Liberal | 33.1 | 31.9 | 38.7 |
| Middle of the road | 16.5 | 20.2 | 19.3 |
| Conservative | 50.4 | 47.9 | 38.5 |

Sources: 1984, 1986, and 1990 derived from St. Norbert College Wisconsin
surveys.

[a] Raw totals do not sum to 100% due to rounding and respondents' citing
alternative ideologies.

Table 9.4.  Trends in Ideology: Wisconsin, 1984–1990

|              | 1984 (%) | 1986 (%) | 1989 (%) | 1990 (%) |
|--------------|----------|----------|----------|----------|
| Liberal      | 37.4     | 37.5     | 34.0     | 41.1     |
| Moderate     | 11.3     | 5.7      | 11.0     | 8.3      |
| Conservative | 51.1     | 56.7     | 55.0     | 50.6     |

Sources: 1984, 1986, and 1990 derived from St. Norbert College Wisconsin surveys; 1989 data derived from Tarrance and Associates Survey.

vatives are the largest ideological group among Republicans. Neither party, however, is ideologically homogenous. The Democratic ranks contain a sizeable proportion of self-perceived conservatives; and the GOP has its share of liberals and moderates, although Republican identifiers do seem to have become more heavily conservative in their orientation.

Whether seen from the perspective of the parties' social group makeup or their identifiers' ideological orientation, Wisconsin parties do not appear to have undergone major changes in the 1980s. Nor do the voters appear to have become more conservative in their self-professed ideological orientation. As table 9.4 indicates, between 1984 and 1990, there was no apparent growth in ideological conservativism within the state.

## PATTERNS OF INTERPARTY COMPETITION

The long period of Republican electoral dominance ended in 1957 with William Proxmire's special election victory in the U.S. Senate contest to replace the deceased Joseph McCarthy. By 1958 the state emerged clearly as a two-party battleground in which the Democrats hold an advantage. A two-tiered electoral system has developed not unlike that which exists at the national level, where the GOP has shown a remarkable ability to win the presidency, while the Democrats have dominated congressional elections. In Wisconsin, the Republicans have shown a capacity to compete effectively in major state-wide races for president, senator, governor, and attorney general; but Democratic dominance of the state legislature has been complete since 1974.

### GUBERNATORIAL ELECTIONS

In the thirteen gubernatorial elections between 1956 and 1990, the Republicans and Democrats have been locked in tight competition,

Table 9.5.  Party Control of State Constitutional Offices: Wisconsin, 1956–1990

|  | Party Winning the Office | | | |
|---|---|---|---|---|
|  | Lt. Gov. | Secy. of State | State Treas. | Atty. Gen. |
| 1956 | R | R | R | R |
| 1958 | D | R | D | D |
| 1960 | R | R | R | D |
| 1962 | R | R | R | R |
| 1964 | D | R | R | D |
| 1966 | R | R | R | D |
| 1968 | R | R | R | R |
| 1970[a] | D[b] | R | D | R |
| 1974 | D | D | D | D |
| 1978 | R | D | D | D |
| 1982 | D | D | D | D |
| 1986 | R | D | D | R |
| 1990 | R | D | R | D |
|  | Party Election Victories | | | |
| Before 1974 | R 5 | R 8 | R 6 | R 4 |
|  | D 3 | D 0 | D 2 | D 4 |
| After 1974 | R 3 | R 0 | R 1 | R 1 |
|  | D 2 | D 5 | D 4 | D 4 |
| Total | R 8 | R 8 | R 7 | R 5 |
|  | D 5 | D 5 | D 6 | D 8 |

[a]Beginning in 1970 all constitutional officers were elected for four-year terms instead of two-year terms.

[b]Beginning in 1970 the lieutenant governor was elected on a combined ticket with the governor. Prior to 1970 the governor and lieutenant governor were elected separately.

with the Republicans winning seven times and the Democrats six. No winning gubernatorial candidate has received more than 58 percent of the major party vote, and the average winning percentage has been 54 percent.

STATE CONSTITUTIONAL OFFICES

After Democrats won the governorship in 1958, it took the party another sixteen years to assert control over the constitutional offices of lieutenant governor, secretary of state, state treasurer, and attorney general (see table 9.5). The state's Republican traditions and well-known GOP incumbents kept those offices under mostly Republican control until 1974. With GOP fortunes at a low ebb in 1974 due to the Watergate scandals in Washington, Democratic governor Patrick Lucey coasted to an easy reelection victory; and a period of sustained Democratic dominance of the constitutional offices was begun. Due to the low public visibility of the constitutional offices below the governor, a well-known political name has been a major asset for candidates of both parties. For example, persons with a last name of Smith were elected state treasurer in all but three elections between 1938 and 1990; and a Zimmerman or La Follette has won the secretary of state's office in every election but two between 1938 and 1990.

STATE LEGISLATIVE ELECTIONS

The Republicans' dominance of both houses of the state legislature ended in 1958, when the Democrats won control of the state assembly (see figure 9.1). The GOP regained the chamber briefly in the 1960, 1962, 1966, and 1968 elections, only to lose it on a continuing basis in 1970. It was not until 1974 that Democrats achieved majority status in the state senate. Since that time, however, the Democrats have maintained uninterrupted control of both chambers of the legislature.

In the years immediately after World War II, there was substantial turnover in the membership of the legislature. Members viewed their positions as part-time jobs, and voluntary retirement was commonplace. Nor was it unusual for incumbents to lose their seats in the primaries or general elections (an average of 17 percent of assembly members were defeated and 13 percent of the senators up for election lost their seats every two years).

The present-day legislature, by contrast, is characterized by low membership turnover. It is a professionalized body, and the job of the legislators has become virtually full time. The advantages of incumbency (staff, mailing allowance, opportunities for constituency service, policy advocacy, and fund-raising) have expanded dramatically. In the five elections between 1980 and 1988, 83 percent of assembly and 79 percent of senate incumbents sought reelection. Incumbents' reelection rates are even more impressive. Both assembly and senate incumbents in the 1980s had a reelection rate of 93 percent (Jewell and Breaux 1988). The tremendous advantages currently enjoyed by incumbents, of course, have substantially impeded shifts in partisan control of the assembly and senate. Like their Democratic counterparts in the U. S. House of Representatives, Wisconsin Democrats appear firmly entrenched in the legislature.

Democratic dominance of the state legislature appears to be a major counterrealigning force in Wisconsin politics. This dominance stems not only from incumbents' electoral advantages, but also from differ-

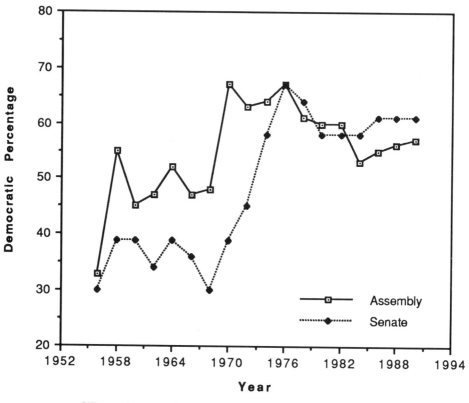

9.1 Wisconsin votes: State assembly and senate seats, 1956–1990

ences in the two parties' abilities to recruit strong legislative candidates. With service in the legislature having become professionalized and practically a full-time position, candidate recruitment has been made more difficult for the GOP. Individuals working the private sector find it increasingly hard to combine a legislative career with managing a small business or practicing a profession. Full-time political careers hold limited appeal for many young Republican-oriented business and professional people. Yet it has been from the ranks of such individuals that the GOP has traditionally recruited its legislative candidates. Potentially strong candidates from among Democratic clientele groups, by contrast, tend to be attracted to the prospect of full-time legislative positions and careers in government. For example, the Democrats have been more effective than the Republicans in using legislative staff positions as training grounds for future legislative candidates (Ehrenhalt 1989, 28–33). After analyzing candidate recruitment in Wisconsin, Alan Ehrenhalt observed: "Within the corridors of the state capital . . . the biennial legislative elections are recognized for what they really are: *a competition to attract candidates who have the skills and energy to win and the desire and resourcefulness to stay in office . . . This is the competition that the Democrats keep winning"* (emphasis added) (1989, 29–30). The seeming advantage that the Democrats hold in legislative candidate recruitment has implications that reach beyond which party controls the legislature. It is from the ranks of state legislators that some of the strongest candidates for governor and U.S. Senator and Representative are often drawn. Thus, in 1990 both the Republican and Democratic candidates for governor and lieutenant governor were former legislators, as was the attorney general and the senior U.S. Senator. In addition, seven of the nine House incumbents were former legislators.

DIVIDED PARTISAN CONTROL OF STATE GOVERNMENT

The pattern of genuine two-party competition for the governorship combined with one-party control of the legislature has made divided partisan control of state government commonplace. In twenty of the thirty-two years between 1958 (when the Democrats captured the governorship for the first time since 1932) and 1990, Wisconsin has had at least one house of the legislature controlled by a different party than that of the governor.

FEDERAL ELECTIONS

*Presidential elections.* Although the Republicans have carried the state for their presidential candidate in four of the last six elections, the party's winning percentage of the vote in Wisconsin has been consistently smaller than its national percentage (see table 9.5). In its presidential voting, Wisconsin has tended to follow national trends and has voted for the winning presidential candidate in seven of the last nine elections (the exceptions were 1960 when the state narrowly supported Nixon over Kennedy, and 1988 when Michael Dukakis won the state's electoral votes against George Bush).

*Senate and House elections.* In Senate and House elections, Wisconsin voters have been decidedly less supportive of the GOP than in presidential elections. Between 1962 and 1980, the Democrats held both Senate seats. It was not until Robert Kasten's defeat of Gaylord Nelson in 1980 and his reelection in 1986 that the Republicans were able to break the Democrats' string of eight consecutive senatorial victories. The narrowness of Kasten's two elections (50.2 percent in 1980; 51 percent in 1986) and Democrat Herbert Kohl's 1988 winning with

Table 9.6. Outcomes of Federal Elections: Wisconsin, 1956–1990

| | % of Popular Vote for President | | No. of Representatives Elected | | % of Popular Vote for Senator | |
|---|---|---|---|---|---|---|
| | R | D | R | D | R | D |
| 1956 | 61.6 | 37.8 | 7 | 3 | 58.6 | 41.2 |
| 1957 | | | | | 40.5[a] | 56.4[a] |
| 1958 | | | 5 | 5 | 42.7 | 57.1 |
| 1960 | 51.8 | 48.1 | 6 | 4 | | |
| 1962 | | | 6 | 4 | 47.2 | 52.6 |
| 1964 | 37.7 | 62.1 | 5 | 5 | 46.6 | 53.3 |
| 1966 | | | 7 | 3 | | |
| 1968 | 47.9 | 44.3 | 7 | 3 | 38.3 | 61.7 |
| 1970 | | | 5 | 5 | 28.5 | 70.8 |
| 1972 | 53.4 | 43.7 | 4 | 5 | | |
| 1974 | | | 2 | 7 | 35.8 | 61.8 |
| 1976 | 47.8 | 49.4 | 2 | 7 | 27.0 | 72.2 |
| 1978 | | | 3 | 6 | | |
| 1980 | 49.9 | 43.2 | 4 | 5 | 50.2 | 48.3 |
| 1982 | | | 4 | 5 | 34.1 | 63.6 |
| 1984 | 54.3 | 45.1 | 4 | 5 | | |
| 1986 | | | 4 | 5 | 51.0 | 49.0 |
| 1988 | 47.8 | 51.6 | 4 | 5 | 47.5 | 52.1 |
| 1990 | | | 5 | 4 | | |
| | *Number of Elections Won* | | | | | |
| | 6 | 3 | 84 | 86 | 3 | 10 |
| | (75%) | (25%) | (49%) | (51%) | (23%) | (77%) |

[a]Special election to fill the vacancy caused by the death of Senator Joseph McCarthy (Rep.). Democrat William Proxmire defeated Walter Kohler, Jr. (Rep.).

52 percent of the vote are testimony to the competitive nature of state-wide elections (see table 9.6).

After decades of Republican dominance of the state's delegation to the House of Representatives, the Democrats achieved majority status in 1972 and continued to control the delegation in the 1980s until the 1990 defeat of thirty-two-year Democratic incumbent Robert Kasteumeir. As is true of congressional elections across the country, an overwhelming proportion of Wisconsin House incumbents win re-election. Between 1970 and 1990, in only five contests out of 102 where an incumbent was seeking reelection was the incumbent de-feated—a 95 percent reelection rate. Not only have House incum-bents been winning reelection, they have been doing so by comfortable margins. The normal pattern is for congressmen to have one or two competitive elections early in their careers and then to solidify their electoral positions. Thus Republican Steve Gundersen, in the potentially competitive Third District in the western part of the state, won his initial election in 1980 with only 51 percent of the vote but in 1986 garnered 64 percent and was up to 68 percent in 1988.

In terms of electoral strength, Wisconsin is quite typical of northern industrial states. The Democrats receive a higher percentage of the vote in presidential elections than they do nationally, statewide races for governor and senator are potentially competitive, a majority of the U.S. House seats have generally been in Democratic hands, congressional incumbents of both parties win handily, and the state legislature is controlled by the Democrats.

## LEADERS AND ISSUES

The early and mid-1980s were a period of severe economic dislocation and adjustment for Wisconsin. Manufacturing jobs declined in the first part of the decade as once stable companies were bought out, closed plants, or moved operations to other states and nations. The economic decisions reverberated throughout the state as voters became increasingly concerned about their own and their children's job prospects. Campaigns for statewide office, therefore, revolved around issues relating to jobs and economic development and the record of the incumbents and their parties in those areas. Democrat Anthony Earl's 1982 election to the governorship with 58 percent of the vote came in the midst of a major recession and Republican disarray after a popular and maverick Republican governor, Lee Sherman Dreyfus, had belatedly bowed out of the race for reelection. Earl was a governor in the tradition of the national Democratic party—an advocate of a high and expanded level of state services, a proponent of strict environmental protection regulations, an outspoken supporter of liberal positions on social issues, and a critic of Reagan foreign policy. He was defeated for reelection in 1986 by the minority leader of the assembly, Tommy Thompson, who had a reputation for being a hard-core conservative. Thompson campaigned effectively on the need for the governor to be a stronger leader in the fight for economic development. In addition to taking advantage of Earl's perceived weakness on the jobs issue, Thompson also benefited from a public perception of Earl's being unusually liberal on social issues.

As governor, Thompson emphasized economic development and

pressed for such things as lower capital gains and taxes. He also involved himself personally and actively in efforts to recruit new businesses to the state and retain or expand existing industries. A major theme of the 1986 Thompson campaign and his administration has been that Wisconsin's expenditures have been increasing more rapidly than its tax capacity. He has, therefore, sought to restrain state and local government spending. Consistent with Wisconsin traditions and its citizens' expectations, however, this conservative Republican governor has supported maintaining a level of state services well above the national norms. In addition, Governor Thompson gained legislative approval for a series of controversial welfare and school reform measures.

Thompson's hyperactivity and his forceful, direct, and unpretentious style resulted in high voter approval ratings throughout his first term (72 percent favorable in January 1990). As a hard-line conservative minority leader of the assembly, Thompson had been dubbed "Dr. No" by Democratic legislators and the capitol press corps. However, his record as governor has been much more that of a pragmatist and activist. Wisconsin's economy picked up during Thompson's administration. As a result, the governor's 1990 reelection campaign stressed an improved job climate, social policy reforms, and his intense personal involvement ("Nobody works harder for Wisconsin") in state policy-making. Thompson's Democratic opponent, Speaker of the Assembly Thomas Loftus, sought early in his campaign to exploit what he considered Thompson's vulnerabilities—rising property taxes, a pro-life abortion stand, support for buisness positions on environmental issues, controversial welfare policies, and the need for increased state funding of education.

However, with the state's economy functioning reasonably well and an unemployment rate well below the national average, Loftus was never able to make those issues salient to the voters. In the latter stages of the campaign, therefore, he focused on Thompson's failure to accept public campaign funds and the governor's $6 million war chest, implying that there had been a shakedown of special interests to raise the money. In the absence of any evidence of wrongdoing or unethical conduct on the part of the governor's campaign organization, that issue also fizzled; and Thompson rolled to an easy reelection victory. Particularly noteworthy were the inroads Thompson made into traditional bastions of Democratic strength. After making fifty-seven public appearances in Milwaukee during the last one hundred days of the campaign, he became the first Republican to carry

Milwaukee County in forty-four years. Douglas County (adjacent to Duluth on Lake Superior) went Republican for the first time since 1952. He also carried the Democratic strongholds of Racine and Kenosha counties in the southeastern corner of the state.

The personality who achieved the greatest continued electoral success in the post-war era has been Senator William Proxmire. His five successive reelection victories by mounting margins were not achieved through partisan appeals or high levels of campaign spending. His campaigns were candidate centered—almost totally devoid of references to his Democratic party affiliation. He stressed his reputation as a person independent of party or interest group connections as he spent every weekend and congressional recess shaking hands with voters in every corner of the state. No one in Wisconsin politics has ever campaigned in such a personal, intense, and sustained manner in the post-war period. He represented, in its most extreme form, Wisconsin maverick and antiparty traditions. He was a Democratic senator, but his remarkable electoral appeal had little to do with partisanship.

CONCLUSION

Like many of the states in the Midwest, Wisconsin was a Republican bastion for most of the post–Civil War era through the middle of the twentieth century. The state's Republicanism was anchored in its small towns, medium-sized cities, and suburban communities. The state, however, had the ingredients for a vibrant Democratic party because of its high level of employment in manufacturing, strong and politicized unions, marginal farming regions in the north, concentrations of Catholic voters of eastern and southern European heritage, and a progressive tradition. The growth of a competitive Democratic party was retarded, however, by the existence of the La Follette Progressive movement within the Republican party prior to 1934 and then as a separate third party from 1934 to 1946. The progressive faction within the GOP and the Progressive party siphoned electoral and organizational strength away from the Democratic party and reduced the Democrats to the status of a minor party in state elections from 1934 through 1944. The decision of the Progressive party to reenter the Republican party in 1946 gave the GOP a transfusion of strength that enabled it to retain its electoral dominance until 1958.

After 1946, the Democratic party's normal electoral coalition came together and achieved a dominant electoral position in the 1960s. Although the Democrats enjoy an advantage in terms of party identification of Wisconsin voters, the Republicans continue to have a strong electoral and organizational base. The additional presence of a large bloc of independents and ticket-splitters means that statewide elections have the potential to be highly competitive. The possibility of the parties achieving rough parity in terms of partisan identifiers exists because of the recent tendency of eighteen to twenty-four-year-olds to prefer the Republicans. The 1980s, however, were not a period of electoral realignment for Wisconsin. The state can, therefore, be expected to continue to be a two-party battleground in statewide elections, with incumbent advantages having a major impact on congressional and legislative races.

# Kansas: Two-Party Competition in a One-Party State

## ALLAN CIGLER AND BURDETT LOOMIS

WITH perhaps the notable exception of Maine, Kansas was the most Republican of all states from the middle of the nineteenth century until well into the 1950s. The Kansas-Nebraska Act in 1854 led to the influx of large numbers of Republican abolitionists from New England into Kansas as the territory became a central battleground for contending free- and slave-state forces. The victory of the former, linked to the establishment of what Daniel Elazar (1972) has termed the "moralistic culture," proved to be the catalyst for the creation in 1861 of a strong Republican-dominated state. Kansas's partisan tendencies survived even the powerful national political forces that brought about the critical realignments of the 1890s and the 1930s. While the agricultural depressions underlying the Populist Revolt and New Deal enabled third parties and Democrats to gain occasional short-run electoral advantages, there were few permanent voter shifts within the Kansas electorate; and the state in each instance quickly returned to its Republican predilections (Harder 1989).

Near the end of the twentieth century, Kansas remains staunchly Republican in its national orientation, particularly in presidential voting; and it stands as the only state not to have elected at least one Democratic senator since the 1930s. Although there is no strong evidence for underlying partisan shifts in voter loyalties, party competition for major state offices has changed markedly in recent decades. As in the rest of the nation, media-dominated campaigns and candidate-centered electioneering have contributed to the declining influence of partisanship as a basis for electoral choice. With greater significance placed on short-term factors such as candidate attractiveness and issue orientation, conservative Democrats have regularly defeated Republicans at the gubernatorial level. The dominant Republican party has had to deal with internal factionalism between its declining rural and growing suburban wings, and the fickleness of the state's large bloc of independent voters.

## THE CONTEXT OF CONTEMPORARY KANSAS POLITICS

When hearing of Kansas today, "usually it's either a tornado one thinks of, or the Wizard of Oz or the inability to get a drink," as former governor John Carlin put it (Ehrenhalt 1985, 559). But the rural, conservative, and agriculture-based image of the state has been overdrawn in the national press. In Kansas today you can buy a drink, play the lottery, and place a bet on either dogs or horses. All those changes came in the 1980s as the state put aside its moralism to seek additional sources of revenue.

Demographic changes over the past few decades, particularly population movements, have contributed to changes in political divisions, which have resulted in a peculiar kind of two-party competition in a state with strong Republican predispositions. Urbanization has taken place at a fairly rapid rate since World War II. In 1940 more than 58 percent of Kansas citizens lived in rural areas; but by the mid-1980s, the figure stood at 33 percent, not far from the national average of 26 percent. Currently, about 1 percent of the state's farms produce nearly 50 percent of the state's agricultural product, and small family farms are far less common than in previous decades as agriculture has become much more capital intensive. In the 1940s farm commodities alone generated 20 percent of the state's economic product, while manufacturing contributed just 8 percent. Today those figures have been reversed; and the Wichita aerospace industry, in particular, is a major component of the state's changing economic base. Wholesale and retail trade now constitute the largest component of the state's economy (Redwood and Krider 1986, 1–2).

Despite diversification, Kansas remains very dependent for economic growth on agriculture and the rural-based oil and gas industry. Indeed, small rural towns suffered tremendously in the 1980s because of depressed grain commodity and energy prices. Many Kansans did not experience the economic boom of the Reagan years. It was not until the second half of 1984, for example, that total employment in Kansas returned to peak 1979 levels (Redwood and Krider 1986, 2), and it has increased little since.

In terms of its socioeconomic mix, Kansas lacks the economic-cultural-racial diversity that often characterizes two-party, competitive politics in other states. Traditional Democratic demographic groups enjoy only a modest presence in the state. Less than 10 percent of the state's residents are members of a racial minority (5 percent black, 2 percent Hispanic, 1 percent Asian, 1 percent American Indian), and only about 10 percent have incomes below the poverty level. Despite an estimated eighty thousand members of organized labor in Kansas, most affiliated with the AFL-CIO, right-to-work laws have impeded the development of a strong union movement that offers substantial support to the Democratic party. Though labor interests are clearly identified with "reform measures and the liberal side of social-welfare issues," they have a record of "intensive involvement with both parties" (Harder and Rampey 1972, 198).

More meaningful for party competition have been patterns of population movement within the state, in-migration, and population clustering in several key areas. Kansas has had one of the slower population growth rates in the nation, and the state has experienced net out-migration in every census decade since 1890. In recent years the migrants have been concentrated among young adults with higher than average education and skill levels. The overall figures, however, hide what have been substantial intrastate variations in population mobility and patterns of regional growth and decline.

Many counties in rural western Kansas have fewer residents than in the 1890s. Most new business activity in the state and its accompanying population growth are concentrated in either the northeastern corridor running from Kansas City to Topeka or the south-central region around Wichita, as occupational opportunities have attracted both in-state and out-of-state migrants. Between 1910 and 1959, for example, Johnson County (suburban Kansas City) experienced a 671 percent growth rate, Shawnee County (Topeka) a growth rate of 109 percent, and Sedgwick County (Wichita) a 388 percent growth rate (Drury and Titus 1960, 32). Population growth in the metropolitan areas, particularly in the Kansas City suburbs, has continued unabated since. In addition, Johnson County has emerged as one of the wealthier counties in the nation.

One upshot of the population and economic developments has been that substantial rural-suburban-urban divisions have steadily changed the face of two-party competition in Kansas, especially for statewide races. Republicans are concentrated in the rural and suburban areas, and their basic fiscal conservatism is regularly registered in support of the national presidential Republican ticket and for U.S. senators and members of Congress. On the state level, however, the rural and suburban wings of the Republican party are often at odds on a number of issues. These include taxes on the oil and gas industry, which almost entirely affect western Kansas; the formula for state aid to public schools, which involves a redistribution of aid from wealthy suburban school districts to the poorer rural school districts; and moral issues, including liquor-by-the-drink and abortion.

In recent decades Democratic candidates have regularly been able to exploit Republican factionism, especially in contests for governor and other statewide offices. The increased competitiveness means that, among other things, people no longer choose to become Republicans because they believe major electoral decisions are made only in Republican primaries, as was the case prior to the 1970s. Nor do activists adopt only the Republican label to further their careers since Democrats have built their own opportunity structure for most state offices.

## THE PARTISAN COMPLEXION OF THE KANSAS ELECTORATE

Data problems are formidable when attempting to assess partisan change in the Kansas electorate. Until the late 1980s, no publicly available polls explored concerns of interest to academic researchers. No time series survey data report patterns of party identification, which makes trend analysis of partisan changes impossible. Basic information on voter registration was not available until 1974, and even now it is not published by the state. We can, however, paint in broad brushstrokes a picture of the certain aspects of partisan change in recent decades and describe the contemporary Kansas electorate in a way that makes some sense of the state's national Republicanism and internal political independence.

Prior to 1974, we can use only indirect measures of the partisan orientations of Kansas voters. For example, one aggregate indicator of partisan orientations is participation in party primaries. Kansas has a version of the closed primary. Voters may declare a party affiliation at the time they register, at any time before the registration rolls close, or at the time of the primary. Voters cannot change their party affiliation at the time of the primary, though unaffiliated voters may register a party preference then and participate in the election. Using aggregate primary participation as an indicator of partisan orientation, Democrats averaged just under 50 percent of Republican participation between 1954 and 1972.

Turning to the party registration figures available since 1974, we see some indication that the Kansas electorate has been responsive to both state and national political forces, but nothing that suggests broad realignment patterns. In general, the proportion of the electorate registered with both parties has increased since the mid-1970s at the expense of independents; but Republicans clearly remain the dominant party. Figure 10.1 plots the voter registration percentages preceding the biennial elections from 1974 through 1990.

In 1974, registered independents composed 44.6 percent of the Kansas electorate, and Republicans outnumbered Democrats nearly three to two. But a popular Democratic governor (Robert Docking), as well as Republican difficulties in the wake of Watergate, evidently affected the state electorate. Between 1974 and 1978, the proportion of the state electorate that registered Democrat increased more than four percent, while both Republican and independent percentages declined; in 1978 Republicans represented less than a third of the state's registered voters. In terms of the total number of party registrants, Republicans gained fewer than nine thousand during this period, while Democratic rolls expanded by almost sixty-five thousand.

The numbers changed dramatically in the late 1980s. In 1980, the state held its first presidential primary, which had the unanticipated effect of prompting many independents to register as partisans. Republicans benefited greatly, with the proportion of GOP registrants jumping from 32.5 percent of the electorate in 1978 to 39.2 percent in 1980, while Democratic registration grew from 25.5 to 29.9 percent. Between 1980 and 1984 both parties experienced slight drops in their proportion of the electorate, but during the later part of the decade the Republican Party increased its registration advantage over the Democrats. By the decade's end, Republicans held a nearly 170,000 statewide registration edge over the Democrats, compared with 129,000 in 1974.

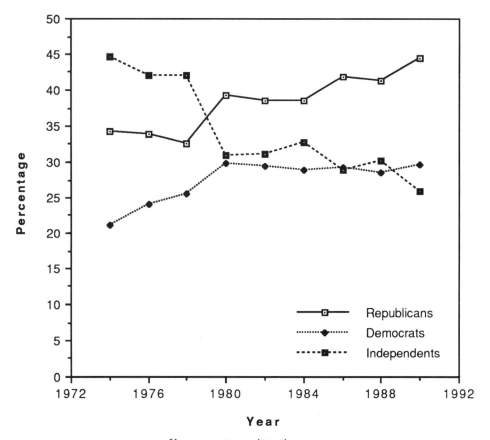

10.1 Kansas voter registration, 1974–1990

　　Republicans continue to hold a registration advantage over Democrats in all but a few counties in the state and in each of the state's five congressional districts. The state has four metropolitan counties; and in only one, Wyandotte (Kansas City), do Democrats hold a registration edge. With a substantial advantage of fifty thousand in the Kansas City suburbs of Johnson County and a narrow margin of ten thousand in Sedgwick County (Wichita), the Republican advantage over Democrats in Kansas is both wide and deep. Of particular importance, the Republican edge has grown considerably in the 1980s. Nevertheless, registration figures do not tell the entire story of partisanship in Kansas. Like many southern states, partisan registration can be misleading, especially when examined in isolation from issues, ideology, and election results.

## THE COMPOSITION OF THE PARTY ELECTORATE

A small number of academic polls commissioned in the late 1980s provides insight into the demographic bases of each party's support among the Kansas electorate. The findings of a 1988 statewide poll relating party identification to a number of respondent background characteristics are presented in table 10.1.

In general, the backgrounds of the party identifiers in Kansas approximate each party's national image along old New Deal lines, but the divisions among the parties are hardly sharp. Kansas Republicans, in particular, fare quite well among traditional elements of the national Democratic coalition. Still, as a group, Kansas Republicans are predominantly white, overwhelmingly Protestant, and overrepresentative of the higher income and educated segments of society. In addition, Republicans do particularly well among the younger Kansans, especially among males. The age data are particularly noteworthy, suggesting that the Republican advantage over the Democrats may continue to grow in the future. Any firm conclusion, however, must await longitudinal data. The Democratic party, as might be expected, appears most attractive to the state's small minority population, non-Protestants, and those with the least education.

The broad base of support of the Republican party in the survey data is impressive. Among respondents, Republican identifiers led Democratic identifiers even in the lowest family income category and among those who resided in urban areas. It is important to realize that in Kansas the Republican party "includes not just rich people and country club members, but the mechanic at the garage and the clerk at the feed store; not just the banker and the lawyers, but the farmer and the minister" (Barone and Ujifusa 1983, 430).

People who consider themselves independents in Kansas appear to come from various demographic backgrounds; and nearly as many survey respondents consider themselves independent as consider themselves Republican, which diverges sharply from the registration data that gives the GOP a substantial edge. The survey data suggest two distinct types of independents in Kansas: one group concentrated among the lesser educated and poorer segments of society, and another group with middle-to-high incomes and at least some college work. A large number of urban residents consider themselves independents, and more Catholics consider themselves independents than Democrats. There is no question that the large number of inde-

Table 10.1.  Characteristics of Party Identifiers: Kansas, 1988

| | Republicans (%) | Democrats (%) | Independents (%) | Other (%) |
|---|---|---|---|---|
| Family income | | | | |
|   Under $15,000 | 30.1 | 25.2 | 39.8 | 3.6 |
|   $15,000–40,000 | 40.1 | 28.8 | 28.2 | 2.8 |
|   $40,001–70,000 | 29.9 | 22.1 | 46.8 | 1.3 |
|   $70,000+ | 63.2 | 0.0 | 31.6 | 5.3 |
| Religion | | | | |
|   Protestant | 44.1 | 23.8 | 29.5 | 2.6 |
|   Catholic | 27.8 | 30.6 | 38.9 | 2.8 |
|   Jewish | 0.0 | 50.0 | 50.0 | 0.0 |
|   Agnostic | 23.4 | 29.8 | 42.6 | 0.0 |
|   Other/not classified | 23.4 | 29.8 | 46.2 | 4.3 |
| Gender | | | | |
|   Female | 31.7 | 27.4 | 38.0 | 1.9 |
|   Male | 42.5 | 22.9 | 32.0 | 2.6 |
| Race | | | | |
|   White | 38.6 | 22.5 | 35.9 | 3.0 |
|   Black | 7.1 | 71.4 | 21.4 | 0.0 |
|   Other | 17.6 | 41.2 | 23.5 | 0.0 |
| Residence | | | | |
|   Rural | 40.3 | 24.4 | 32.6 | 2.7 |
|   Urban | 30.0 | 27.1 | 40.0 | 2.9 |
| Education | | | | |
|   Less than high school | 25.6 | 33.3 | 38.5 | 2.6 |
|   High school | 36.2 | 38.8 | 23.3 | 1.6 |
|   Some college | 36.8 | 21.1 | 40.0 | 2.1 |
|   B.A./B.S. | 41.2 | 27.9 | 27.9 | 2.9 |
|   Graduate degree | 32.0 | 12.1 | 56.0 | 0.0 |
| Age | | | | |
|   Under 30 | 37.2 | 19.2 | 42.3 | 1.3 |
|   30–40 | 31.7 | 23.2 | 42.7 | 2.4 |
|   41–50 | 44.9 | 22.5 | 30.6 | 2.0 |
|   51–65 | 41.1 | 28.8 | 26.0 | 4.1 |
|   65+ | 41.1 | 31.6 | 23.3 | 4.1 |

Source: Institute for Public Policy and Business Research, University of Kansas.

N = 362.

pendents in Kansas constitutes a continuing barrier to a would-be Republican hegemony.

The ideological composition of the various categories of party identifiers illustrate the Republican problems. Survey respondents were asked to classify themselves along a scale ranging from very liberal to very conservative. As one might surmise, there are clear aggregate ideological differences between Democrats and Republicans. Almost half (46 percent) of the Republican identifiers consider themselves conservative, while more than 40 percent of the Democratic respondents consider themselves liberal. More than a third in each party see themselves as moderate. Independent identifiers, however, look more like Democrats than Republicans. Of self-identified independents, nearly one-third consider themselves liberals, while a little more than one-fifth label themselves conservatives.

Overall, the survey data make clear that Kansas is hardly the extreme conservative bastion that many think (there were actually more self-identified liberals in the survey than conservatives). A plurality of Kansans considers itself moderate, and even self-identified conservatives and liberals did not place themselves at the extreme end of the ideological measure.

Finally, although the state has a reputation for sending to Washington legislators who are fiscally conservative, perhaps epitomized in recent years by Republican senator Robert Dole, Kansas citizens are not likely to reject substantial federal spending and governmental intervention in the economy. With one of the highest median age populations in the nation and a stagnant economy that relies heavily on government spending for defense and agriculture, Kansans support many of the foundations of large, expensive federal programs (Social Security, defense spending, and farm subsidies, among others). Indeed, the political values in the state have always run along the lines of populism (Pierce 1973, 221–22), with a potential for political volatility. The apparently dominant Republican party must confront this element of its own makeup, as it seeks to bridge the urban-suburban-rural divisions among its own partisans and activists.

## PARTY COMPETITION: NOW YOU SEE IT, NOW YOU DON'T

Beyond registration and party identification, two major criteria reflect long-term trends in party competition: relative strength in voting and office holding. Although interparty competition has not been uniform across eras and offices, in general Kansas politics has steadily grown more competitive since the 1950s. At the same time, in many ways it remains a most Republican state.

Nevertheless, Democrats have made many significant advances over the past thirty years. Although Democratic politicians often face uphill climbs in their bids for public office, since the 1960s it has been possible for minority-party officeholders to build careers in Kansas politics and government.

VOTES

Presidential years do not make for splashy, expensive campaigns in Kansas. Republicans and Democrats alike assume that the state will vote reflexively for the GOP candidate, as it has in all but one election (1964) since 1936, when it rejected native son Alf Landon. Evidence is increasing that presidential elections could be competitive, but national Democrats have not yet been willing to test the possibility by committing adequate resources to produce a major effort in a relatively small state.

Conversely, since 1956, gubernatorial elections have generated strong efforts from both parties. Indeed, beginning with George Docking's breakthrough triumph in 1956, Democratic candidates for governor have won more often and have accumulated more votes than their Republican opponents (see figure 10.2). Democrats have succeeded by espousing relatively conservative governing philosophies (often echoing Robert Docking's "austere but adequate" formula) and by taking advantage of factional divisions within the Republican majority. In part, GOP factionalism is exacerbated by the weakness of Kansas party organizations. As Mayhew notes, "Nowhere in the slim literature on Kansas does traditional organization make an appearance" (Mayhew 1986, 170; Harder 1959; Averyt 1970). Over the past thirty-five years, Kansans have grown comfortable with the possibility of a Democratic governor, and this has frequently overcome their ordinary partisan leanings.

Republicans have maintained their majority status in elections for the U.S. House and Senate, but their advantage in votes has been translated into seats in very different ways. Since 1956, Republican U.S. Senate candidates have won an average of 62.5 percent of the two-party vote. The percentages surged in the 1980s when Senator Dole and Kassebaum obtained an average of 71.5 percent in their four contests. In U.S. House races, the 1956–88 mean GOP percentage stands at 57.2 percent, with an average of 55.4 percent over the five elections of the 1980s. Democrats captured two of Kansas's five House seats in all but two elections since 1970. Democratic congressmen Dan Glickman and Jim Slattery have both ministered to their potentially marginal districts to produce safe districts; although if either were to abandon his respective seat, it would be highly competitive. Indeed,

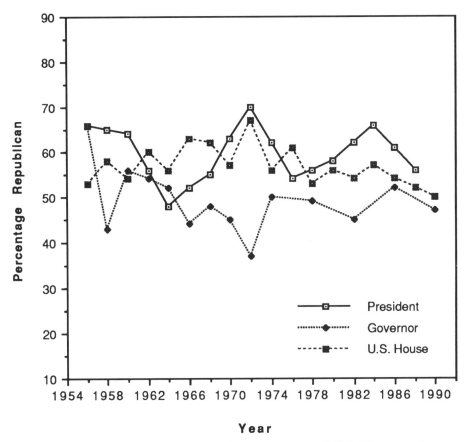

10.2  Kansas: Percent GOP vote for president, governor, and U.S. House, 1956–1990

the Republican candidate might well be favored. Despite the fact that Kansas will lose a seat in the wake of the 1990 census, Glickman and Slattery will be strong favorites to retain their positions (see figure 10.2).

The development of strong two-party competition for some offices, in the face of continuing Republican advantages in party identification and registration, begs for explanation. Both national and state-specific forces are at work (Heil 1983). A wealth of information is available to an increasingly urban and suburban Kansas electorate. Reflexive Republican identification has decreased, and split-ticket voting has risen dramatically. In 1972, for example, Richard Nixon won 68 percent of the Kansas presidential vote, and Republican incumbent James Pearson obtained 71 percent of the U.S. Senate vote.

At the same time, Democrats Robert Docking and Vern Miller were winning reelection as governor and attorney general with 62 percent and 68 percent of the vote, respectively (Heil 1983, 135–36). Democrats such as Docking and Miller succeeded by running as relative conservatives, within a state context that encouraged such a tack.

Finally, the state's reactions to the Supreme Court's one-person, one-vote mandates of the 1960s opened up the party system to greater competition (Cigler and Drury 1981). As noted earlier, Kansas has become increasingly urban throughout this century, and especially in the post–World War II era. Equitable representation has given Democrats both a stronger base in the state legislature and the opportunity to develop issues that can capitalize on urban-rural differences. For instance, in his 1978 gubernatorial campaign, Democrat John Carlin received only 32 percent of the vote in Johnson County, a populous, affluent, heavily Republican suburb of Kansas City. Four years later, with an emphasis on imposing a severance tax on oil and other minerals, which would negatively affect the central and western parts of the state, Carlin won 55 percent. In the 1990 gubernatorial campaign, incumbent Republican Mike Hayden faced some of his most virulent opposition among his fellow partisans in Johnson County, who felt the impact of state-mandated property tax increases in residential areas while agriculture assessments declined. Facing Democratic state treasurer Joan Finney, Hayden could not overcome the property tax negatives, and he lost his bid for reelection. In short, Democrats continue to use differences among majority Republicans to field credible candidates in gubernatorial races. But Republican dominance remains in races for the U.S. Senate and the presidency.

## SEATS

Directly related to voting patterns is the conversion of votes to seats. Despite their inability to make any real headway in presidential or U.S. Senate elections, Kansas Democrats have moved into competitive status in most other statewide offices and within the legislature. Indeed, Democratic governors have become more the rule than the exception since George Docking's 1956 victory.

Still, the broadest indicators of increasing interparty competition come in the evolutionary changes within both houses of the Kansas legislature. Although Democrats are ordinarily the minority party in the house and senate, they have achieved a competitive status over the past fifteen years that leaves them within grasp of winning control of the chambers (see figure 10.3). Prior to the 1990 elections, Democrats

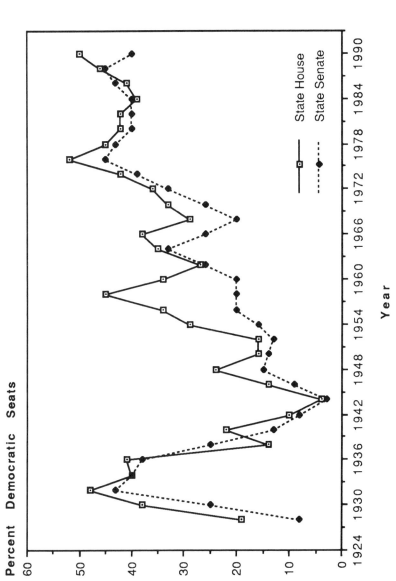

Percent Democratic Seats

State House
State Senate

Year

10.3 Kansas Democratic seats: State legislature, 1926–1990

have held majorities for only four years in each house. In 1912, taking advantage of Theodore Roosevelt's Bull Moose challenge to the Republican party, Democrats won both chambers, only to lose control in the next election. The sole other Democratic majority came in the 1977–78 period. Democrats also did well in the New Deal era, winning more than forty percent of the house seats and slightly fewer in the senate during the 1930–38 period.

After the 1930s, Democratic numbers plummeted, and the story of statehouse competition in Kansas since has been one of steady, secular progress over the past five decades. The previous bursts of competition (1912–16, 1930–38) depended on national events as translated to state politics. The post-1974 level of competitiveness, with Democrats consistently winning more than forty percent of the seats in both houses, derives from solid grass roots gains in an equitably apportioned legislature, where the majority party challenges for almost all seats.

### ELECTORAL AND POLICY IMPLICATIONS

With the success of Democratic candidates for governor (since 1956), for the U.S. House (since 1970), and the legislature (generally since 1956 and especially since 1974), Kansas Democrats have contructed a legitimate "structure of opportunity" that allows ambitious politicians to climb toward statewide and national office (Schlesinger 1966). Although credit for this development can legitimately go to various individuals, the most important figures were Governors George and Robert Docking. George Docking won election in 1956 without an effective party organization; he took advantage of a bitter Republican division, which is a recurring theme for Democratic success in Kansas (Harder 1959; Heil 1983). His son, Robert, won four consecutive two-year terms, starting with his initial victory in 1966. During the Dockings' era (1956–74), Democrats became increasingly competitive in the legislature, and the post-Watergate election of 1976 elevated statehouse Democrats to overall levels of success that they have roughly maintained ever since. This should continue for the foreseeable future, given the state-mandated 1989 reapportionment that redistributed several seats into growing suburban Republican areas. Democrats succeeded in protecting most of their incumbents and challenged Republicans effectively in 1990 to the extent that they captured control of the lower house by a single seat.

Regarding policy implications, on occasion Kansas parties will define policy positions within the state. Normally, however, regional and urban-rural differences dominate the policy process. Given their majority status, Republicans stand to lose the most by such divisions. To the extent that Democrats can remain reasonably well unified—especially in gubernatorial elections and within the legislature—they can have a disproportionate influence on the state policies.

Before Democrats became a significant presence in statehouse politics, Republican factions would struggle internally to establish state policy. Since the 1950s, however, with their gubernatorial success and their growing legislative presence, Democrats have frequently contributed substantially to policy outcomes. Republican governor Mike Hayden relied heavily on Democratic support in both the house and senate to pass a major highway package ($2.65 billion) in 1989; this backing was especially significant since many suburban Kansas City Republicans opposed the legislation.

CONCLUSION

The evidence seems clear that Kansas, while still predominantly a Republican state, has undergone some significant political transformations over the past few decades. A variety of forces, ranging from changes in the rural-urban population mix to the roles played by a generation of skillful, moderate-to-conservative Democratic politicians, has contributed to a situation in which the Republican hegemony in the state has been broken. Although little suggests that a realignment within the state's electorate has occurred, especially in terms of indications that Kansas voters have moved in great numbers from one party to the other, evidence does indicate that some form of dealignment is under way. While the number of independent voters has decreased since 1974, divisions along rural-urban lines have made Republican identifiers and registrants increasingly apt to defect in support of centrist Democrats. The Kansas vote is less firmly anchored by party than before the era of Democratic governors George and Robert Docking (1956–74). As a consequence, even though Democrats remain outnumbered by both Republicans and independents, minority-party candidates have greatly improved their electoral performance.

In a very real sense, Kansas has generated a form of two-tiered electoral behavior, somewhat the reverse of the American South, which has been characterized in recent decades by strong support for Democrats at the subpresidential level, coupled with an inclination to support conservative candidates, most often Republicans, in presidential races. Kansans, on the other hand, are committed Republicans in national politics but frequently behave like nonaligned voters in state elections. The Kansas experience appears similar to patterns found in several other midwestern states, where "the waning pull of partisanship on the voters has enabled gubernatorial candidates of both parties to win races in states previously considered strongholds of the opposition" (Bibby 1989, 13). One result in Kansas has been a strong tendency toward divided party control of state government in twenty-four of the thirty-six years between 1957 and 1992. Again, this reflects an increasingly common pattern in a number of midwestern states (Jewell and Olson 1988). More generally, Democrats enjoy an enhanced and highly visible role in state policy-making. Without question, the Democratic party is now considered a serious opposition.

Kansas's pattern of Republican voting in national-level races and relative independence in statewide contests will likely continue. The national Democratic policy agenda, as defined in recent elections, appears too liberal to attract a majority of Kansans, but Republican divisions at the state level should provide continuing opportunities for moderate Democratic politicians.

# Iowa and the Drift to the Democrats

## PEVERILL SQUIRE

IN 1885 Jonathan P. Dolliver, a U.S. senator from Iowa, uttered one of the more memorable comments on the partisan predilection of his home state. He asserted, "Iowa will go Democratic when Hell goes Methodist." The senator's hyperbolic forecast was based on Iowa's solid support for Republicans in the period since the Civil War and proved prophetic about the course of party politics for the next fifty years. But by the mid-1940s, American chronicler John Gunther (1947, 336) observed, "Iowa is an extremely conservative state, but it is not quite so overwhelmingly Republican as most outsiders believe." The drift toward the Democrats intensified during the next forty years to the point where, in the 1980s, another sounding of the state's political leanings noted, "Iowa is by instinct and normal voting pattern Republican, although it has become a closely divided state in recent years" (Peirce and Hagstrom 1984, 572). Certainly it is beyond the scope of this chapter to speculate about the current state of Hades, but it is reasonable to determine to what extent Iowa is on its way to becoming Democratic and why it might be headed in that direction.

I am grateful to Blake Wood and Tisha Tallman for research assistance. Thomas C. Mans of Creighton University generously shared some of his Iowa Poll data, and my colleague, Russell Ross, gave me the benefit of his expertise on Iowa politics. Any errors are, of course, my own.

## POLITICAL CULTURE AND CONTEXT

Iowa's political image has, at least during this century, always been one of clean, honest politics. Elazar characterizes the state's political culture as moralistic with a strong individualistic strain (1972). Similarly, Mayhew gives Iowa the lowest possible score on his traditional party organization measure (1986). What we can infer from both studies is that Iowa has been devoid of the political machines or strong party organizations and the corruption and harsh politics associated with them that many other states once had or still have. Patterson, in a recent survey of Iowa, observes: "If the style of Iowa politics had to be distilled into a single term, it would be bland. Iowa's political leaders . . . generally are people of high quality who carry a sense of public service to their political or governmental roles. Political conflict in Iowa is remarkably civil and high-minded" (1984, 89). This is not to claim that there are no skeletons in the state's political closet; but, with few exceptions, partisan political competition has been open and aboveboard.

Voter turnout in Iowa is usually among the highest in the nation. In 1988, 59 percent of the state's voting-age population cast a ballot for president, ranking eighth in the country. The high level of turnout is due, in part, to the state's relatively easy registration system. Since the mid-1970s Iowans have been allowed to register using postcards and also have benefited from deputy registrars found in many locations (Larew 1980, 131).

The demographic characteristics of the state's population also contribute to high turnout. As of 1980, 72 percent of the persons twenty-five years or older had at least four years of high school, and 14 percent had four or more years of college. The population is among the oldest in the nation; in 1987 almost 15 percent of the population was sixty-five years or older, ranking second in the nation. Because older and better educated people are more likely to vote (Wolfinger and Rosenstone 1980), Iowa's high level of turnout is not surprising, even in the apparent absence of strong party organizations to mobilize voters.

A significant proportion of the state's population—59 percent in 1980—lives in urban areas. Although Iowa is strongly identified with agriculture, farmers comprise less than 10 percent of the state's population. Twice as many Iowans are employed in manufacturing—particularly of heavy machinery—and a similar number work in the service sector. Certainly agriculture is central to the state's economy because much of the manufacturing and service industires are, at least indirectly, tied to it. But the state's economy is diverse, and the composition of the work force suggests at least one important political fact: the Farm Bureau may have a strong population base, but so do labor unions.

Iowa's population, then, lives in both rural and urban areas, and is employed in a number of different industries. This diversity has accelerated over the last several decades. In 1950, for example, more than 52 percent of Iowans lived in rural areas; by 1980 that number had declined to about 41 percent. Likewise, the number of people living and working on farms has decreased. The percentage of the population which is over sixty-five years of age has also increased during the last thirty years. All of the demographic changes are, of course, likely to have consequences for party politics in Iowa.

## ELECTION OUTCOMES AND PARTY FORTUNES

For most of its first one hundred years, Iowa was a rock-solid Republican state. From 1856 to 1928, a span of nineteen presidential elections, Iowa's electoral votes always went to the GOP candidate with one exception: 1912, when Taft and Theodore Roosevelt split the Republican base, allowing Wilson to win with just 40 percent of the vote. Franklin Roosevelt took the state in 1932 and 1936, but Iowa went for Wilkie and Dewey in the next two contests. Truman won in 1948, but by a very small margin.

A similar story holds for the governorship. From 1858 to 1948, Democrats won five out of forty-five elections for the then two-year position. The only periods when the Republicans lost were when the party was not doing well nationally: 1890–94 and 1933–39. Elections for other national and state offices produced the same extremely high level of support for the GOP.

After 1948, the Democrat's prospects began to improve, although the evidence for this at the presidential and gubernatorial level is skimpy. The only Democratic presidential candidates to carry the state since 1948 were Lyndon Johnson in 1964 and Michael Dukakis in 1988. During that forty-year period, only two Democrats were elected governor: Herschel Loveless (1957–61) and Harold Hughes (1963–69). Republicans enjoyed the same relative level of success in contests for other statewide offices.

The one-sided results at the presidential and gubernatorial levels are somewhat deceiving in that they mask some movement toward the Democrats. While the GOP has been successful at winning Iowa's electoral votes in recent years, they usually do so by smaller margins than in the rest of the nation (Squire 1989). Similarly, Terry E. Branstad won his first two bids for office in fairly close elections. It is possible that had not Branstad's first opponent, Roxanne Conlin, committed a major campaign blunder over the issue of her tax payments, she would have won the 1982 race. However, in the 1990 election, Branstad was reelected for a third term by a comfortable 61 percent of the vote.

Democrats have been more successful in contesting U.S. Senate and House seats. Since 1948 the party has elected six of its candidates to the Senate. Republicans, however, were able to defeat three of the Democrats after a single term (Gillette, Clark, and Culver). Of the other two, Harold Hughes retired after a single term—although he was expected to be reelected without much trouble—and Tom Harkin was reelected for a second term in 1990.

The situation in House races is somewhat promising for the Democrats. In 1956 Iowans elected their first Democratic congressman since 1940. Over the last three decades, the state's House delegation has tended to have a majority of Republicans, but the Democrats have dominated in two periods: 1965–71, and 1975–79. Each of those success, of course, was consistent with overwhelming Democratic successes nationally. Democrats, however, had held at least two of the six House seats in every election since 1965; and in the 1990 election, the two Democratic seats were uncontested.

Perhaps the best evidence for the Democrats' resurgence is their success in winning state legislative seats. As can be seen in figure 11.1, in the late 1940s the Democrats controlled very few seats in either house. The general trend from that point to the present is increasing Democratic success in winning seats. After every major increase in Democratic seats—1958, 1964, and 1974–the Republicans won back seats in the next election. The GOP also made gains in 1990, but overall the increase in Democratic success has continued in a fairly linear fashion. Moreover, while Democratic control of both the senate and house in the mid-1960s and mid-1970s might be considered aberrations resulting from extraordinary national electoral forces, the party's majority from 1983 on reflects its expanded base of support.

The findings regarding Democratic success in gaining seats in the General Assembly are important because most people know very little about the people who serve in that institution. Only 36 percent of

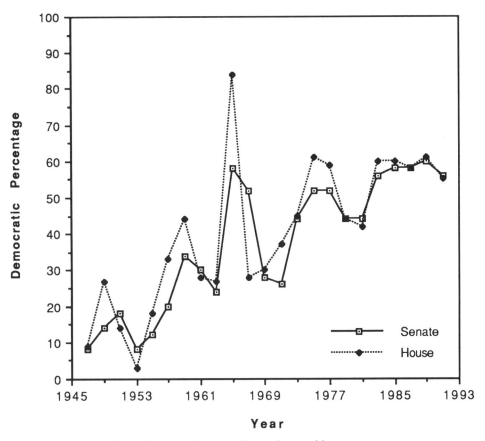

11.1 Iowa Democratic seats: General assembly, 1947–1991

Iowans even claim to know who represents them in the legislature (*Des Moines Register* 1986). No doubt they know even less about challengers for those seats. What this means is that voting for state legislator is a good measure of party preference at the time of the election, because it is unlikely that voters will be influenced by information about the candidates other than the party label appearing on the ballot.

Overall, evidence from election outcomes in Iowa shows that in the last forty years the Democrats have been transformed from a party that rarely won any election to one which is, at minimum, competitive with the Republicans. Before attempting to explain why this change has occurred, party support at the voter level needs to be examined. The election outcomes presented above reveal only which party won, and not by how much. We cannot be sure, therefore, if the

basically steady increase in Democratic success evidenced in state legislative races reflects movement at the individual level or if people
have moved away from the GOP and to the Democrats at specific
points in time in response to national forces, such as the Goldwater
candidacy or Watergate, or short-term, state-level influences, such as
the popular Democrat Harold Hughes' gubernatorial campaigns and
tenure.

## CHANGING PARTY IDENTIFICATION IN IOWA

How, if at all, has party identification changed in Iowa over the last
forty years? Fortunately, data are available to address this question.
The *Des Moines Register*'s highly regarded Iowa Poll has asked Iowans
about their party preferences on a regular basis since 1948. Unfortunately for our purposes here, the Iowa Poll has twice changed the
question asked about which party a respondent supports.

The original question used from 1948 to 1964 was:

Will you please tell me confidentially whether you regard yourself as generally a:
  1. Republican, definitely (usually vote straight ticket)
  2. Independent Republican (split ticket and vote either party)
  3. Democrat, definitely (usually vote straight ticket)
  4. Independent Democrat (split ticket and vote either party)
  5. Other
  6. Declined to answer

This question was replaced by a two-part probe:

In politics, as of today, do you generally consider yourself a Republican,
Democrat, or independent?

(If independent or other ask:) As of today, do you lean more to the Republican party or more toward the Democratic party?

The last set of questions was changed in 1975 by dropping the second
question.

The varying question formats produce somewhat different answers.
As can be seen in table 11.1, the number of independent party identifiers, or closet partisans, is higher under the first question than the
second. The most recent question does not allow leaners to be distin-
guished from pure independents. Thus the numbers in table 11.1
must be interpreted with some care. But they can reveal to what extent, if at all, the party preferences of Iowans have changed over the
last four decades.

Table 11.1. Trends in Party Identification: Iowa, 1948–1987

| | Republican (%) | Independent Republican (%) | Independent Democrat (%) | Democrat (%) | Other (%) | N |
|---|---|---|---|---|---|---|
| Nov. 1948 | 17 | 36 | 25 | 17 | 5 | 655 |
| Aug. 1950 | 16 | 34 | 26 | 12 | 9 | 538 |
| Nov. 1952 | 19 | 37 | 23 | 12 | 8 | 595 |
| Sept. 1954 | 17 | 35 | 25 | 14 | 9 | 893 |
| Feb. 1957 | 16 | 34 | 26 | 17 | 7 | 577 |
| Sept. 1958 | 18 | 31 | 27 | 17 | 7 | 578 |
| Sept. 1960 | 20 | 30 | 25 | 17 | 8 | 602 |
| Oct. 1962 | 18 | 30 | 25 | 17 | 11 | 1,181 |
| Oct. 1966[a] | 36 | 7 | 8 | 39 | 10 | 1,126 |
| Oct. 1968 | 38 | 10 | 8 | 34 | 11 | 1,190 |
| Feb. 1971 | 36 | 10 | 13 | 32 | 9 | 591 |
| Sept. 1972 | 42 | 10 | 8 | 30 | 10 | 599 |
| Sept. 1973 | 29 | 7 | 11 | 38 | 13 | 1,180 |
| Sept. 1975[a] | 34 | — | — | 32 | 34 | 595 |
| Jan. 1980 | 30 | | | 31 | 38 | 987 |
| Jan. 1986 | 30 | | | 29 | 40 | 790 |
| Apr. 1987 | 29 | | | 30 | 41 | 1,194 |

Source: Various *Des Moines Register* Iowa Polls.
[a] Wording of question changed.

Examination of table 11.1 shows that Republicans were clearly the majority party well into the 1970s. Combining identifiers with leaners gives Republicans anywhere from a five- to twenty-one-point advantage during the years from 1948 to 1962. The Goldwater debacle, which hurt the GOP nationwide, gave Iowa Democrats a short-lived lead. A 1964 survey with leaners lumped with pure independents shows the Democrats with a ten-point advantage (computed from information in table 11.3). That lead still held in 1966, but by 1968 the Republicans were again the majority party in the state.

Beginning with the Nixon administration, the GOP lead began to decay. Adverse reaction in Iowa to the McGovern candidacy provided Republicans a brief resurgence, but Watergate turned the tide in the Democrats' favor. Since the mid-1970s, the Republicans have not enjoyed the dominance in party identification they previously held.

The recent data, however, indicate that the Democrats have only a very slight edge over the GOP. The question format employed by the Iowa Poll and the sparse number of surveys to analyze make it difficult to discern exactly what has happened in the last fifteen years.

Table 11.2.　Trends in Party Registration: Iowa, 1980–1988

|      | Republicans (%) | Democrats (%) | Independents (%) | Total Number of Voters |
|------|-----------------|---------------|------------------|------------------------|
| 1980 | 30 | 34 | 36 | 1,551,756 |
| 1981 | 32 | 32 | 36 | 1,743,278 |
| 1982 | 32 | 32 | 36 | 1,593,847 |
| 1983 | 32 | 35 | 34 | 1,605,601 |
| 1984 | 32 | 34 | 34 | 1,563,072 |
| 1985 | 31 | 35 | 35 | 1,753,796 |
| 1986 | 31 | 35 | 34 | 1,605,354 |
| 1987 | 31 | 35 | 34 | 1,619,469 |
| 1988 | 31 | 36 | 33 | 1,690,093 |

Source: Information on 1980 to 1987 is from the State Registrar of Voters; 1988 is from "Democrats the Winners in Registering Iowans" (*Des Moines Register*, 5 Nov 1988). The figures are for the month of January for each year except 1986, when only the December 1985 numbers were available, and 1988, when the November number was used.

Party registration figures, provided for the years 1980 to 1988 in table 11.2, help fill in the gaps. These figures are consistent with the survey results. They show that the Democrats have a small, and perhaps growing, lead over the Republicans.

Overall, the data presented in the tables demonstrate that over the last two decades Iowa has been transformed from a heavily Republican state to a competitive one in which the Democrats enjoy a growing advantage. How can this change be explained?

## EXPLAINING DEMOCRATIC RESURGENCE

Several explanations have been advanced to account for the resurgence of the Democratic party in Iowa. Hahn (1971) points to increasing urbanization as the source of the change, although others (Gold and Schmidhauser 1960; Ryan 1981) have found no relationship. Changes in other demographic and economic characteristics might produce a shift in party allegiance, as suggested earlier in this chapter. Stronger party organization is stressed by Larew (1980) in explaining the Democrats' success. Finally, in examining the period from 1950 to 1956, Ryan (1981) dismisses increasing urbanization and improved party organization in favor of Republican factionalism as the cause of the Democrats' revival.

It should be noted that the different explanations need not be exclusive; there is no reason that they cannot be made compatible with each other. For example, the Democratic party may have been strengthened organizationally at the same time as the population became more urban, each of which occurred independently and improved the party's fortunes. The available data cannot determine conclusively which of the explanations is correct, or even their relative importance. But the information we can analyze can help us improve our understanding of the dynamics behind the Democrats' improved political standing.

Iowa's changing economy is likely to have political consequences. Since farmers are traditionally Republican, as their numbers decline Democratic prospects should improve—particularly if those who leave the farm move to urban areas and become blue collar workers. Table 11.3 presents Iowa Poll data on party identification by occupation from 1955 to 1987. These data show that, over time, Republican support has declined among every occupational category except farmers. Democrats have become the preferred party of "others"— retirees, housewifes, students, and the like. Service workers are split evenly between the two parties; and even among those in the professions or management, the gap between the two parties has narrowed substantially. Blue collar workers have continued to be in the Democrats' fold, although not to the overwhelming extent many might expect.

The full import of the results is reflected in the second part of table 11.3, which shows the percentage of each sample that is accounted for by a particular occupational group. Farmers, the most solidly Republican group, are declining as a percentage of the state's population. Those in the residual "other" category have shifted to the Democrats at the same time their numbers in the population have been swelling. Thus the changes in Iowa's economy have favored the Democrats. Moreover, the data suggest that as the state becomes more urbanized, the Democrats will, on balance, benefit.

Another striking change in each party's support base is presented in table 11.4, which gives party identification by age for selected years from 1965 to 1986. In January 1965, when Democratic support in the state was still enjoying its anti-Goldwater induced peak, those over fifty-six years of age were strong Republicans; but those who were younger were very Democratic. By 1971 when party identification levels had returned to more typical levels (see table 11.1), those fifty-six and older were still the only group tilting toward the GOP; but the

Table 11.3. Party Identification by Occupation: Iowa, 1955–1987

| | Professional and Management | | Service | | Blue Collar | | Farm | | Other | | |
|---|---|---|---|---|---|---|---|---|---|---|---|
| | Rep (%) | Dem (%) | Rep (%) | Dem (%) | Rep (%) | Dem (%) | Rep (%) | Dem (%) | Rep (%) | Dem (%) | N |
| 1955 | 78 | 20 | 63 | 37 | 46 | 51 | 57 | 41 | 57 | 40 | 552 |
| 1962 | 60 | 29 | 52 | 38 | 37 | 51 | 50 | 41 | 47 | 40 | 1,181 |
| 1964[a] | 44 | 28 | 36 | 43 | 19 | 54 | 39 | 44 | 41 | 40 | 1,181 |
| 1972 | 62 | 27 | 56 | 28 | 41 | 49 | 54 | 36 | 54 | 39 | 575 |
| 1975[b] | 24 | 32 | 30 | 28 | 24 | 37 | 58 | 19 | 37 | 35 | 583 |
| 1987 | 33 | 23 | 31 | 31 | 20 | 31 | 37 | 18 | 31 | 39 | 1,203 |

| | Occupation Percent in Sample | | | | |
|---|---|---|---|---|---|
| | Professional and Management | Service | Blue Collar | Farm | Other |
| 1955 | 19 | 16 | 29 | 29 | 6 |
| 1962 | 16 | 13 | 31 | 34 | 6 |
| 1964 | 12 | 11 | 29 | 21 | 27 |
| 1972 | 17 | 14 | 24 | 18 | 27 |
| 1975 | 19 | 10 | 30 | 15 | 26 |
| 1987 | 24 | 15 | 30 | 7 | 23 |

Source: Iowa Poll numbers 138, 169, 177, 205, 218, 284.
Note: The Iowa Poll has asked the same basic open-ended question on occupation over time. It is not clear, however, who gets placed in which category. The increase in "others" in 1964 and after appears to be the result of a change in coding, which placed homemakers and retirees in their own categories rather than placing them in the category of the head of household's occupation or former occupation.
[a] Party leaners not included.
[b] Question wording change.

Table 11.4. Party Identification by Age: Iowa, 1965–1986

| | Age | | | | | | | | | |
|---|---|---|---|---|---|---|---|---|---|---|
| | 18–29 | | | 30–55 | | | 55+ | | | |
| | Rep (%) | Dem (%) | Ind (%) | Rep (%) | Dem (%) | Ind (%) | Rep (%) | Dem (%) | Ind (%) | N |
| 1965 | 27 | 65 | 7 | 39 | 56 | 5 | 52 | 43 | 5 | 577 |
| 1971 | 30 | 57 | 11 | 42 | 46 | 11 | 53 | 38 | 8 | 579 |
| 1976[a] | 24 | 29 | 47 | 30 | 30 | 40 | 35 | 36 | 29 | 461 |
| 1986 | 31 | 17 | 51 | 26 | 29 | 43 | 31 | 39 | 30 | 677 |

Source: Iowa Poll numbers 178, 200, 218, and 272.
[a] Wording of question changed for party identification.

gap between the two parties among the other age groups had narrowed some. But starting in the mid-1970s, the support patterns changed dramatically. Those fifty-six and older in 1987 were more likely to be Democrats than Republicans, and Iowans under the age of thirty were much more apt to be Republican than Democrat.

The impressive changes in party support by age could work to the disadvantage of the Republicans. As noted earlier, the state's population is getting older. The results in table 11.4 show that the older an Iowan is, the more likely he or she is to identify with the Democrats. Moreover, it is well established that the likelihood an individual will vote increases with age. In Iowa, this could compound the GOP's problems; their support is strongest among those least apt to vote. Democrats benefit from the fact that their supporters are much more likely to go to the polls.

Finally, as Larew documented (1980), the Democratic party has developed increased organizational strength. Until the 1970s the Democratic state party had little in the way of permanent staff, raised very little money, and was chronically in debt. Revival of the party structure was generated from lower levels. Democrats in Polk County (Des Moines) organized with great success in the 1950s, and later John Culver and his assistant, Dick Clark, were able to give the party a base of organization in the second Congressional District after Culver was elected its representative in 1964. Still, analyses of party organization strength at both the state and local level in 1979 to 1980 considered Iowa Democrats to be moderately weak at each tier (Cotter et al. 1984; Jewell and Olson 1988, 64–65).

Prospects for the Democratic state party, however, improved with the passage in 1973 of a state income tax checkoff law allowing taxpayers to direct one dollar of what they owed to one of the state party organizations. The funds generated by that law allowed the Democrats to get out of debt and to participate more vigorously in electoral activities. In the 1988 campaign the Democratic party in Iowa was better financed than its Republican counterpart, and its impressive voter registration and turnout programs were credited for the party's success. The election left the Democrats in solid control not only of the state legislature, but also of the ninety-nine county courthouses (*Des Moines Register* 1988a). Indeed the tables had shifted to the extent that David Yepsen, the state's leading political journalist, titled a post-election analysis "What Iowa GOP Must Do Now to Survive" (*Des Moines Register* 1988b).

## POLITICAL SHIFTS AND SECULAR REALIGNMENT

The individual level and electoral outcome evidence presented here point to a single, clear conclusion: during the last forty years Iowa has undergone a secular realignment (Key 1959). That there has been a realignment is beyond dispute; the Democrats entered the period with little support among the voters and almost no elected officials at the state and federal level and have emerged as the strong party in a competitive system.

The timing of the shift also seems clear. Key (1959) considered a secular realignment to be a long, slow change in the distribution of party loyalties. This characterization fits the evidence in Iowa. No single, cataclysmic event or election seems to have reshaped the nature of party competition in the state. Certain elections, particularly 1958, 1964, and 1974, did produce significant changes in support for the two parties; but those shifts were, for the most part, short-lived. Similarly, no single candidate or issue appears to account for the realignment. Perhaps Harold Hughes's service as governor and U.S. Senator during the 1960s and early 1970s improved the electorate's image of the Democratic party and inspired increased organizational activity. But Hughes's success and popularity did not precipitate a massive movement to his party. Moreover, as figure 11.1 and table 11.1 demonstrate, the Democrats' prospects had begun to improve before Hughes and continued to brighten after he retired from political life. Indeed, the shift in Democratic support in the General Assembly mirrors what was happening in other Midwest states (Smith and Squire 1987, 47). Party leaders and organizational improvements no doubt contributed to the realignment; but given that the shift was secular, changes in the state's demographic and economic characteristics were the primary dynamic forces behind it.

## FUTURE TRENDS

Currently, partisan politics in Iowa is best described as competitive, with the Democrats ascending. Looking to the future, experts disagree as to whether the state will lose population or grow slightly over the next few decades; but there is consensus that the economy and the composition of the population will continue to undergo significant changes (*Des Moines Register* 1988c). In particular, the number of people directly involved in agriculture is expected to decline, further eroding the Republicans' traditional political base. But the number of manufacturing jobs also is predicted to drop, diminishing the Democrats' prospects for attaining dominant status in the state. Only the service economy is expected to grow, and those working in that sector appear to be evenly split between the two parties. On that score, then, partisan politics in Iowa should continue much as they are today.

Some potential wild cards are, of course, in the forecast. For instance, abortion could become the most divisive electoral issue in recent history. That issue, about which many people have passionate and uncompromising views, became a major issue in the 1990 gubernatorial and senate races. Pro-choice Democrats were pitted against pro-life Republicans as outside groups poured money and workers into the contests, creating considerable volatility in those elections. Although most polls showed Iowans tilting toward a pro-choice position, in the end the 1990 results were split in favor of incumbents. Senate abortion rights supporter Democrat Tom Harkin was reelected and abortion opponent Republican Terry Branstad regained the statehouse.

If there is anything about the Iowa political scene that might work to one party's advantage, it is the Democrats' increasing dominance at the local level. This is important because lower level officeholders constitute a pool of potential candidates for higher office. It may be that in a few years Democrats will increase their lead over the Republicans because they will be able to field more experienced candidates. Overall, however, there is little reason to expect Iowa will become dominated by either the GOP or the Democrats.

# Ohio: Party Change without Realignment

## LAWRENCE BAUM AND SAMUEL C. PATTERSON

**12**

WHAT changes have taken place in the partisan loyalties of Ohioans since the 1960s? Have the electoral fortunes of the Democratic and Republican parties been transformed in the last two or three decades? Can we detect shifts in the basic partisan attachments of Ohio's citizens? What implications, if any, do such changes have for politics in one of the nation's large, urban, industrial states?

Ohio is an urbanized and industrialized midwestern state that has suffered in recent years from a weakening of its industrial sector and slow population growth. Those characteristics are hardly unique to Ohio. But the state has a political history that distinguishes it from states such as Illinois and Michigan, and that heritage provides a special context for political change in the recent past and the present.

### THE POLITICAL CONTEXT

Ohio is a populous and highly urbanized state. Unlike many other states, it has no dominant city. Cleveland has the largest metropolitan area, but

We are grateful for discussions about Ohio politics with Thomas A. Flinn, Cleveland State University, and Herbert B. Asher, The Ohio State University. We appreciate the help of Stephen Quinlan of Ohio State University's Polimetrics Laboratory with the analysis of the 1984, 1986, and 1988 Ohio State surveys. We thank Alfred J. Tuchfarber, the director of the Institute for Policy Research at the University of Cincinnati, for providing us party identification data from the Ohio Poll from 1981 to 1990.

Cincinnati and Columbus also are sizeable, and the state includes several other major cities. Like Illinois and Indiana, Ohio drew its nineteenth-century population from both the North and the South, with settlers from different regions predominating in different parts of the state. Industrialization brought new populations to the state, including blacks and whites from the South and immigrants from southern and eastern Europe. The new populations settled most heavily in Cleveland and other cities of the state's northeast. Notably, however, the number of immigrants was more limited than in most other industrial states.

As the United States became industrialized, Ohio benefited from its natural resources and its pivotal location in the nation's transportation system (Hunker 1984). In the years after World War II, Ohio was one of the leading industrial states in the nation. Its agricultural sector was also relatively prosperous. In its wealth and the economic status of its people, Ohio ranked well above average.

Gradually, however, Ohio's economic status began to erode. Changes in the nation's economy reduced the value of the state's strengths and exposed weaknesses such as a work force ill-trained for new economic developments. Steel and other heavy industries important to the state declined, with a major negative impact on Ohioans. Those trends accelerated in the late 1970s and 1980s. Between 1979 and 1982, a period of two recessions, manufacturing employment declined by 23 percent in the durable goods sector and 13 percent in the nondurable goods sector. Lost jobs were not recovered later; manufacturing employment remained flat during the remainder of the 1980s (Ohio Bureau of Employment Services 1989, 48, 50). Ohio's unemployment rate was well above the national average during the first half of the 1980s and remained above the national average nearly every month during the second half of the decade (Ohio Bureau of Employment Services 1989, 69). Growth in personal income failed to keep pace with that in the nation as a whole, dropping Ohio per capita income below the national average (*Survey of Current Business* 1989, 34).

Changes in Ohio's economy have been paralleled by striking transformations of its political life as well. Having remained a predominantly Republican state for three decades after the New Deal, Ohio has become politically competitive, with a record in the 1970s and 1980s of significant Democratic political successes.

Beginning in the 1940s, Ohio's politics took on a distinctive pattern.

While the New Deal realignment produced majority status for the Democrats in most northern industrial states, the Republicans retained an advantage in winning Ohio elections as late as the 1960s. Democratic candidates competed fairly well for the presidency and governorship, but the Republicans were far more successful in winning other offices. Between 1941 and 1970, for instance, the Democrats controlled the state legislature only twice (Fenton 1966, 146).

The Republican party's success in Ohio stemmed from several factors (Fenton 1966, 117–54; Flinn 1960, 1962). Part of the explanation is that the state's socioeconomic characteristics were more favorable to the Republicans than in states such as Illinois and New York. The ethnic and racial composition of the state as a whole aided the Republicans. The relative absence of industry in Columbus and Cincinnati helped the Republicans gain a level of strength unusual for cities of such size, and the Republicans enjoyed considerable success in many of the state's medium-sized cities as well. Settlement patterns, prosperity, and alienation of ethnic Germans from the Democratic party during the two world wars made rural areas even more Republican and conservative than in most other northern states.

State characteristics also benefited the Republicans in party organization. The absence of a dominant big city and the relative weakness of labor unions limited the organizational base for the Democrats. Further, the party suffered from internal divisions among organizations of the various cities and ideological differences between liberal big-city Democrats and more conservative rural Democrats. In contrast to the Democrats, the Republican party built a highly effective organization, largely through the efforts of long-time party chairman Ray Bliss, who served from 1949 to 1965. The effectiveness of Republican organization undoubtedly helped foster a considerably higher turnout rate for Republican identifiers (Fenton 1966, 133).

Republican strength both reflected and fostered a greater degree of conservatism than that of most industrial states. In the post–World War II era, government spending in Ohio was relatively low, especially in relation to the state's wealth; Ohio's tax effort generally ranked at or near the lowest among the states. Significantly, the most successful Democratic politician in this era, Governor and Senator Frank Lausche, was a conservative who helped establish a tradition of frugal state spending (Fenton 1966, 148–49). The most powerful interest groups in Ohio have represented the business sector, with less of a countervailing force from the labor movement than in most other industrial states (Morehouse 1981, 110).

In the 1960s, John Fenton (1966, 117) characterized Ohio's politics as issueless. Though clearly overstated, that depiction carried a degree of truth. In part because of differences in political culture, activists in Ohio were less concerned with issues than their counterparts in upper midwest states such as Wisconsin and Michigan. The ideological division within the Democratic party and the absence of a labor movement with a broad policy agenda limited the Democrats' issue orientation, and the Republican party deliberately avoided issues to help maintain its electoral advantage.

By the late 1950s the Democrats began to catch up with the Republicans in their ability to win elections. That process continued in the 1960s and 1970s, and we will discuss those events and the current electoral fortunes of the two parties later in this chapter.

The economic downturn of the late 1970s and early 1980s inevitably influenced Ohio politics, accelerating change processes that already were occurring. The state's government and its politicians focused on economic development even more than in the past, a focus reflected in an active effort to attract business investment from other states and nations. Faced with a mounting budget deficit when he came into office in 1983, in his first year Democratic governor Richard Celeste secured a sizeable increase in the state income tax. While the increase aroused major opposition in the state, two tax-limitation initiative measures were defeated in 1983. That outcome, in a state where the two most recent Democratic governors had been defeated for reelection after raising taxes, suggested that the attitudes of the state's citizens were changing. Ohioans of the 1980s were somewhat more progressive than in the past, with more of them willing to support the economic development programs their leaders proposed even if the programs meant increases in taxes. But the change should not be exaggerated. The tax issue weakened Celeste, and it helped the Republicans regain control of the state senate in 1984 and maintain that control in 1986, 1988, and 1990.

## TRENDS IN PARTY IDENTIFICATION

As far back as 1958, a good year for Ohio Democrats, a survey found that the party enjoyed a forty-two to thirty-one advantage in party identification (Fenton 1966, 133). Table 12.1 provides data from 1968 through 1990. In 1968 the breakdown of party loyalties was almost exactly the same as in 1958. The Democrats retained their advantage during the 1980s.

Table 12.1.  Trends in Party Identification: Ohio, 1968–1990

|      | Strong Demo-crat (%) | Weak Demo-crat (%) | Leaning Demo-crat (%) | Indepen-dent (%) | Leaning Repub-lican (%) | Weak Repub-lican (%) | Strong Repub-lican (%) | Total[a] |
|------|------|------|------|------|------|------|------|------|
| 1968 | 21 | 20 | 12 | 8  | 7  | 17 | 14 | 99  |
| 1981 | 15 | 20 | 15 | 13 | 11 | 15 | 11 | 100 |
| 1982 | 17 | 18 | 14 | 16 | 11 | 14 | 10 | 100 |
| 1983 | 15 | 19 | 15 | 18 | 9  | 14 | 9  | 99  |
| 1984 | 16 | 18 | 12 | 18 | 12 | 12 | 13 | 101 |
| 1985 | 18 | 17 | 10 | 19 | 10 | 14 | 12 | 100 |
| 1986 | 15 | 19 | 12 | 18 | 11 | 16 | 10 | 101 |
| 1987 | 14 | 18 | 11 | 18 | 12 | 16 | 11 | 100 |
| 1988 | 17 | 17 | 11 | 10 | 12 | 18 | 14 | 99  |
| 1989 | 16 | 17 | 9  | 16 | 10 | 18 | 15 | 101 |
| 1990 | 17 | 16 | 11 | 16 | 13 | 16 | 12 | 101 |

Sources: For 1968, Thomas A. Flinn, "Ohio," in David M. Kovenock, James W. Pro-thro and associates, *Explaining the Vote: Presidential Choices in the Nation and the States, 1968* (Chapel Hill: Institute for Research in Social Science, University of North Caro-lina, 1973), 11–210; for 1981–88, data are from the Ohio Poll (University of Cincinnati) and the Ohio State Survey (Ohio State University). For 1989 and 1990, data are from the Ohio Poll (University of Cincinnati), for which we especially thank Alfred J. Tuchfarber, director of the Institute for Policy Research at the University of Cincinnati.

Note: Data for party identification over time come from three different survey sources, so some inconsistencies may occur. Even minor differences in sampling schemes and question wording can affect the reported distribution of party identifica-tion. Accordingly, the patterns over time should be interpreted with some caution.

[a]Totals may differ slightly from 100% because of rounding.

In general, the distribution of party identification has been mark-edly stable. Throughout the 1980s, Democratic party strength held at roughly a third of the citizenry, and Republican party loyalty ordi-narily has remained firm at about one-fourth of the electorate. The 1988 presidential year underscored the stability of Democratic party attach-ment in the Ohio electorate and evidenced some increase in Republi-can party identification, as about a third of Ohioans characterized themselves as either weak or strong Republicans. The phlegmatic growth in Republican strength, if it continues, provides potential for statewide partisan change sometime in the future.

On the average over the years, proportionally somewhat fewer Ohioans have identified as Democrats and Republicans than has been true for the nation as a whole. But in 1988, distributions of party iden-tification for Ohio and the nation were very similar (see Abramson, Aldrich, and Rohde 1990, 204).

One indirect but comprehensive measure of party loyalties is the enrollment of voters in the two parties. In Ohio, a closed primary state, voters are not required to register as party adherents prior to primary elections. Rather, when Ohio voters go to vote in a primary election they make a statement of party affiliation and support that determines in which party primary they will vote. Those partisan declarations, reflected in the vote for candidates in the Democratic and Republican primaries, are sometimes reported as party registration in Ohio. Registered voters who do not participate in the primaries are counted as independents. For the 1980s, that indicator of Democratic and Republican party strength in Ohio looks like this:

|      | *Democrats* | *Republicans* | *Independents* |
|------|-------------|---------------|----------------|
| 1980 | 26%         | 18%           | 56%            |
| 1984 | 30%         | 20%           | 49%            |
| 1986 | 31%         | 20%           | 49%            |
| 1988 | 32%         | 21%           | 47%            |

Because Ohio's practices regarding party registration are rather peculiar, these proportions are not really comparable to registration figures in the twenty-six states that have party registration of the usual variety. Nevertheless, the Ohio percentages suggest the stability of partisan activation in recent primary elections.

From the perspective of the party identifications of Ohioans, the story of the 1980s is as much one of dealignment as realignment. Republican presidential successes in the 1980s brought no surge of new recruits to Ohio Republican ranks, although Republican party identification edged upward. Nor have the improved fortunes of Democratic party candidates for state offices engendered steady growth in the corps of Democratic identifiers. Instead, the percentage of independents in the electorate doubled between 1968 and 1982 and then climbed a bit higher, to 18 percent. There the proportion of independents remained until 1988, when more Ohioans declared a party affiliation. Ohioans took the "flight from partisanship" in substantial measure, and apparently most who did have remained aloft (see Beck 1984, 252).

## COMPOSITION OF PARTY GROUPS

For at least the last half-century, most Democratic party identifiers in the country as a whole have seen themselves as liberal politically,

Table 12.2. Ideology of Party Identifiers: Ohio, 1986 and 1988

| | Liberal | | Middle of the Road | | Conservative | | Nonideological | | Total[a] | |
|---|---|---|---|---|---|---|---|---|---|---|
| | 1986 | 1988 | 1986 | 1988 | 1986 | 1988 | 1986 | 1988 | 1986 | 1988 |
| Strong Democrat | 22 | 32 | 31 | 28 | 22 | 19 | 26 | 22 | 101 | 101 |
| Weak Democrat | 18 | 24 | 36 | 37 | 20 | 21 | 26 | 18 | 100 | 100 |
| Leaning Democrat | 19 | 12 | 46 | 58 | 14 | 17 | 21 | 14 | 100 | 101 |
| Independent | 10 | 7 | 32 | 34 | 15 | 25 | 44 | 34 | 101 | 100 |
| Leaning Republican | 5 | 5 | 35 | 35 | 36 | 33 | 24 | 27 | 100 | 100 |
| Weak Republican | 5 | 3 | 39 | 30 | 36 | 51 | 21 | 16 | 101 | 100 |
| Strong Republican | 2 | 2 | 18 | 15 | 62 | 67 | 19 | 15 | 101 | 99 |
| Total | 12 | 13 | 34 | 32 | 29 | 35 | 26 | 20 | 101 | 100 |
| Number of cases | 90 | 74 | 263 | 189 | 221 | 208 | 202 | 120 | 776 | 591 |

Source: Ohio State Survey (The Ohio State University).
[a] Totals may differ slightly from 100% because of rounding.

and Republican party identifiers have thought of themselves as conservative. This has generally held true in Ohio, although Ohio's Democrats have always included a substantial proportion of political conservatives. In 1968 Flinn found Ohio Republicans to be much more homogenous ideologically than their Democratic counterparts (Flinn 1973, 216). That homogeneity, as we noted earlier, helped strengthen the Republican party as an organization and electoral force.

The 1986 and 1988 surveys show a similar pattern, depicted in table 12.2. Conservatives continue to predominate: about 12 to 13 percent of Ohioans think of themselves as liberals and roughly a third as conservatives. The largest number reported that they were middle-of-the-road ideologically or indicated that they were nonideological. Democrats are quite sharply divided between people who label themselves liberals and those who think of themselves as conservatives. Republicans are overwhelmingly conservative. About two-thirds of the strong Republicans were self-styled conservatives in both 1986 and 1988. In contrast, in 1986 as many strong Democrats characterized themselves liberal as conservative, although liberals outnumbered conservatives in 1988 among strong Democrats.

In their mix of ideological positions, Ohio Republicans basically mirror national Republicans, while conservative Democrats are considerably more common in Ohio than they are nationally—even with the inclusion of southern Democrats. To that extent, the Ohio Democratic party has not overcome its historic problem of ideological diversity. The large numbers of conservative Democrats would seem to provide a basis for a shift of identifications toward the Republican party, but that longstanding condition has not yet produced a dependable, stable shift.

Beyond ideological differences, Ohio party identifiers exhibit various similarities and differences in their social composition and political behavior. Table 12.3, based on the Ohio State Survey for 1988, breaks down party identifications in that year by a variety of social, economic, and political characteristics. If we leave age aside for further consideration, the results are as expected in every respect. The social and economic correlates of Republican and Democratic identification differ little from those in 1968 (Flinn 1973, 210–211); even the gender gap favoring the Democratic party existed in the late 1960s. The stability over two decades in the correlates of party loyalties provides further evidence against the existence of a strong Ohio realignment. The Republican party has not been able to gain sufficiently within any group to create a different pattern of party identifications for Ohio's social and economic groups.

The party loyalties of different age cohorts offer a somewhat different picture. In 1968, the Democrats enjoyed a substantial lead among young voters, just as they did among other cohorts below the age of 65. But in 1988, very nearly half of young Ohioans (between ages eighteen and twenty-five) identified as strong or weak Republicans. If leaners are included, well over half of the youngest age cohorts thought of themselves as Republican in 1988 compared to only 29 percent who were strong, weak, or leaning Democratic. Interestingly, the young Republican recruits were not coming mainly from conservatives who found a new partisan home, as occurred in Florida (see Beck 1982, 432). The largest shift to the Republican side among young Ohioans in the mid-1980s occurred among self-styled liberals.

The presence of the young Republicans may presage a movement toward the Republicans in the electorate as a whole (see Norpoth 1987). But analysis of the partisan attachments of young voters in the 1980s indicates a mixed story. The proportion of strong and weak Republicans among voters who were eighteen to twenty-five-years-old has fluctuated fairly strikingly, declining between 1984 and 1986 and then rising in 1988. The fluctuations reflect the political volatility of new entrants into the electorate. Young Ohioans as a group tend to exhibit partisan loyalty more fervently in presidential election years.

Table 12.3. Characteristics of Party Identifiers: Ohio, 1988

| | Strong Repub- lican (%) | Weak Repub- lican (%) | Leaning Repub- lican (%) | Indepen- dent (%) | Leaning Demo- crat (%) | Weak Demo- crat (%) | Strong Demo- crat (%) |
|---|---|---|---|---|---|---|---|
| Education | | | | | | | |
| Some high school | 9 | 8 | 6 | 11 | 14 | 16 | 36 |
| High school | 11 | 21 | 13 | 10 | 11 | 16 | 18 |
| Some college | 14 | 0 | 29 | 0 | 14 | 0 | 43 |
| College graduate | 29 | 11 | 17 | 11 | 9 | 14 | 10 |
| Income | | | | | | | |
| Under $20,000 | 15 | 15 | 11 | 11 | 8 | 18 | 23 |
| $20,000–45,000 | 18 | 16 | 16 | 8 | 12 | 13 | 17 |
| $45,000+ | 21 | 17 | 21 | 7 | 8 | 20 | 8 |
| Race | | | | | | | |
| White | 18 | 19 | 15 | 9 | 10 | 15 | 15 |
| Black | 0 | 0 | 4 | 13 | 11 | 19 | 53 |
| Other | 0 | 11 | 11 | 11 | 11 | 11 | 44 |
| Religion | | | | | | | |
| Protestant | 21 | 19 | 13 | 9 | 9 | 13 | 17 |
| Catholic | 9 | 16 | 19 | 7 | 10 | 19 | 19 |
| Jewish | 0 | 20 | 0 | 0 | 40 | 0 | 40 |
| Other | 9 | 11 | 9 | 20 | 11 | 17 | 23 |
| None | 6 | 19 | 13 | 19 | 16 | 16 | 13 |
| Age | | | | | | | |
| 18–25 | 21 | 28 | 13 | 10 | 10 | 10 | 9 |
| 26–35 | 14 | 21 | 22 | 9 | 6 | 13 | 15 |
| 36–65 | 15 | 14 | 11 | 10 | 12 | 17 | 22 |
| 65+ | 22 | 13 | 9 | 8 | 11 | 17 | 20 |
| Gender | | | | | | | |
| Female | 17 | 15 | 12 | 10 | 10 | 16 | 20 |
| Male | 16 | 20 | 16 | 9 | 10 | 14 | 15 |
| Union Membership | | | | | | | |
| Union member in household | 6 | 11 | 11 | 10 | 18 | 18 | 26 |
| No member | 16 | 18 | 13 | 10 | 9 | 14 | 17 |
| Economic Conditions | | | | | | | |
| Better off | 19 | 24 | 17 | 8 | 8 | 14 | 10 |
| Same | 22 | 10 | 10 | 11 | 12 | 15 | 20 |
| Worse off | 4 | 12 | 12 | 10 | 12 | 19 | 32 |

Source: Ohio State Survey, 1988 (The Ohio State University).
Note: Percentages add to 100 by rows.

And in the 1980s both Republican presidential candidates—Ronald Reagan and George Bush—won victories in Ohio with significant support from young voters.

The Ohio survey data indicate an electorate in a quite steady state, edging toward party dealignment due more than anything else to shifts among young Ohioans. It may be significant that Democratic losses in party loyalties since the late 1960s have not been more substantial, given the traditional bastions of Republican strength in Ohio and the national influences of the Reagan presidential victories.

## THE ELECTORAL STRENGTH OF THE PARTIES

In the three decades following the New Deal realignment, the Republicans did better at the polls in Ohio than in most comparable states. We might expect that the Republican party would maintain an advantage in winning elections in the last two decades, despite the plurality of Democratic identifiers—particularly with the signs of erosion in that plurality in recent years.

At the presidential level, the Republicans have been very successful. Since 1964, only one Democratic candidate has won Ohio's electoral votes, and that victory—by Jimmy Carter in 1976—came by a margin of eleven thousand votes out of four million. Republican victories in 1972, 1980, and 1984 came by more than 10 percent of the vote. In 1988, Republican George Bush won over Democrat Michael Dukakis by just 10 percent of the vote. Of course, Republican dominance is hardly unique to Ohio; as figure 12.1 shows, Ohio voting in presidential elections since 1960 has tracked national trends fairly closely. Indeed, in both 1984 and 1988, Ohio ranked above the median in the Democratic proportion of the vote—nineteenth in 1984, twenty-fourth in 1988. But most northern industrial states ranked higher, and in that sense Ohio can be considered Republican territory at the national level.

In state elections, the reality has been something quite different. Ohio is a prime example of what Paul Beck in chapter 16 calls "a decoupling of presidential and subpresidential voting." Since the early 1970s Democratic candidates have tended to win statewide elections for governor, auditor, and other executive offices below the governorship. They have also sustained majorities in the lower house of the state legislature.

The division of the two-party vote cast in elections for the Ohio House of Representatives provides an especially good gauge of basic

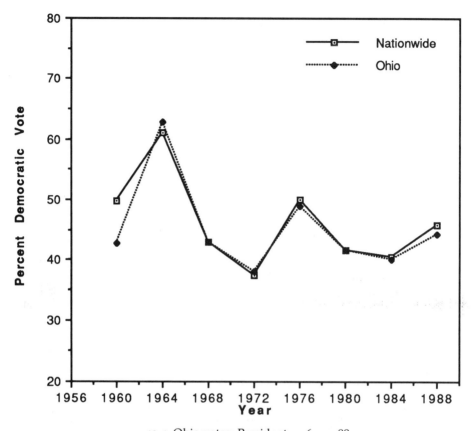

12.1 Ohio votes: President, 1960–1988

partisan voting; the aggregate Democratic vote for house candidates grew from 1966 to 1974 and then leveled off to constitute a solid majority. Here are the Democratic percentages of the two-party vote for Ohio house candidates for selected years:

| 1966 | 1970 | 1974 | 1978 | 1982 | 1986 | 1988 |
|------|------|------|------|------|------|------|
| 46.1% | 50.6% | 55.3% | 54.3% | 56.2% | 54.9% | 54.7% |

The Democrats moved from a minority position in 1966 to equity in 1970 and a fairly stable majority of about 10 percent since that time. By that measure, the Democrats have gained substantially in their ability to win votes despite the slightly negative trend for them in party loyalties.

The picture is similar if we look at election outcomes for various

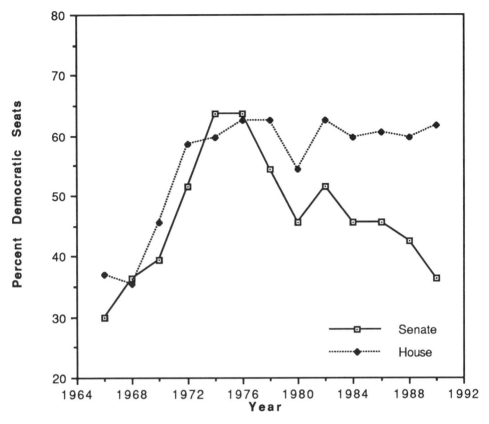

12.2 Ohio seats: State legislative elections, 1966–1990

state executive offices. At that level, the Democrats have won more often since 1970. In the six elections for governor from 1970 through 1990, the Democrats won three, including two victories by Democrat Richard Celeste, and lost two races by close margins to Republican James Rhodes. During the same period Democrats elected the secretary of state three times; and their candidates for attorney general, treasurer, and auditor have won consistently since 1970. Even in 1990 when the Republicans recaptured the governorship, the Democrats retained three of the other four executive offices.

The division of seats in the state legislature, depicted in figure 12.2, also illustrates the Democratic party's gains in Ohio. The Democrats' long period of minority status in the legislature continued in the elections of 1964 through 1970. But in 1972 the Democrats won a solid majority in the house, and since then they have maintained a majority averaging fifteen to twenty seats in a ninety-nine-member house. In

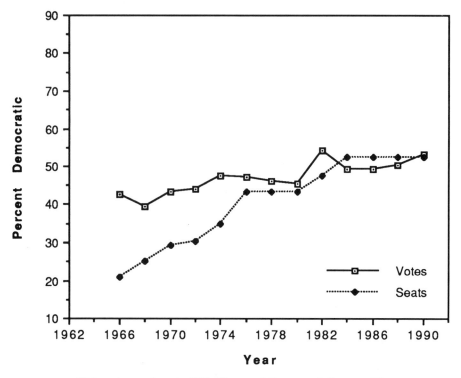

12.3 Ohio votes and seats: U.S. House of Representatives, 1966–1990

the state senate, Democrats fell just short of a majority in 1972, but they followed with two large majorities in 1974 and 1976. From 1978 through 1986, each election produced a small senate majority for one or the other party. The Republicans then gained several seats, holding a twenty-one to twelve majority after the 1990 election and slightly exceeding in proportional terms the Democrats' sixty-one to thirty-eight majority in the Ohio House of Representatives.

Ohio Democrats have made similar gains in congressional elections, as shown in figure 12.3. In the 1966 election, the Republicans won nineteen of the state's twenty-four seats in the U.S. House of Representatives. But the Democrats reached near parity by 1976, and in 1984 they finally achieved an eleven to ten majority—a ratio that was maintained in the elections from 1986 through 1990. Of course, as figure 12.3 indicates, the Democratic gain in *votes* in House elections has been far more modest. The Democrats also have held a monopoly of the state's seats in the U.S. Senate since 1976. The landslide victory of Democratic senator Howard M. Metzenbaum in 1988 over a strong challenger (then Cleveland mayor George V. Voinovich) and in the face of George Bush's 55 percent vote in Ohio, underlined the ability of Democrats to achieve successes in the state despite their weaknesses at the presidential level (Patterson and Kephart 1991).

## THE GEOGRAPHY OF PARTY STRENGTH

Recent electoral trends also can be considered geographically. The historic pattern of the distribution of the Democratic and Republican vote over Ohio's geography is highly correlated with the pattern of settlement (Flinn 1960, 709). Southeastern Ohio was settled by New Englanders who supported John Q. Adams in 1824 and the Whigs in 1848, and it remains generally Republican. Northeastern Ohio, once the Western Reserve of Connecticut, was predominantly Republican for many decades until it was "overtaken by the effects of industrialization and of the New Deal revolution" (Flinn 1960, 709). Several easternmost counties continue a Democratic voting tradition begun by the Pennsylvania Dutch and Germans who first settled there (Flinn 1962, 525–26).

Democratic voting patterns in south-central Ohio counties stem from the settlement of that area by Virginians and Kentuckians (in an area once called the Virginia Military District). A tier of counties roughly running from northwest to southeast generally has been Republican since the 1920s, and many of the counties before that, depending on their proportion of Germans and farmers (Fenton 1966, 119–24). Republican organizational strength was always greatest in Hamilton County (Cincinnati) and the other western counties. Democratic electoral clout grew as northern and northeastern counties industrialized, and centered in Cuyahoga County (Cleveland).

Figure 12.4 shows Ohio counties' voting in elections for governor over three decades—from 1956 to 1986. The areas of relative Democratic and Republican strength are similar to those that existed throughout the post–New Deal era. Democrats are still most successful in the industrialized northeast of the state, other industrial counties, and some traditionally Democratic rural counties in the south and southeast. Republicans generally win majorities in the great preponderance of rural counties and continue to hold majority positions in Franklin (Columbus) and Hamilton (Cincinnati) counties. The Democratic gains in strength in the past two decades have not upset the traditional geographic sources of the two parties' votes in state elections.

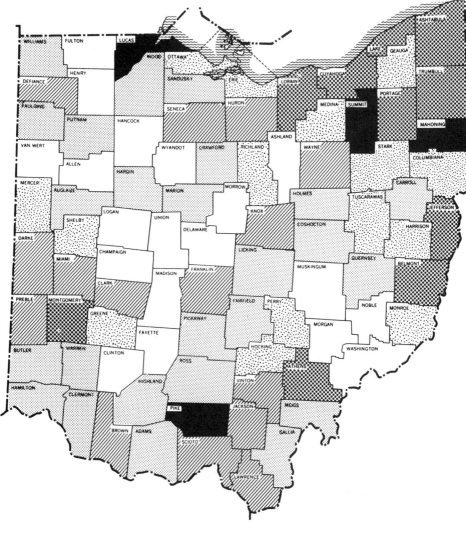

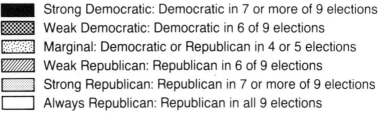

Strong Democratic: Democratic in 7 or more of 9 elections
Weak Democratic: Democratic in 6 of 9 elections
Marginal: Democratic or Republican in 4 or 5 elections
Weak Republican: Republican in 6 of 9 elections
Strong Republican: Republican in 7 or more of 9 elections
Always Republican: Republican in all 9 elections

12.4 Ohio geography of party strength, 1956–1986

ISSUES AND LEADERSHIP

Close observers have often described Ohio politics as a paradox (Flinn 1973, 209). A heavily industrial state, it generally went to the Republicans in presidential elections before and after the New Deal era. But Democrats have come increasingly to capture state offices. The improvement in Democratic fortunes has come in the decided absence of a pro-Democratic realignment in party loyalties. How can this paradox be resolved?

We can begin by largely dismissing national forces as a source of new Democratic strength. The Democrats have developed and maintained a majority position in Ohio elections during a period of Republican presidential dominance at the national level. Further, that dominance is reflected in overwhelming Republican success in presidential voting in Ohio. The divergence between presidential and state elections in the past two decades is hardly unique to Ohio—it has been considerably wider in most southern states—but it is nonetheless noteworthy.

National trends may have favored the Democrats in Ohio in a few respects. National Republican party policies have been most favorable to the South and West in the 1980s, and that is where Republican strength has grown (see Beck 1982; Dyer, Vedlitz, and Hill 1988; Galderisi et al. 1987). In the Northeast and Midwest, Democratic candidates for governor may benefit from the perception that the Republican party is unsympathetic to state interests. Further, the economic troubles suffered by Ohio, particularly during the early 1980s, provided a basis for attacks on the Republican party by Democratic candidates. But those factors seem relatively limited in their impact. Certainly an explanation for Democratic electoral successes in Ohio must focus on the state level.

Democratic successes can be considered a belated result of the Democratic plurality in voter loyalties that extends as far back as 1958. Democratic candidates were slow to benefit from that advantage because of the Republican edge in party organization, compounded by the electoral advantage enjoyed by many Republican incumbents. Some of the Democratic electoral gains of the 1970s were inevitable, given growing Democratic party identification, though their timing was not.

Further, the Democratic party gained organizational strength in the 1970s and 1980s (see Asher n.d.). Although still weaker than the Republicans at the state level, Ohio Democrats have scored organizational gains at the local level (see Cotter et al. 1984, 28–29, 52–53). The labor movement became a more effective pillar for the Democrats, and more leaders appeared who were interested in building a stronger organization. The Democratic party at the elite level became more unified ideologically, largely accepting the liberal agenda of the national party—even while rank-and-file Democrats remained ideologically divided. While Republicans retained important organizational advantages, the gap between the two parties narrowed. As a result, the Democratic party became better equipped to capitalize on growing Democratic attachments among voters. And once Democrats began to win executive offices and legislative majorities, the party gained the various advantages of incumbency: name recognition, patronage, and control over legislative reapportionment.

In that respect, the two Democratic governors who served in the 1970s and 1980s were quite important (Asher n.d.; Larson 1982). John Gilligan was governor from 1971 to 1975. In the 1968 Democratic primary, Gilligan had defeated conservative incumbent Frank Lausche for the senatorial nomination, thereby removing from power the most important exemplar of the party's traditional orientation. Gilligan lost the Senate race to William B. Saxbe. But he then ran successfully for governor in 1970 on a liberal platform, one that included advocacy of a new income tax to improve public services. His campaign and term in office brought young, liberal activists into the state's government and politics; and he also helped to solidify the labor movement as a sturdy component of the Democratic coalition.

Richard Celeste, a former state legislator and lieutenant governor, won the governorship in 1982 after an unsuccessful campaign for that office in 1978. His main rival for the gubernatorial nomination in 1982 was state attorney general William Brown, who campaigned as a conservative Democrat. Celeste adopted liberal positions on a range of economic and social issues, and his defeat of Brown confirmed the party's increasingly liberal orientation. Like Gilligan, Celeste achieved a sizeable tax increase. More impressively, he helped build a coalition that defeated a tax rollback initiative measure. That success allowed the state government to avoid substantial cutbacks in services. Celeste's overwhelming reelection victory over four-term governor James Rhodes in 1986 let him continue to use the governor's office to strengthen the state Democratic party.

The 1990 election brought a reminder—if one was needed—that the Republicans remain a very strong competitor for power in Ohio. While they lost two additional seats in the Ohio house, their majority in the senate was enhanced by two seats. Republican George V. Voinovich was elected governor, and one of the many Republican Tafts who have run successfully for office in Ohio was elected secretary of state. Those two victories gave the Republican party control over the apportionment of legislative seats in 1991 under Ohio's unusual system. Moreover, as governor, Voinovich will have the same opportunities to strengthen the Republican party that Richard Celeste exploited during the preceding eight years to strengthen the Democratic party.

If the Republicans continue to gain marginally in the balance of party identifications, those gains may combine with the party's successes in 1990 to give it a clear advantage in winning Ohio offices over the next decade. But the Democratic party can be expected to maintain the competitive position that it gained with so much difficulty over the preceding quarter century. That the Democrats achieved this position in the face of unfavorable trends in party identification is a striking reminder of the complexities of party change in the states.

# New York's Selective Majority

## JOHN KENNETH WHITE

13

EVER since its founding, New York State has been a caldron of political emotions. Fifty years ago, for example, urban-based Catholic ethnics clashed with rural white Anglo-Saxon Protestants over three issues: immigration, Prohibition, and the enlargement of government bureaucracies. Catholics favored a liberal immigration policy, while Protestants envisioned a "conquest by the immigrant" if the large migration from the Catholic-dominated countries of Europe continued unabated (Brewer 1926). Protestants supported a constitutional amendment forbidding the sale of liquor, damning their Catholic rivals as "wringing wet." But the issue that drove a lasting wedge between New York's downstate Catholics and upstate Protestants was the Catholic belief that government had a responsibility to help those who could not help themselves. Protestants disagreed, noting the danger to individual liberties from an oversized federal establishment.

Back then the political parties provided a forum to debate those issues. Catholics made good use of their Democratic platform, five times nominating one of their own, Alfred E. Smith, for governor. To succeed Smith, Catholics supported someone who, while not one of them, thought like they did—an upstate patrician named Franklin D. Roosevelt. The Catholic-Protestant political rivalries had consequences far beyond the New York borders. Both Smith and Roosevelt were nominated by the national Democratic party for president. Each was a catalyst for a great party realignment, one that produced what became known as the New Deal party system, which was organized, in part, around Protestant-Catholic tensions. For three generations, a kind of us-versus-them politics prevailed in New York and much of the rest of the country. And in the folklore of the New York Democratic party, Smith and Roosevelt were lionized as heroes in that struggle.

What of the New York party system as the twentieth century nears its end? Some lingering tensions remain between Catholics and Protestants, but the issues that gave them sustenance no longer hold sway. In the land that gave birth to the New Deal party system, the New Deal coalition is dead. New ethnic and ideological animosities have arisen; and, as in the days of old, the political parties provide a stage on which the new conflicts are fought. Today, blacks in New York City are engaged in a bitter struggle for control of the Democratic party organization and a new kind of us-versus-them politics has emerged: black versus white.

Meanwhile, a feud between liberals and conservatives has raged within the Republican party. After the New Deal, New York Republicans believed that they too must accede to the electorate's desire for a larger, more proactive government. At the same time, Republicans promised to administer the state government more efficiently than their Democratic opponents. Nelson Rockefeller and Jacob Javits symbolized what conservative critics called "me-too Republicanism." After the deaths of Rockefeller in 1978 and Javits in 1986, liberal Republicans in New York State were placed on an endangered species list. Ronald Reagan carried the state in 1980 and 1984; and conservative Republican Alfonse D'Amato twice won election to the U.S. Senate, first in 1980 and again in 1986. Liberal Republicans challenged both when they ran the first time and were unenthusiastic about their subsequent victories. But the Reagan and D'Amato wins signaled something more than adept campaigning by two pros. To the dismay of liberal Republicans, conservatives are now the dominant faction within New York State's Republican party.

The many third parties in the Empire State provide another dimension to partisan conflict. An unusual New York law known as cross-endorsement allows a minor party to endorse a major party candidate. Cross-endorsement gives New York's third parties—Liberal, Conservative, and Right-to-Life—considerable clout. Thus, in 1988 the Conservative party endorsed Republican George Bush for president, and Conservatives voted for him without squandering their votes on some unknown candidate. Since the Liberal party obtained a ballot line in 1946, no Democratic candidate for governor has won without its support. Similarly, Republicans view Conservative party backing as a prerequisite for victory. The minor parties are the "tail that wags the dog" in New York politics (Spitzer 1989). Conservatives are currently listed third on the election ballot, after the Democratic and Republican parties. The Right-to-Life party is next, as the abortion issue has become an important social issue. And the once-glorious Liberal Party stands dead last in the rankings, as its members squabble over the party's future.

## POLITICAL CONTENT

Us-versus-them politics stems in part from the large geographic hunk of United States that we call New York. In many ways, New York is not one state but many. It was settled by the Dutch in the early 1600s. The center of power in the colony, then called New Netherland, was New Amsterdam, today the site of New York City. From the port of New Amsterdam, merchants and traders shipped goods to Europe, the Dutch settlements, and outposts in the Hudson Valley. In 1644 the British established dominion over the colony. As more English immigrants settled in New Amsterdam, an upstate-downstate feud began. English farmers in Long Island and Westchester County protested the terms of trade set by the Dutch West India Trade Company located in New Amsterdam.

The Revolutionary War added to the us-versus-them dimension of New York politics. From September 1776 until the end of the revolution, the British occupied New York City. Meanwhile, the war raged in upstate New York, as one-third of the battles were fought there. After the war, the military conflicts became political ones as upstaters, led by Governor George Clinton, favored harsh actions against the Tories.

The state's central location in the new nation and the early development of New York City as a port made it a focal point for commerce, transportation, and immigration. By the 1800s, New York City had become the nation's economic and cultural capital. Upstate also changed from a rural backwater to a string of burgeoning cities and industries along the Hudson River north to Albany and through the Mohawk Valley to Buffalo. The Erie Canal and railroads linked the cities with the rest of the nation, further enhancing economic growth.

The relatively populous upstate cities, which might have mitigated the differences between New York City and upstate, did nothing to diminish the us-versus-them feelings of upstaters and downstaters. Democrats were viewed by upstaters as the protectors of New York City; New York City residents saw the GOP defending upstate interests. Two related events in the 1890s were crucial in institutionalizing the rivalry. New York City, which then consisted of what is now Manhattan and part of the Bronx, consolidated with Brooklyn, Queens, and Staten Island and annexed the rest of the Bronx. This doubled the population and established borders that remain to this day. Upstate fears of New York City's growing political and economic power increased; and, in reaction to the consolidation, the 1894 State Constitutional Convention endorsed several provisions that virtually guaranteed upstate Republican majorities in both houses of the state legislature. George Washington Plunkitt, best remembered as one of the bosses of the Tammany Hall machine, derisively called the upstaters "hayseeds," saying of their legislative dominance: "The hayseeds think we are like the Indians to the National Government—that is, sort of wards of the state, who don't know how to look after ourselves and have to be taken care of by the Republicans of St. Lawrence, Ontario, and other backwoods counties" (Riordan 1963, 21).

This image of rural upstate is outdated. Only one-sixth of New York State's population lives in the forty-four rural counties with fewer than two hundred thousand residents each. Nonetheless, social and cultural differences remain. New York City is home to the vast majority of the state's blacks, Hispanics, and Jews, thus reinforcing ethnic differences between upstaters and city dwellers. To those disparities have been added several bread-and-butter issues: legislative apportionment, taxes, and disbursement of state revenues. Some of the disputes are geographic, such as spending for roads upstate versus dollars for mass transit downstate. Other issues arise from differing demographics. The state's assumption of local government's medicaid expenditures is viewed by many as a bailout of New York City, which has a disproportionate share of the state's poor.

## TRENDS IN PARTY IDENTIFICATION

Conventional wisdom has it that New York is solidly Democratic. After all, the state produced such illustrious Democrats as Alfred E. Smith and Franklin D. Roosevelt. Those two New Yorkers precipitated a historic party realignment, one that reshaped politics in New York State and the rest of the nation. At the heart of the New Deal, was the belief that big government works. For most Americans, the

1930s were years of economic deprivation. The next decade saw the United States fighting the Germans and Japanese. In both instances, the federal government was successful in accomplishing stated objectives. The New Deal transformed many have-nots into haves. World War II produced the unconditional surrender of the Germans and Japanese, prompting social historian Studs Terkel to call it "the good war" (Terkel 1984).

Success bred success. As the party that accomplished its missions, Democrats were seen as favoring the common man, while Republicans became the party of privilege. Democrats used that formula to capture the presidency in seven of the nine elections held from 1932 to 1964.

But the Republicans were not finished. GOP presidential candidate Dwight Eisenhower won in 1952 and again in 1956. In New York, Republicans captured the governorship, first with Thomas E. Dewey in 1942 and then with Nelson Rockefeller in 1958. Together they ruled New York State for twenty-eight years. But neither Eisenhower, Dewey, nor Rockefeller could alter the us-versus-them politics of the New Deal. Instead, each became a me-too Republican, promising that government would do even more for the people. Nelson Rockefeller became the epitome of a me-too Republican, expanding government to unprecedented levels. From 1970 to 1975, state government employment rose by 9.1 percent (Carey 1981, 13). While manufacturing and other industries were losing jobs, state government continued to be New York's growth industry.

The emergence of a major Democratic player on the national stage in the 1980s, Governor Mario M. Cuomo, reinforces the perception that New York is a predominantly Democratic stronghold. Voter registration figures show Democrats outnumbering Republicans by 1,264,696 voters. Moreover, Democrats in 1990 won all but one of the state offices, a reversal from 1966 when Republicans held all but one. Democrats also maintained a comfortable majority in the State Assembly, currently holding ninety-five of 150 seats (figure 13.1). Democrats also captured twenty-one of New York's thirty-four congressional seats in 1990—unchanged from the 1988 totals.

The Democratic victories are somewhat deceiving. In 1990, Republicans won a majority in the state senate, controlling thirty-five of the sixty-one seats. But the GOP victories were not party-oriented, as they were personal triumphs for incumbent legislators. Of the 127 members of the state assembly and the fifty-two members of the state senate who sought reelection in 1990, 97.8 percent were successful—

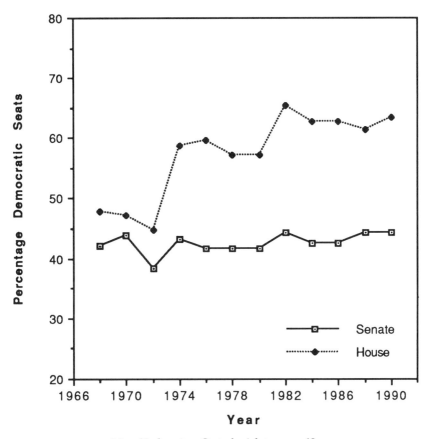

13.1 New York votes: State legislature, 1968–1990

a percentage that surpasses the return rate for the U.S. Congress (*The New York Times* 1990). Since most incumbents in New York are Democrats, the victories are usually Democratic ones. And they have helped their party. Since 1988, Democrats have added nearly four hundred thousand people to their rolls, bringing the number of registered Democrats to an all-time high since 1966. Republicans, on the other hand, have lost 174,032 enrolled party members since 1966. Meanwhile, the ranks of the unaffiliated grew nearly twofold. As far as the minor parties were concerned, Conservatives experienced the greatest growth, having more than doubled their registrants since 1966. Liberals, meanwhile, have had their registrants cut by one-third. Right-to-Lifers have increased their small numbers by 60 percent since 1978 when they were listed on New York's ballot (table 13.1).

Table 13.1. Trends in Party Registration: New York State, 1966–1990

|      | Democrat | Republican | Conservative | Right-to-Life | Liberal | Democratic Advantage |
|------|----------|-----------|-------------|---------------|---------|----------------------|
| 1966 | 3,616,775 | 2,794,320 | 54,127 | NA[a] | 87,596 | 822,455 |
| 1968 | 3,676,714 | 3,053,398 | 106,207 | NA | 94,000 | 623,316 |
| 1970 | 3,540,174 | 2,870,467 | 117,307 | NA | 112,893 | 669,707 |
| 1972 | 4,226,604 | 3,201,059 | 147,685 | NA | 159,669 | 1,025,545 |
| 1974 | 3,619,732 | 2,774,250 | 121,393 | NA | 114,861 | 845,482 |
| 1976 | 3,703,357 | 2,705,523 | 120,025 | NA | 104,429 | 997,834 |
| 1978 | 3,349,182 | 2,406,337 | 104,002 | 90 | 75,938 | 942,845 |
| 1980 | 3,455,596 | 2,467,472 | 106,777 | 15,282 | 70,010 | 988,434 |
| 1982 | 3,330,566 | 2,438,997 | 105,273 | 15,739 | 65,558 | 891,569 |
| 1984 | 3,548,858 | 2,460,836 | 107,995 | 18,933 | 65,031 | 1,088,022 |
| 1986 | 3,820,085 | 2,602,782 | 110,485 | 21,606 | 62,540 | 1,217,303 |
| 1988 | 3,494,050 | 2,472,438 | 107,421 | 20,981 | 55,678 | 1,021,612 |
| 1990 | 3,884,984 | 2,620,288 | 112,786 | 24,204 | 59,176 | 1,264,696 |

Source: New York State Board of Elections. This table excludes those who are independents. The State Board of Elections lists them as blank and combines the registrations with those that are void and missing.

[a]NA = not applicable. The Right-to-Life party was formed in 1978.

Party registration figures tell only part of the story. Indeed, party registration is often a lagging indicator of political change. When voters are asked with which party they identify, as opposed to with which party they are registered, a different portrait of the New York electorate emerges. There we find some significant Republican gains. Many of the new Republicans are younger voters who, historically, are in the vanguard of any realignment of the party system (Burnham 1970; Jennings and Niemi 1975). As the data in table 13.2 show, younger New Yorkers were much more inclined to say they are Republicans in 1988 than in 1980.

Other groups also had a proclivity to move to the GOP. Protestants provide one example. In 1980, they were evenly divided in their partisan affiliations, reflecting an erosion of Republican support after Watergate. By 1988, the GOP had a ten-point advantage over the Democrats among that religious cohort.

Democrats received strong backing from Jewish voters, as they have since the days of Smith and Roosevelt. However, their leads diminished from forty-eight points in 1980 to thirty-seven points in 1988.

Catholics were a different story. Catholic Democrats shrank from 48 percent in 1980 to 39 percent in 1988. New York Times/CBS News exit polls gave the Catholic Democrats a twenty-six-point edge over the

Table 13.2. Characteristics of Party Identifiers: New York State, 1980–1988

| | 1980 | | | 1984 | | | 1988 | | |
| --- | --- | --- | --- | --- | --- | --- | --- | --- | --- |
| | Dem (%) | Rep (%) | Ind (%) | Dem (%) | Rep (%) | Ind (%) | Dem (%) | Rep (%) | Ind (%) |
| Totals | 43 | 29 | 25 | 38 | 35 | 26 | 37 | 34 | 26 |
| Sex | | | | | | | | | |
| Male | 40 | 30 | 27 | 36 | 35 | 29 | 33 | 38 | 27 |
| Female | 46 | 28 | 23 | 41 | 35 | 23 | 41 | 32 | 24 |
| Age | | | | | | | | | |
| 18–21 | 43 | 31 | 23 | 34 | 40 | 26[a] | | | |
| 22–29 | 43 | 26 | 30 | 40 | 35 | 26[c] | 37 | 37 | 23[b] |
| 30–44 | 40 | 27 | 30 | 38 | 31 | 30 | 36 | 34 | 28 |
| 45–59 | 45 | 29 | 23 | 38 | 34 | 27 | 35 | 33 | 28 |
| 60+ | 45 | 35 | 17 | 40 | 40 | 19 | 41 | 34 | 21 |
| Religion | | | | | | | | | |
| Protestant | 37 | 37 | 23 | 32 | 44 | 25 | 32 | 42 | 23 |
| Catholic | 48 | 22 | 28 | 45 | 27 | 28 | 39 | 31 | 28 |
| Jewish | 62 | 14 | 22 | 60 | 16 | 24 | 54 | 17 | 26 |
| Other | 51 | 22 | 24 | 46 | 23 | 30 | 50 | 19 | 30 |
| Education | | | | | | | | | |
| Less than high school | 53 | 25 | 17 | 53 | 30 | 17 | 53 | 25 | 19 |
| High school graduate | 48 | 27 | 22 | 41 | 34 | 25 | 44 | 31 | 22 |
| Some college | 39 | 30 | 29 | 36 | 37 | 29 | 34 | 35 | 28 |
| College graduate | 37 | 32 | 30 | 34 | 37 | 29 | 28 | 43 | 27 |

Source: *New York Times*/CBS News exit polls 1980, 1984, and 1988. Text of question: "Do you usually think of yourself as a Republican, a Democrat, or an independent?" Percentages do not add up to 100 because of rounding.

[a] Age range is 18–24.
[b] Age range is 18–29.
[c] Age range is 25–29.

Republicans in 1980. Eight years later Catholic voters still preferred the Democrats, but this time by only an eight-point advantage. This represents a remarkable desertion by Catholics from the party that once nominated two of their own, Alfred E. Smith and John F. Kennedy, for president. Clearly, many Catholics have converted from the Democratic to the Republican party. Such a conversion is also associated with a party realignment (Burnham 1970; Erikson and Tedin 1981; Ladd and Hadley 1975; Sundquist 1983).

Class divisions were somewhat more muted in the 1980s. Low-income New Yorkers making less than $12,000 gave the Democrats overwhelming support. Likewise, those earing more than $50,000 preferred the Republicans by a substantial margin. But the middle class had a change of heart. In 1984, those earning between $15,000 and $25,000 favored the Democrats 38 percent to 33 percent. By 1988 the margin narrowed, with the Democrats holding a slender 36 to 35 percent lead.

The gender gap was readily apparent. In 1980, both sexes were inclined to say they were Democrats—men by two points, women by eighteen points. By 1988, Republicans had a five-point lead among New York males, even though the percentage of men who said they were Republicans was unchanged from 1980. Women gave the Democrats a nine-point advantage, even though the number of New York females who called themselves Democrats had fallen five points since 1980.

## ELECTORAL TRENDS

As the data above indicate, the conventional wisdom that New York is solidly Democratic has become increasingly error-prone. In 1980, conservative Republicans Ronald Reagan and Alfonse D'Amato scored upset victories, prompting veteran *New York Times* political reporter Frank Lynn to write that the wins "rang down the final curtain on the Dewey-Rockefeller-Javits era of liberal Republicanism in New York" (*The New York Times* 1980). Democrat Michael Dukakis barely carried New York State in 1988, defeating Republican George Bush by 52 to 48 percent. Bush strategists gloated that they had forced the hapless Democrat to spend considerable time campaigning in the supposedly safe Democratic state (Germond and Witcover 1989, 416). Just two years later, Democrat Mario M. Cuomo won only 53 percent support in his bid for reelection against two relatively unknown Republican and Conservative opponents.

As these ballots suggest, elections since 1980 have given birth to a new era in New York State politics. New Right conservatives like Reagan and D'Amato were in vogue, while the old liberalism was passe. New York City mayor Edward Koch saw the rising conservative tide in 1979 and adjusted his positions accordingly, calling his fellow Democrats "knee-jerk liberals."

The old liberalism became so passe that the Liberal party itself fell into disrepair. Even *The New York Times* questioned its purpose: "If in the shadow of a conservative era, they are truly intent on promoting liberal values, should they not bring their energy and dedication into the ranks of the major parties?" (*The New York Times* 1985b) In 1986 and again in 1990, the bottom dropped out, as the Liberal party finished last in the race for governor. Mario Cuomo, as the Liberal candidate in both contests (and the Democratic party's also), did not receive enough votes to beat the Right-to-Life nominees.

Change has not been limited to party position. The old upstate-downstate rivalry still exists. In 1988, for instance, Democrat Michael Dukakis defeated Republican George Bush in New York City by 645,637 votes while Bush won the rest of the state by 392,609 votes. But many analysts now argue that the growth and maturation of the suburbs surrounding New York City are dividing the state into three regions rather than two (Colby and White 1989; Marcus 1983; Miringoff and Carvalho 1986). Today, one-fourth of the New York electorate is located in the suburbs. The 1982 election of Mario Cuomo as governor points to their importance. When the election is analyzed in terms of city, suburbs, and upstate, the suburbs (Nassau, Suffolk, Rockland, and Westchester counties) emerge as important political battle-grounds. Cuomo won 68 percent of the city vote; his opponent, Republican Lewis Lehrman, got 58 percent of the upstate vote; and the suburban counties split almost evenly. Eight years later a similar split emerged. Cuomo was challenged by Republican Pierre Rinfret and Conservative Herbert London. Rinfret was chosen by a desperate Republican party that believed Cuomo was immune to serious challenge. Conservatives, including Jack Kemp, did not like Rinfret's repudiation of Reaganomics and backed Herbert London. Although Cuomo faced a divided opposition, the three battlegrounds of city, suburbs, and upstate gave very different results. Cuomo won nearly 72 percent of the votes cast in New York City, while Rinfret and London won just 11 and 13 percent of the votes, respectively. But in the four suburban counties surrounding New York City—Suffolk, Nassau, Westchester, and Rockland—Cuomo dropped to 50 percent, while Rinfret and London won 45 percent of the suburban vote. In the rest of the state, Cuomo received 45 percent of the vote to Rinfret's and London's 51 percent.

Dividing the state into three regions provides a useful framework for analysis. The appeal of particular candidates and issues differs from election to election but the image of a Democratic New York City, Republican suburbs, and Republican upstate remains fairly well-drawn (table 13.3).

But instead of using the political parties as catalysts for the changes I have so far described, New Yorkers have transcended them. The contrast between the last two statewide Democratic landslides—Lyndon Johnson's in 1964 and Mario Cuomo's in 1986—makes the point. Both Johnson and Cuomo devastated their GOP opponents, respec-

Table 13.3.  Percentage Deviation of Two-Party Total Vote for President: New York City, Suburbs, and Upstate, 1952–1988

|        | New York City (%) | Suburbs[a] (%) | Upstate (%) |
|--------|-------------------|----------------|-------------|
| 1952   | +10.4 D           | +13.8 R        | +9.0 R      |
| 1956   | +12.3 D           | +10.4 R        | +9.6 R      |
| 1960   | +10.2 D           | +9.2 R         | +6.7 R      |
| 1964   | +4.4 D            | +8.6 R         | +0.5 R      |
| 1968   | +11.2 D           | +9.2 R         | +5.8 R      |
| 1972   | +10.3 D           | +6.6 R         | +5.9 R      |
| 1976   | +14.6 D           | +4.5 R         | +7.9 R      |
| 1980   | +10.9 D           | +10.3 R        | +1.8 R      |
| 1984   | +15.0 D           | +8.0 R         | +6.8 R      |
| 1988   | +14.7 D           | +9.8 R         | +5.0 R      |

Source: Peter W. Colby and John K. White, eds. *New York State Today: Politics, Government and Public Policy* (Albany: State University of New York Press, 1989).

Note: For example, in 1988 Republican George Bush received 47.9 percent of the two-party vote in New York State as a whole, but only 33.2 percent of the New York City vote. Thus, the city deviated from the statewide pattern by 14.7 percent in favor of Democratic candidate Michael Dukakis.

[a] Suburbs includes Nassau, Suffolk, Rockland, and Westchester counties.

tively winning 68.6 and 64.6 percent of the votes cast. In each case the Democratic margins exceeded the Republican totals.

But the similarity between the Johnson and Cuomo landslides ends here. Johnson had coattails that reached to the lowliest Democrat. The result was a Democratic recapturing of both houses of the New York State legislature, something that had not happened since 1958. Mario Cuomo's 1986 coattails, however, were nonexistent. The popular governor did not alter a single outcome in the Republican-controlled state senate, where no seat changed hands. In the state assembly, Democrats added just one seat to their majority. Those results, coupled with Cuomo's unwillingness to come to the aid of his party, left many Democrats unhappy. Senate minority leader Manfred Ohrenstein said of Cuomo: "He embarked on a strategy to win by a huge margin, and he did it. Not everyone liked the strategy. It is a controversial strategy, but it worked enormously well" (*The New York Times* 1986).

New York's selective majority manifested itself in 1988. Democrats Michael Dukakis and Daniel Patrick Moynihan may have been in alignment on the ballot, but not in their respective vote totals. Statewide, Dukakis barely scraped by with a four-point victory, but Moynihan overwhelmed his Republican opponent by thirty-two points—the largest margin ever recorded in a New York U.S. Senate contest. The suburbs that ring New York City illustrate the selective nature of the New York electorate. Republican Bush won them by 243,614 votes, while Democrat Moynihan amassed a whopping 273,487 plurality there.

In 1990, New York voters, once again, showed their penchant for selective purchasing. Democrats and Republicans had something to crow about. Mario Cuomo won reelection to a third term, but with a substantially reduced margin than he accumulated four years before. Republican state comptroller Ned Regan also won another term with just 52 percent of the vote in a tight contest with Democrat Carol Bellamy, who captured 48 percent of the ballots. Republicans rejoiced that they retained the state senate, even adding one more to their ranks. But Democrats pointed to a comfortable win by their candidate for attorney general. Democrats also took comfort in the fact that they increased their majority in the state assembly by three seats.

## ISSUES AND LEADERSHIP

Clearly, there has been no party realignment in New York State akin to that produced by Alfred E. Smith and Franklin D. Roosevelt. Rather, the political changes that occurred during the 1980s might be termed a rhetorical realignment. Beginning with Ronald Reagan's election in 1980, the tone of political conversation changed. Instead of promising to increase the size of government, politicians in both parties now suggest ways of limiting its growth. Mario Cuomo in late 1990 proposed cutting the New York State workforce by some ten thousand employees.

Rhetorical conservatives are winning elections in New York. Rather than voting randomly New Yorkers are selective, choosing rhetorical conservatives from both parties. Those who do not speak the new language face rejection by a fickle electorate.

No one is better at playing the game of rhetorical conservatism than Mario Cuomo. The day after the 1984 presidential election he told an interviewer:

> One of the Senators . . . is supposed to have said, "We have read all of Governor Cuomo's speeches and they are New Deal." I laughed. What are you

when you reduce public employees by 9,000? What are you when you say [that] need should be the criterion [for welfare benefits]? What are you when you come out for a tax cut? What are you when you refuse to raise the basic taxes? What are you when you spend more on your defense budget, which we call corrections, than any governor in history? (Barnes 1985, 18).

Cuomo's aversion to the New Deal liberal tag has earned him a new appellation: the New Deal refusnik. His popularity has been enhanced by a perception shared by many New Yorkers that it is the Republican Party that "taxes and spends, taxes and spends." Ronald Reagan and George Bush used that shibboleth effectively against Democrats in three presidential elections. But in New York it was former four-term GOP governor Nelson Rockefeller whose name and party became synonymous with higher taxes. As Rockefeller once said, "You could plop me down in a town of two hundred people, and the first thing I'd do is try to start solving their problems." Often, that meant spending more money. One voter, less than enthralled with that approach, wrote Rockefeller, "Thank God our town is too small for your plopping" (Persico 1982, 201).

Mario Cuomo has tried to pin the tax and spend label on the Republicans. Accepting renomination in 1986, he recalled Rockefeller's profligate spending:

> For sixteen years, from 1959 to 1974, the Republicans dominated the government in Albany. During that period they took us from twenty-second in the United States, in terms of per capita taxes, to first. They raised the state income tax to a nearly incredible 17½ percent rate. In the process we lost hundreds of thousands of jobs. . . . By 1983 we were still suffering from the after effects of sixteen years of crippling Republican tax increases (Cuomo 1986).

In his three gubernatorial campaigns, Cuomo reminded New Yorkers, "You campaign in poetry and you govern in prose." As to the prose of Cuomo's governance, the conservative rhetoric has sometimes matched the reality. During his first term, tax rates were cut to their lowest point in twenty-seven years. But the hallmark of the Cuomo years lies in the vast amounts of money spent to house convicted criminals. From 1983 to 1990, Cuomo added nearly thirty thousand beds to a prison system that already was one of the largest in the nation. Moreover, those incarcerated nearly doubled, growing to fifty-five thousand (*The New York Times* 1990). Prisons have become the greatest physical legacy of the Cuomo years.

CONCLUSION: THE END OF LIBERALISM?

Clearly, the poetry of the Empire State has changed, but has the prose lost its Rockefeller-like liberalism? Certainly Cuomo and other successful candidates for state office (both Democratic and Republican) have emulated the conservative rhetoric of Ronald Reagan to win election. But do New Yorkers really want a conservative government? The answer may be surprising. From 1982 to 1986, disbursements from New York State's general fund increased 30 percent (*New York State Statistical Yearbook* 1987, 350). Patrick J. Buchanan, director of communications for the Reagan White House in 1985, attacked Cuomo's proclivity to spend: "Mario Cuomo's incessant invocations of the poor, the downtrodden, [and] the ill almost invariably turn up as preambles to budget requests that would augment the power of his own political class—the Welfare Statists" (*The New York Times* 1985).

But using the power of government to help the poor, the downtrodden, and sick is not without appeal—especially after a decade of making do with less. During the 1970s New York lost 684,103 residents, according to U.S. Census figures. Many of those who left migrated to southern and western states, taking their jobs with them. Fewer jobs meant a shrinking tax base. Governor Hugh Carey declared in his 1975 inaugural address that "the days of wine and roses are over" (Colby and White 1989, 235). As if to punctuate Carey's remark, New York City hovered on the brink of bankruptcy. An expensive city government, high taxes and stiff regulations, fewer businesses and jobs, and a shrinking population were to blame. The conditions were also instrumental in restructuring policy-making in the state at large.

By the 1980s the idea that big government works fell into disrepair. Candidates who questioned that premise often found themselves garnering more votes than their opponents. But New Yorkers wanted to have their cake and eat it too. Voters, though skeptical of government, want it to do more. In 1983 a $1.25 billion Rebuild New York bond issue won easy approval. The new money was used to fix the state's crumbling roads. As New York's economy improved with the rest of the nation during the 1980s, state government was in a position to do more.

But the improved economy did not translate into a return to normalcy as far as government was concerned. Voters wanted state government to address the challenges of the 1990s. When asked by the

Marist Institute whether they would be willing to pay an additional one hundred dollars in taxes to increase funding for several government programs, New Yorkers were largely supportive: 72 percent would use the additional money to pay for the education of the mentally retarded and handicapped, 67 percent would pay more to house the homeless, 60 percent would favor budgeting the new money to care for patients with Acquired Immune Deficiency Syndrome, 56 percent would give the money to the public schools, and 54 percent would favor spending the money to rebuild New York's roads and bridges (Marist Institute for Public Opinion 1990).

Thus, when it comes to bread and butter issues like education, health care, the problems of the mentally ill, and mass transportation, most New Yorkers have not abandoned the old liberalism. Party elites, however, have a different view. They believe voters want a tight-fisted, fiscally conservative government. For Cuomo, the impression is so real that it has become a hallmark of his governorship.

But the voters are ahead of the politicians. Their support for Cuomo derives from the belief that he is both a conservative and a liberal. Voters like the fact that he has built so many jail cells while remaining a spokesperson for the welfare state. Cuomo himself recognizes the contradictory aspects of his electoral appeal. The governor often describes himself as a progressive pragmatist.

Once on hearing reports of his death, Mark Twain pugnaciously denounced them as premature. It is not premature to say that the New Deal party system is dead in New York. Alfred E. Smith and Franklin D. Roosevelt have faded into the mystic chords of memory for most New Yorkers. But it is premature to argue that a party realignment, like that engineered by Smith and Roosevelt, has occurred. Clearly there have been significant partisan changes. But voters have managed to transcend the parties in making government do the things they want. Old tensions have been replaced by new ones. And the political parties are but one stage upon which the new conflicts are fought. Neither the Democrats nor the Republicans have established superiority on the new political battlefield. The next decade will determine if either one can become New York's new majority party.

# Secular Realignment in New Jersey

## MAUREEN MOAKLEY

**14**

IN January 1990 Democrat Jim Florio, a congressman from a working-class background with roots in the Camden County Democratic party, took office as the forty-ninth governor of New Jersey. Florio won office in a landslide election, regaining the governor's office and the state assembly for the Democrats. Those events might suggest politics as usual in New Jersey. The state is generally considered a Democratic one, where the traditional constituencies of the New Deal coalition came to power after the election of Franklin Roosevelt and have continued to dominate the political life of the state. Hence, after a period of Republican success in the 1980s, which coincided with the Reagan years, the election of Florio signaled a return to the New Deal fold.

This chapter offers two different perspectives on those events. One is that the New Deal coalition, to the extent that it came to dominate politics in the Garden State, has eroded, and New Jersey is in the midst of a long-term secular realignment. The second perspective is that the secular pattern of change is similar to political transitions that have occurred in the state over the past century. In a state with a history of strong and competitive parties, the eventual ascendency of the Democrats after the New Deal era was a long, cumulative process that began before the election

The author would like to thank Gerry Pomper and Alan Rosenthal of Rutgers University, Drew Goldman of Connecticut College, and especially Barbara Salmore of Drew University for their helpful comments on earlier drafts of this chapter.

of FDR. Similarly, the current changes are rooted in long-term shifts in voter allegiance toward the parties that have the potential to produce Republican dominance.

## THE POLITICAL CONTEXT

However one judges the specific policy initiatives of his administration, the popular two-term Republican governor Tom Kean (1981–89) will be remembered as the governor who changed the image of New Jersey (Sinding 1989). That somewhat curious legacy illustrates the broad social, economic, and political transformations that have occurred in New Jersey since the Second World War. Kean, in fact, presided over the tail end of a transition in which the state evolved from a county-based, machine-dominated political system—in a locale that to many appeared to be little more than a polluted corridor between New York and Philadelphia—into a prosperous and economically developed state with modern, progressive government. While the changes have been ongoing, stereotypes die hard. The fact that Kean was able to put the old images to rest suggests that the transition, at least at the level of state politics, is complete.

Demographic and economic trends since the Civil War laid the groundwork for change. From 1860 to 1940, industrialization and urban growth, fueled by successive waves of European immigration, changed the character of this once rural state. New Jersey, given the proximity of New York and Philadelphia, never developed any major cities. Yet by 1940, 60 percent of all jobs in the state were related to manufacturing; and 30 percent of the population lived in the six smaller cities of Newark, Jersey City, Trenton, Camden, Elizabeth, and Paterson (Sternlieb and Hughes 1986). The depression, however, caused an economic squeeze and a housing shortage that pinched the vastly expanding middle class.

The post-war building boom that created massive housing developments throughout the state eased those tensions and facilitated the rapid suburbanization of New Jersey. The demographic changes precipitated an economic transition. As the state's infrastructure expanded, businesses developed along suburban areas of growth; and New Jersey made the successful transition from a manufacturing to a service economy (Sternlieb and Hughes 1986). Through the early 1980s, the state experienced unprecedented growth and prosperity; New Jersey became and remains an affluent state. It ranks second in the country in per capita income and, as of 1990, households that annually earn $50,000 or more constitute about one-quarter of the population.

The post-war economic and demographic changes, in turn, precipitated a political transition. The late 1960s marked the beginning. Until that time, politics in the Garden State was controlled by strong, country-based party organizations. Most of the twenty-one counties in New Jersey were solidly one-sided in partisan distribution, providing the dominant party with a firm base of voter support in a noncompetitive political environment. Hence, those organizations were akin to autonomous political fiefs controlled by the leadership; and informal, shifting and competitive coalitions of those organizations dominated the political life of the state (Moakley 1984). Since most public jobs and services were administered at the county level, with local property taxes representing the core of the tax base, the party organizations developed and enjoyed a vast patronage system controlled by the dominant party's leadership.

County organizations extended their influence to the statehouse through the electoral system. Until the reapportionment decisions of the late 1960s and early 1970s, members of the state senate and assembly were elected at large from within each county. County parties essentially controlled nomination and elections to the state legislature; and, for the most part, legislators in office did the bidding of the county leaders. The organizations and their leaders also played a key role in nominating and electing the state's chief executive. Through the early 1970s, even the most prestigious candidate for governor needed the backing, money, votes, and campaign workers the party organizations controlled in order to make a bid for office (Moakley 1986). Moreover, once elected, sitting governors had to work through these leaders to secure legislative support for most policy initiatives.

This parochial system, along with the inefficiency and corruption it engendered, eroded quickly throughout the 1970s. During suburbanization, politics within counties became more competitive. Many voters—particularly those from urban areas—took their partisan inclinations with them; and eventually county organizations no longer enjoyed solid, one-party constituencies and political control. Moreover, an expanding middle class no longer supported the machinations of the old-style patronage organizations as voters demanded more professional and open government.

Reapportionment decisions, in tandem with a more competitive political environment, gave state legislators a measure of independence from county leaders. More competent candidates were encour-

aged to run for office (Rosenthal 1986); and a more professional legislature initiated a series of reforms aimed at dismantling the old
county-based patronage system and creating effective authority at the
state level.

In the office of the governor, the transition occurred in significant
ways during the tenure of Democrat Brendan Byrne (1973–81). Although Byrne probably owed less to the county bosses for his nomination and election in 1973 than his predecessors, he acknowledged
he would not have made his first bid for office without the support of
key county leaders. During his first term, however, the more progressive proclivities of his administration alienated the Democratic county
leaders, and they turned against him. They were not able, however,
to deny Byrne renomination (as Republican party leaders were able to
do to sitting Republican governor William Cahill in 1973). Byrne's successful reelection in 1977, without party leaders' support, signaled
the end of the county parties' influence in the statehouse.

Moreover, during that election, Byrne campaigned for a permanent
enactment of a statewide income tax, a temporary version of which
had been forced on the legislature by the state supreme court. For all
intents and purposes, the election became a mandate on the tax; and
the fact that voters supported Byrne indicated that New Jerseyans
were ready for some measure of programmatic government. The im-
plementation of the tax shifted monies, services, and authority away
from the counties and toward state government. As a result of his second administration, Byrne left a legacy of progressive statewide initiatives that laid the groundwork for modern state government and
nurtured the economic boom of the late 1970s. By the mid-1980s, the
image of the state finally began to change. New Jersey had entered
the modern era.

PARTISAN TRENDS

How did the long-term political trends affect the partisan balance in
the state? First, one should note that political parties were formed
early in New Jersey; and, since the Civil War, both major parties have
enjoyed a strong presence in the state. Around the election of 1896,
however, the voters rejected the populist position of the Democratic
national ticket, and the state became quite solidly Republican. More
conservative Democrats, however, made statewide breakthroughs as
early as 1907, as coalitions of poor, urban, and largely immigrant
voters began to mobilize around emerging Democratic political ma-

chines. They enjoyed some striking successes, particularly as the huge pluralities from Hudson County allowed the Democrats, under the leadership of Frank Hague, to take control of the governor's office and occasionally gain a majority in the lower house of the legislature.

Franklin Roosevelt's election as president certainly enhanced the position of the Democrats; the party enjoyed a brief period of hegemony around the election of 1932. But the Republicans did not fade from the electoral scene. In fact after that critical election, the GOP regained control of the state legislature and the congressional delegation after only one term.

The period from the 1950s through the 1970s, however, was a time of growing Democratic strength. Certainly the ascendency of the Democrats was slowed by structural factors. In the state legislature, the continued dominance of the Republicans was aided by New Jersey's off-year electoral cycle and by a malapportioned state senate that favored rural Republicans (Salmore 1986). Representation to county freeholder boards also favored Republicans, as Democratic strength was concentrated in fewer, but more densely populated counties. By the early 1970s, however, New Jersey was a solidly Democratic state. The Democrats controlled both houses of the state legislature, dominated the congressional delegation, captured more than 60 percent of the local county freeholder seats throughout the state, and enjoyed a solid twenty-two-point advantage in polls on partisan support.

Democratic gains began to erode throughout the 1980s. A Republican governor, Tom Kean, who squeaked into office in 1981 with less than a two-hundred-vote edge, began to enjoy unprecedented public approval levels. That was during the peak of the economic boom, when budget surpluses and a surge of state chauvinism—which were the aftermath of the changes of the previous decade—really hit home. During that period, polls indicated that Democrats were losing their advantage among some key constituencies. By 1985, the Republicans, in conjunction with Kean's landslide reelection, were able to take control of the lower house of the legislature and score impressive victories in local county elections.

By the end of the 1980s and Kean's tenure, political and social problems associated with growth and development began to emerge. The economy slowed, population growth leveled off, and the population aged. While the long-term economic footing of the state appears relatively sound, social problems are less tractable. The focus on business growth failed to accommodate the social and educational needs of

many sectors of the changing society. The cities, despite efforts at renewal, continued to decline: by 1990 less than 15 percent of the population resided there. The city population is largely poor, disadvan-
taged, and without the tax base to support adequate educational and
social services.

Even in middle-class suburban areas, educational funding formu-
las, which were still linked to property tax revenues, produced gross
inequities in per capita spending. The unexpected pace of growth—
which was geared toward roads and not mass transit—taxed the
state's infrastructure, producing congestion, pollution, and the highest insurance rates in the country. In addition the growth of the senior
population, along with the potential health care services they would
require, loomed on the horizon.

It was in that context that Democrat Jim Florio was able to regain, in
1989, the statehouse for the Democrats. The 1991 elections, however,
gave the GOP majorities in both houses, and the state is now, by any
measure, highly competitive.

What do the historical patterns of partisan change say about party
realignment? First, they indicate that since the turn of the century,
there have been neither sharp nor synchronized transitions in the
partisan character of the state. Looking at trends over the long haul, it
would seem that while FDR's election and tenure certainly gave the
party a boost and probably had a profound socializing effect on
younger generations of voters, there has not been a critical realignment in New Jersey—at least since 1896. Rather, as V. O. Key (1959)
suggested, the state experienced a secular realignment that favored
the Democrats. During that time, long-term demographic and social
change, encouraged by various short-term political forces, eventually
created a solid Democratic majority. And, after a period of Democratic
hegemony, it appears that other changes are again altering the political complexion of the state.

The critical difference, of course, is that the era of party dominance
is over. Like their counterparts in the rest of the country, few New
Jerseyans manifest unquestioning loyalty to either political party or its
candidates. Given the nature of modern campaigns and the influence
of television, visible statewide races are likely to remain strongly influenced by short-term forces. Further, the demands of more programmatic state government and the professionalization it requires
has dismantled the old patronage system, an incentive structure on
which older, more enduring loyalties were built.

On the other hand, the trend toward voter independence, which was so evident in the 1970s, appears to have leveled off, and partisan support is increasing, particularly among younger voters. And even within the context of more professionalized government, politics in New Jersey remains highly partisan. Parties within the state legislature are highly developed and, as national research has indicated, local county organizations in both New Jersey parties are still among the strongest in the country (Cotter et al. 1984). While the organizations have changed their structure and organizational base, they remain a key factor in most legislative and local elections.

In this changed milieu of weakened party loyalties, how can we evaluate current partisan shifts? As Paul Beck notes in the concluding chapter of this book, there are different perspectives on what constitutes a realignment, each emphasizing different levels of voter support. One view argues that realignments represent enduring shifts in the loyalties of groups of voters (Beck 1988). Another perspective requires that the shifts produce a new electoral majority (Pomper 1967), while a third supports the view that realignments occur only when a dominant majority party controls all or most elected offices (Clubb, Flanigan, and Zingale 1980).

In terms of the first perspective—shifts in the loyalties of groups of voters—we can only speculate about how and when changes occurred during the period of the New Deal. But extensive survey data for the *Star-Ledger*/Eagleton Poll at Rutgers University allow us to plot and evaluate contemporary shifts in voters' support for the parties.

## TRENDS IN PARTY IDENTIFICATION

Although we have no accurate measures of partisan identification in New Jersey before 1978, electoral returns indicate that the 1970s were a period of Democratic dominance amid growing dealignment. Polls from 1978 support this view. As table 14.1 shows, in that year

Table 14.1. Trends in Party Identification: New Jersey, 1978–1990

|      | Democrat | Lean Democrat | Independent | Lean Republican | Republican | Democrat Advantage |
|------|----------|---------------|-------------|-----------------|------------|--------------------|
| 1978 | 35 | 17 | 12 | 11 | 19 | 22 |
| 1983 | 36 | 15 | 10 | 15 | 22 | 14 |
| 1984 | 34 | 13 | 11 | 15 | 23 | 9 |
| 1985 | 32 | 13 | 9 | 16 | 26 | 3 |
| 1986 | 34 | 13 | 8 | 12 | 27 | 8 |
| 1990 | 36 | 14 | 8 | 11 | 28 | 11 |

Source: *The Star-Ledger*/Eagleton Poll.

Table 14.2.  Characteristics of Party Identifiers: New Jersey, 1978–1990

|  | 1978 | | | 1990 | | |
|---|---|---|---|---|---|---|
|  | Demo-crat[a] (%) | Indepen-dent (%) | Repub-lican (%) | Demo-crat (%) | Indepen-dent (%) | Repub-lican (%) |
| Occupation[b] | | | | | | |
| Blue collar | 66 | 13 | 17 | 52 | 8 | 37 |
| White collar | 48 | 16 | 31 | 46 | 9 | 44 |
| Retired | 39 | 22 | 36 | 55 | 9 | 32 |
| Not employed | 70 | 12 | 12 | 47 | 6 | 41 |
| Income[c] | | | | | | |
| Low | 61 | 15 | 19 | 59 | 8 | 30 |
| Medium | 55 | 16 | 26 | 49 | 7 | 41 |
| High | 51 | 13 | 33 | 40 | 10 | 49 |
| Education | | | | | | |
| Less than high school graduate | 56 | 13 | 26 | 64 | 4 | 28 |
| High school graduate | 56 | 16 | 22 | 46 | 9 | 39 |
| More than high school | 48 | 18 | 32 | 44 | 8 | 45 |
| Ideology | | | | | | |
| Liberal | 70 | 11 | 15 | 68 | 5 | 15 |
| Moderate | 54 | 18 | 22 | 51 | 9 | 37 |
| Conservative | 40 | 14 | 44 | 35 | 9 | 55 |
| Region | | | | | | |
| North | 56 | 14 | 26 | 53 | 6 | 38 |
| Central | 53 | 19 | 25 | 45 | 8 | 40 |
| South | 48 | 29 | 27 | 48 | 11 | 38 |
| Length of Residence | | | | | | |
| Under 10 years | 53 | 15 | 29 | 49 | 3 | 45 |
| 10 Years or more | 53 | 13 | 28 | 45 | 10 | 43 |
| Lifelong | 54 | 17 | 25 | 53 | 7 | 34 |

Democrats enjoyed a twenty-two-point advantage over Republicans, and the number of pure independents, who are defined as those who do not lean toward either party, was 12 percent.

Trends since that time show an overall erosion of the Democratic advantage to eleven points in 1990. While the number of Democrats in the electorate has remained relatively constant over these years, the number of independents has declined and the number of voters who identify with the Republican party has continually increased.

The data indicate that although the Democrats are still the majority, patterns of change seldom favor them. They have held their own among such constituencies as women and blacks and have made some marginal gains among a few groups, like the retired. They have,

Table 14.2. (continued)

| | 1978 | | | 1990 | | |
|---|---|---|---|---|---|---|
| | Demo-crat[a] (%) | Indepen-dent (%) | Repub-lican (%) | Demo-crat (%) | Indepen-dent (%) | Repub-lican (%) |
| Race | | | | | | |
| White | 52 | 16 | 28 | 45 | 9 | 43 |
| Nonwhite | 69 | 6 | 13 | — | — | — |
| Black | — | — | — | 77 | 6 | 15 |
| Hispanic | — | — | — | 54 | 2 | 44 |
| Age | | | | | | |
| 18–29 | 57 | 15 | 22 | 49 | 6 | 42 |
| 30–49 | 56 | 15 | 26 | 50 | 9 | 37 |
| 50–64 | 56 | 14 | 26 | 50 | 6 | 40 |
| 65+ | 41 | 20 | 36 | 50 | 9 | 38 |
| Religion | | | | | | |
| Protestant | 41 | 16 | 38 | 45 | 8 | 44 |
| Catholic | 63 | 13 | 20 | 48 | 8 | 42 |
| Jewish | 59 | 20 | 15 | NA | — | — |
| Other | 54 | 17 | 25 | 58 | 8 | 28 |
| Gender | | | | | | |
| Female | 53 | 12 | 28 | 54 | 7 | 35 |
| Male | 54 | 19 | 24 | 45 | 9 | 43 |

Source: Selected Eagleton Polls, 1978–90.
[a]Leaners included with partisans. Margin of error +/− 3.5%.
[b]Occupation of chief wage earner in household.
[c]Income Categories: 1978: low = under $15,000, medium = $15,000–20,000, high = over $20,000; 1990: low = under $20,000, medium = $20,000–50,000, high = over $50,000.

however, suffered substantial losses among other key constituencies, such as the young, blue collar workers, men, and Catholics. Over the years, those groups have become more Republican. Table 14.2 provides a more detailed picture.

Among occupational groups, blue collar workers have become more Republican while retirees are more Democratic. Republicans have picked up support among white collar workers and the unemployed. Figures on educational groups indicate gains for the Republicans among those with higher levels of education. In terms of income, Republicans made gains in all income categories and, as one might expect, are now a plurality among those in the higher-income categories.

Questions on ideology are difficult to interpret; but within the context of New Jersey politics, the electorate is generally considered liberal on some social questions (like abortion) but conservative on fiscal issues (Salmore 1986). Within that framework, polls suggest that the electorate has remained relatively stable and moderate in its ideological predispositions between 1978 and 1990. Republicans, however, have picked up support among all ideological groups, even those that consider themselves liberal.

Figures on party identification by race indicate a continued commitment to the Democrats among blacks, who number about 11 percent of the population. Among Hispanics, patterns are mixed, with growing support for the Republicans in this constituency. The data need to be considered with caution, however, since Hispanics are themselves a varied group who comprise only about 5 percent of most samples.

No significant regional variation in party support appears across the state, although Republicans have made gains in all regions. While newcomers to the Garden State are more Republican than they were in 1978, in-migration no longer appears to be a factor in voters' orientations. Now there is little party variation by length of residence except among lifelong residents of the state, who still tend to be more Democratic.

What seem to be important are religion, age, and gender. Table 14.2 indicates that, consistent with national trends, the GOP has made significant gains among younger voters (Norpoth and Kagay 1989). While in 1990 the distribution of partisans varies little across age groups, the notable losses for the Democrats and gains for the GOP have occurred among eighteen- to twenty-nine-year-olds. In terms of religion, support among Catholics for the Democrats has eroded severely and has grown steadily for the Republican party. This is highly significant, because Catholics represent about 45 percent of the state's population and traditionally had been strong supporters of the Democratic party.

A gender gap exists in New Jersey given the greater variation among women in their orientations toward the parties and the proclivity of women to be much more Democratic than men. However, as figure 14.1 illustrates, the most significant changes over the years have occurred among men. In 1978 men and women differed little in their support for the parties, except that men tended to be slightly more independent than women. Since that time, support for the Democratic party among women has remained strong and consistent. Support among men for the Democrats has eroded; they have become

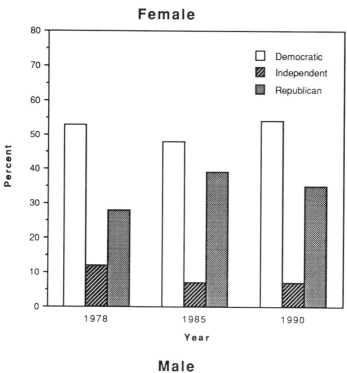

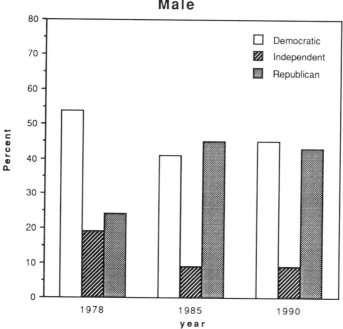

14.1 New Jersey party identification by gender, 1978–1990

less independent and more Republican. Similar patterns of change by gender have also been documented at the national level (Wirls 1986).

The data present a picture of a highly competitive state in which the partisan edge still favors the Democrats, but where key demographic trends bode well for the Republicans. In that sense New Jersey is experiencing long-term secular change as traditional constituencies of the Democratic party are converting to the GOP while patterns of generational replacement also favor the Republicans. Given weakened partisan loyalties, it is difficult to know if or when the shifts will manifest themselves in a changed electoral order. But the data do provide a picture of the unraveling of a coalition, which could eventually yield Republican dominance.

ELECTORAL TRENDS

If one considers realignment from the perspective of electoral trends and uses a standard of either a party majority or unified party control of government, New Jersey has become a competitive state where Republicans have scored recent gains because of the tax issue. Looking at patterns of electoral control from around the time of the New Deal, however, suggests that in a state with two vigorous political parties, one-party dominance has always been difficult to achieve.

The results of presidential elections in New Jersey indicate a strong Republican presence in the state since the turn of the century. The Civil War encouraged a north-south split in party loyalties within the state, with southern New Jersey favoring the Democrats and the north supporting the Republicans. Overall, from 1856 to 1892, the state was relatively competitive, with a Democratic tilt. The state fell quite clearly into the Republican fold, however, around the elections of 1896.

In presidential elections from that time until 1932, New Jersey voted only once for a Democrat: in a three-way race in 1912 when the state voted for Woodrow Wilson, who was the sitting governor. Even so, it did not support Wilson's reelection bid in 1916. As figure 14.2 illustrates, New Jersey supported FDR from 1932 through 1944 but during that time remained less Democratic than the country at large. After 1944, the state cast its electoral votes for a Democrat only twice: once for Kennedy in 1960 and then for Johnson in 1964. Since that time, New Jersey has consistently supported Republican candidates

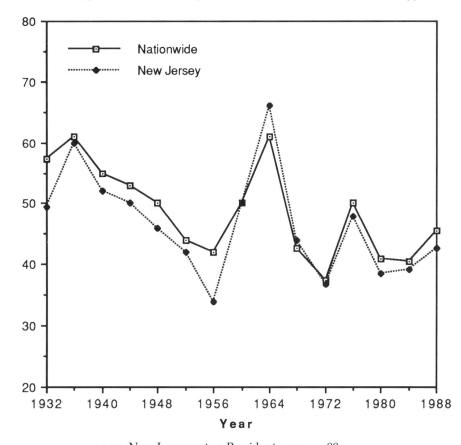

14.2 New Jersey votes: President, 1932–1988

and remains less Democratic than the rest of the nation at the presidential level.

In congressional elections for the U.S. House, the Republicans continued to dominate from the turn of the century until 1964, when the Democrats finally achieved majority status in the delegation. Democrats made a brief breakthrough in 1936, when they won just half of the congressional seats, followed by decades of Republican dominance (see figure 14.3).

The total Democratic statewide vote indicates a fairly competitive electoral environment from 1928 to 1990. Until 1962, the disparities between the total Democratic vote and the number of Democratic seats reflect the politics of apportionment, which favored the Republicans, as well as the tendency of Democrats to be centered in urban areas. After that time, apportionment politics favored the Democrats.

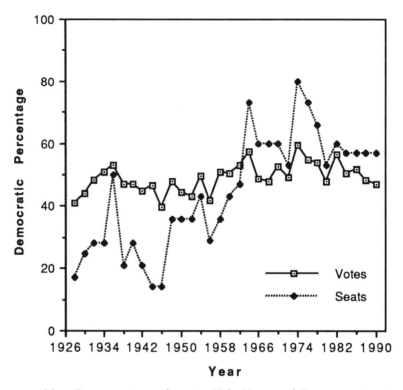

14.3 New Jersey votes and seats: U.S. House of Representatives, 1928–1990

By 1988, although the Democrats were still able to hold an eight to six edge over the Republicans in House seats, they received only 48 percent of the statewide vote.

Results from gubernatorial elections indicate Democratic strength early in this century. In statewide elections, huge pluralities out of the urban counties allowed the Democrats to take the office as early as 1910. From the early 1920s through 1943, the office was dominated by the Democrats. During that time the Hudson County machine and Frank Hague of Jersey City enjoyed their heyday. (In most elections Hague would virtually anoint Democrats *and* Republicans as governor!) As figure 14.4 indicates, Republicans whom Hague backed were elected only in 1916, 1928, and 1934. The GOP then controlled the office during the 1940s, briefly in the late 1960s, and then during the 1980s.

A striking aspect in gubernatorial elections has been their volatility, which has been more evident recently. While the most closely con-

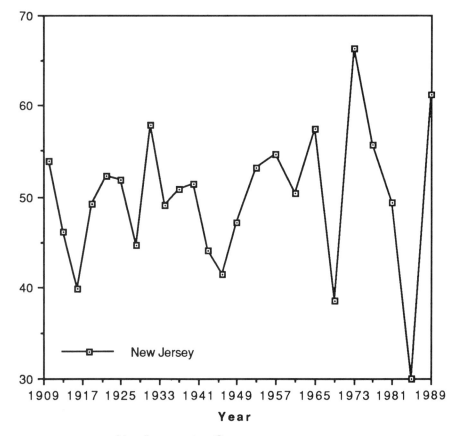

14.4 New Jersey votes: Governor, 1910–1990

tested election in the state's history was held in 1981, when a Republican was elected by less than two thousand votes, overall patterns indicate considerable fluctuation, even during times that are considered strong party eras. The pattern of fluctuation becomes more pronounced by the early 1970s, indicating not only weakened loyalties of voters but also the disengagement of the gubernatorial race from the parties' organizational structure. Since 1977, when public financing of that race was initiated, the contest for governor has become a visible and personalized contest where candidates distance themselves from the party and run individualized, media-based campaigns. In that sense, more reliable indicators of party strength in recent years may be the less visible races for the state legislature and the county freeholder boards.

Until the reapportionment decisions of the early 1970s, control of

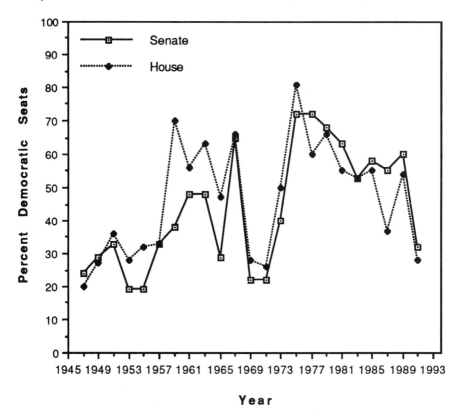

14.5 New Jersey seats: State legislative elections, 1947–1991

the state legislature reflected a structural bias that favored the Republicans, especially in the state senate. Up through 1965, representation to the senate was based on one representative from each of the twenty-one counties. Until 1973 legislative districts, although apportioned essentially according to population, were still drawn within each county. Those provisions tended to favor the Republicans, who dominated in more counties. Democratic support was concentrated in fewer but more densely populated urban counties.

The history of legislative control in New Jersey from the turn of the century to the late 1960s is one of Republican dominance. From 1900 to 1947, when the state senate was elected every two years and the state assembly every year, the Democrats took control of the assembly for a single year only in 1907, 1911, 1913, 1914, 1932, and 1937. They scored a majority in the state senate only during the 1913–14 term and achieved a tie in 1937. (Interestingly, the Democrats did better before than after the election of 1932.)

Figure 14.5 charts the results of legislative elections after 1947, when terms were changed to four years in the senate and to two in the assembly. The Democrats made a breakthrough in the assembly in the 1957 election and began to score majorities in that body throughout the 1960s. They gained seats in the state senate in the late 1960s and from 1973 through 1985 enjoyed unified control of the legislature. They lost the assembly in 1985, regained control in 1989, and lost both houses in 1991.

Another useful indicator of party strength, particularly in recent times, is representation on county freeholder boards. Freeholders in New Jersey are elected county representatives; and within each of the state's twenty-one counties, seats on the three- to nine-member boards are the focus of intense organizational effort and competition. Although the power of the county parties has severely diminished in statewide politics, the party organizations are still highly active and influential at the county and local level; and seats on the freeholder boards are still the bread and butter of party influence.

As with elections to the state legislature, Democrats were slow in making inroads on many freeholder boards until demographic trends allowed them to capture a majority of seats. Their high-water mark came in 1980, when they controlled 62 percent of the board seats and had managed to place at least one Democrat in every county but one. As of 1990, the parties were just about even, with each controlling half of the state's freeholder seats. Burlington, Cape May, Morris, and Somerset are heavily Republican, while Union, Middlesex, Hudson, and Essex are Democratic territory. The rest are generally competitive.

These uneven patterns of electoral control have characterized the politics of the past century. While presidential elections indicate Republican strength in the state since 1896, gubernatorial elections show the formation of a competitive political environment and Democratic influence as early as 1910. The initial transition appears to have been the result of long-term demographic changes related to the mobilization of poor urban immigrants (who aligned with the Democratic party) and their descendents (who moved to the suburbs and took their party affiliation with them).

Thus, as in the case in some other states that are explored in this book, the logic of party change was in place long before either FDR or Reagan came on the scene. In New Jersey the fortunes of the Democratic party were surely boosted by the New Deal; the party made brief but marked breakthroughs around the election of 1932. Lacking survey data, we can only guess at the socialization effect that Roosevelt's presidency and the articulation of his agenda had on a younger generation of voters, who would then align with the Democratic party. Nonetheless, electoral returns in the Garden State do not synchronize neatly along the time frame of the New Deal. Although structural factors account for some of the delay, Democratic control and unity in a state with two vigorous parties was a long-term transition.

Current patterns in New Jersey indicate an electoral environment wherein neither party is likely to achieve dominance or unity over the next decade. Although the Republicans are making gains in the loyalties of the voters, tight competition and weakened party loyalty mitigate against sustained electoral control for either party in the near term. The character of current state leadership and the issue of state taxes, however, have the potential to alter the balance.

## LEADERSHIP AND ISSUES

Only recently have scholars begun to consider the impact of elites on realignment. Presidential leadership appears to have some influence on the partisan inclinations of voters, and governors can also influence state party fortunes. While they do not appear to have much impact on the enduring loyalties on the voters, governors in some states are able either to build strong party organizations or, using a salient issue, establish networks of support that sustain the electoral dominance of a party even in the face of weakening voter loyalties.

New Jersey governors traditionally have had little influence on party fortunes. First, governors generally have not been highly visible or well known. The major television media outlets in New Jersey are either New York or Philadelphia stations; hence, sitting governors get little daily media coverage from the networks. In various areas of the state, voters know more about political leaders in New York and Pennsylvania than they do about their own elected officials. The first popular and visible governor was Tom Kean (1981–89), and although the Republicans' electoral standing improved during that time, his tenure did not realize any long-term gains for the GOP.

Second, public financing of gubernatorial elections has removed candidates from the organizational structure of the parties. Winners tend to see their agenda in terms of shifting power away from paro-

chial county and local levels and toward more centralized and professionalized state activities. Thus, it is not in the political interest of a
sitting governor to strengthen local party organizations; and recent
governors have done little to build the state party organization, which
they do control. Even the popular Tom Kean, who operated with considerable political capital, did little during his tenure to build a statewide Republican organization and failed to provide leadership in the
nomination of his successor.

In terms of issues, the last debate that polarized the electorate and
capped the heyday of Democratic dominance in the state was the
ratification of the state income tax. The issue was fought out during
the 1977 reelection campaign of Democrat Brendan Byrne. The initial
income tax had been forced on the state legislature by the state supreme court decision on the property tax formula for school funding;
it was to self-destruct after the election. Byrne campaigned on making
the income tax a permanent base of tax revenues and won the election
by large margins. It should be noted that during that period the state
was in the midst of an economic boom, and the Democrats were the
popular majority party. Moreover, the tax was a moderate one; and in
the context of the 1977 election, there was an air of inevitability about
the tax. The courts initiated the debate and took a tough stance on the
issue of school funding. The tax was already in place; and since the
Republican opposition could not come up with a viable alternative,
voters went along.

The 1990s will see another version of the tax drama play itself out,
and the issue has the potential to change the electoral balance in the
state. Democrat Jim Florio has effected a sweeping restructuring of
the state's tax structure. The package he pushed through the legislature in 1990 raises the marginal income tax rate to 7 percent for individuals who make more than $35,000 and for couples who earn more
than $70,000. It also increases the sales tax to 7 percent and extends
the tax to a host of consumer items. Perhaps most contentiously, part
of the plan radically restructures the public school funding formula,
capping funds for the top 220 school districts and redistributing considerable monies to 358 less prosperous school districts. The effort is
intended to redress inequities by giving tax relief to poor and lower
middle-class communities by creating better opportunities for public
education, especially in impoverished urban school districts.

Jim Florio may be the exception in New Jersey politics in that he is
now a highly visible governor. The national media have given him extensive coverage, and New Jersey voters know who he is and what he

has done. However, the politics of redistribution has not sat well with the voters; and Florio's initiatives have been met with outrage not only by high-income voters but from members of the middle class as well. A 1991 poll found that 77 percent of the voters think Florio's tax package will hurt not the wealthy but the middle class.

How the issue plays out in the politically competitive, fiscally conservative, and affluent state is likely to shape party fortunes over the next decade. In the short term, the tax issue has produced divided government, giving the Republicans veto-proof majorities in the legislature. It will also probably fuel organizational factionalization among the Democratic party, as legislators and other elected Democrats attempt to distance themselves from the administration.

In the long term, Florio's leadership on the tax issue has the potential to encourage the ongoing secular shifts in the loyalties of the voters. Recent polls that show further decline in the Democratic constituency may be only a temporary reflection of the voters' anger. But an underlying motif in the political debate on the issue was illustrated in one letter to the editor from a resident of a middle-class community. Reflecting on how he and his wife had struggled to buy a house in a town with a first-rate school system that now faces severe school funding cutbacks, he concluded, "It's just too tough to be a Democrat anymore." If the voters make that connection—particularly as it relates to party—it could spell eventual Republican dominance and mark another era of secular change in the political history of New Jersey.

# Stalled Realignment: Party Change in Rhode Island

## DARRELL M. WEST

"Rhode Island," George Washington remarked from the Constitutional Convention after the state refused to send a delegate, "still perseveres in that impolitic—unjust—and . . . scandalous conduct, which seems to have marked all her public counsels. . . ." (Barone and Ujifusa 1987, 1059)

DURABLE changes in partisan attitudes and behavior constitute the classic definition of party realignment (Sundquist 1983; Burnham 1970). Most commonly studied at the national level, there has in recent years been increasing interest in realignment at the state level (see Galderisi et al. 1987). The diversity of state economic and political settings gives analysts a much better chance to investigate the process of party change under different institutional structures and political conditions. Furthermore, the rise in a number of state survey operations facilitates the study of realignment in the American states.

Yet not all locales represent the same type of opportunity for research. This chapter examines realignment in the Democratic bastion of Rhode Island. The Ocean State is one of the last places scholars would envision a Republican realignment. Dating back to the Green Revolution of 1935, when a Democratic governor staged a palace coup to gain control of the legislature, Rhode Island has been a strongly Democratic state. Democrats have dominated state legislative and

An earlier version of this chapter was presented at the annual meeting of the American Political Science Association, Chicago, 3–6 September 1987. My thanks to Maureen Moakley for helpful comments on preliminary drafts of this manuscript.

executive offices for most of the time since the 1930s. And Rhode Island was one of six states plus the District of Columbia carried by President Jimmy Carter in 1980.

However, Rhode Island represents an interesting place to examine party change because of significant Republican gains in the 1980s. Using data from 1966 to 1990 on party control of major offices and aggregate voting patterns for national and state offices as well as survey evidence from 1978 to 1990, it is apparent that Republicans had new opportunities because of scandal and short-term political events in 1982 and 1984. While those opportunities led to surprising Republican electoral gains, the GOP successes that developed during the period now appear to be receding. This chapter will discuss some of the reasons behind the stalled realignment and what this period tells us more broadly about the process of party change at the state level.

## THE ECONOMIC AND POLITICAL CONTEXT

Rhode Island has a rich and complex history. Founded by Roger Williams in 1636 as a sanctuary for religious heretics, it quickly became a haven for rebels, malcontents, and social misfits. Those origins as well as its colorful history led to its nickname of Rogues' Island among neighboring colonies (see McLoughlin 1986).

The state experienced the classic case of a critical realignment in the 1930s. Like much of New England, Rhode Island for a long time had been dominated by Yankee Republicans. A few wealthy families controlled the state, monopolizing industrial enterprises (mainly textile mills) and keeping political control firmly in the hands of the economic establishment (Whittemore 1988).

However, the need for workers in the textile mills led to an influx of immigrants. Generally shut out of politics and often facing clear ethnic discrimination, those groups were able to organize in the 1930s, win elections, and ultimately wrest control of government from the dominant Republicans (McLoughlin 1986). Taking advantage of President Roosevelt's popularity and the election of a Democratic governor (Theodore Green), a 1935 palace revolution in the general assembly led by Governor Green forced a recount in two state senate districts. That resulted in the expulsion of two Republicans and the election of two Democrats, which was just enough to give Democrats control of the legislature. They then used their power to seize control of the government and redistribute public benefits to a broad range of supporters around the state.

Democrats have controlled state and national offices within Rhode Island since 1935. The lack of a sizeable middle class and highly educated citizenry in following decades helped limit Republican gains and also worked to maintain the strength of the Democratic party. Ethnic groups and labor unions representing blue-collar workers were quite strong, and old-style political machines were set up to turn out the votes.

Politics during that time had the rough-and-tumble element often associated with machine politics. Groups fought for their share of government jobs and contracts, and allegations of scandal and corruption were quite common. With the exception of the dominant state newspaper, *The Providence Journal*, good government forces were weak.

Yet in the 1980s, the state went through demographic changes and economic development that began to undermine old patterns. Census figures from 1980 to 1988 indicate that in terms of per capita income, Rhode Island went from twenty-sixth to fourteenth in the nation. Attracted by the financial opportunities of the booming Northeast, better educated people moved into the state and were more oriented to good government than machine politics. Scandals received extensive coverage from the *Providence Journal*, and the publicity began to generate more of a backlash against corruption.

For the first time in years, the Republican party started to mount credible challengers to Democratic officeholders and actually won victories in a number of races. Among federal offices, the 1980s featured parity between the parties—one Republican senator and one Democratic senator as well as one Republican representative and one Democratic member. In 1988, Republicans even won one of the remaining federal offices with Ron Machtley's upset victory over Ferdinand St. Germain in a congressional race, giving them three of the four congressional seats.

At the state level, the GOP made significant inroads during the 1980s. A Republican governor, Edward DiPrete, was elected in 1984; and there were Republican victories in races for secretary of state and attorney general. That gave the GOP control over three of five state offices. Republicans also went from seven to twenty-one in the state senate, a gain that put them within striking distance of majority status in the fifty-member body.

Those improvements, along with the widely publicized Republican gains at the national level during the Reagan presidency, stimulated discussion about whether the state was undergoing the type of funda-

mental change in the political landscape associated with realignments
(Sundquist 1983; Burnham 1970). But while Rhode Island politics has
undergone significant changes, many of the Republican gains now
appear to have become stalled. The study of state voting patterns
demonstrates how Republicans gained and then lost opportunities
for enduring party change.

## PARTY CONTROL OF STATE OFFICES

Party control of leading offices often is used to measure party fortunes. The hypothesis is that if there is enduring change in public attitudes and voting behavior, it should translate into shifts in the
partisan balance of executive and legislative offices.

Figure 15.1 charts the percentage of Democrats between 1966 and
1990 in control of state offices—the five elected executive offices—the
five elected executive offices (governor, lieutenant governor, secretary
of state, attorney general, and treasurer), the state senate (which contains fifty districts), and the state house of representatives (which
seats one hundred members). The early part of this period in the
1960s shows a bifurcated state: some Republican successes on the
executive side but substantial Democratic majorities both in the house
(67 percent of members) and senate (70 percent of senators).

This pattern reverted to Democratic dominance shortly after that
time. Democrats maintained their hold on the legislature, but they
also gained control of state executive offices. In fact, in the period
from 1974 to 1982, Democrats controlled all five of the statewide elected offices, a position that in conjunction with their decisive legislative majorities of more than 80 percent in both chambers gave them
undisputed influence within the state.

However, Republicans made significant inroads within the state
starting in 1982. After a partisan Democratic gerrymander of the state
senate plus numerous cases of scandal and corruption, voters turned
against the Democratic party and elected Republicans in much larger
numbers. The state senate, which was the focus of the redistricting
controversy, went from seven to twenty-one Republicans; and the
GOP followed those gains in 1984 by taking three of five statewide
races.

At that point that many wondered whether the elections of 1982
and 1984 heralded permanent gains for the Republican party. While
long-term generalizing would be premature, the elections of 1986,
1988, and 1990 seem to cast doubt on those claims. In 1986, Democrats

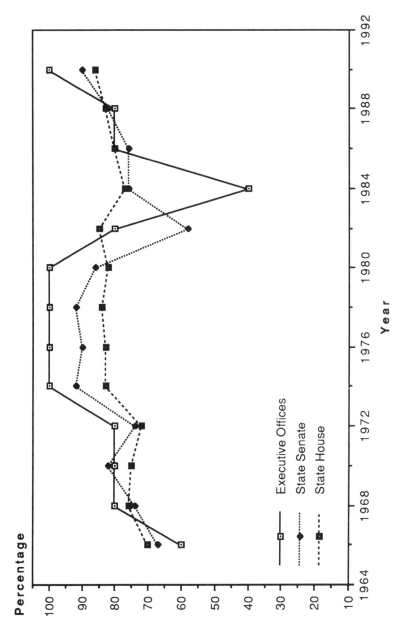

15.1 Rhode Island Democratic control of state offices: Executive offices, state senate, and state house, 1968–1990

regained control over four of five state offices. That left only a Republican governor in place of the prior GOP gains. Democrats also increased their majority in the house of representatives to 80 percent of the overall membership. Similarly, in 1988, Democrats retained four of the five statewide offices and came very close to recapturing the governorship. Their margin in the house was eighty-two to eighteen and they also had a forty-one to nine edge in the senate.

The election of 1990 represented a Democratic sweep. The Democrats took all statewide offices and Democrat Bruce Sundlen, who had been defeated two years earlier, was elected governor with 74 percent of the vote. In the congressional races, U.S. Senator Claiborne Pell defeated House challenger Claudine Schneider winning 62 percent of the vote; and the open seat vacated by Republican Schneider went to Democrat Jack Reed. In the state legislature the Democrats also picked up four senate and three house seats.

This would seem to dovetail with patterns at the national level, where after six years as the minority party in the U.S. Senate, Democrats regained control in 1986 and did well in the 1988 and 1990 congressional elections. These results demonstrate the difficulties of forging long-term changes based on short-term electoral events.

## PARTISAN VOTING

Another indicator of party change is aggregate voting patterns between the two parties. Figures 15.2 and 15.3 list the Democratic percentage of the major party vote in a series of races between 1966 and 1990. Figure 15.2 examines voting patterns in the high profile offices of the presidency, U.S. Senate, and governor's races. Figure 15.3 focuses on the less visible statewide offices—lieutenant governor, secretary of state, attorney general, and treasurer.

It is clear from figure 15.2 that Democrats have been advantaged during much of this period. They have run well statewide and, in fact, only rarely has their percentage of the overall vote in the three offices dropped below 50 percent.

But beneath this seeming sanctuary of Democratic strength, there has been considerable volatility in voting margins. In all three offices (but especially in the governor's and Senate races), there have been wide swings from election to election in Democratic pluralities. For example, in the 1970s, Rhode Islanders gave big margins to Governor Garrahy and Senator Pell, both Democrats. But Democrats in the

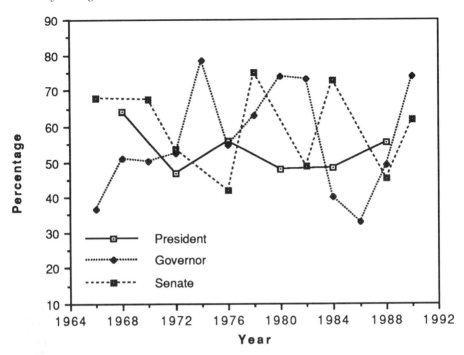

15.2 Rhode Island Democratic vote: President, governor, and U.S. Senate, 1966–1990

1980s were unable to unseat Republican Chafee and lost the governorship to DiPrete in 1984.

The electoral successes of President Ronald Reagan, Senator John Chafee, and Governor Edward DiPrete during the 1980s show that Republicans have from time to time managed to carve out political niches for themselves in Rhode Island. A prosperous economy boosted the fortunes of DiPrete and Reagan in 1984. With the state economy doing quite well and voters alarmed at Democratic improprieties in the redistricting process, Republicans were able to use short-term forces to capture and retain the top elective offices.

Figure 15.3 makes this case even more dramatically. Democrats did very well in the low visibility offices during the 1970s. But there was a slight trend toward competitiveness between the two parties beginning in the mid-1970s. In some of the races, the trend lines cluster around the crucial 50 percent mark, showing that Republicans have made inroads in voting power within the state. And most importantly, in the 1980s, Republicans actually won several statewide offices.

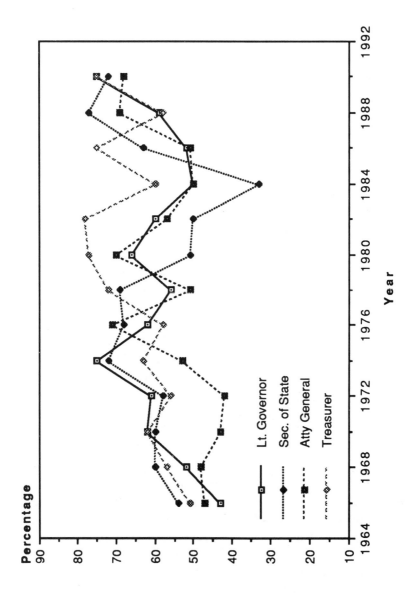

15.3 Rhode Island Democratic vote: Lieutenant governor, secretary of state, attorney general, and treasurer, 1966–1990

However, those gains seem to have been reversed in the big Democratic year of 1986. Democrats regained two of the three statewide offices (secretary of state and attorney general), but they lost the governor's race by a two-to-one margin. In 1988 the state supported Dukakis over Bush, and the Democrats won four of the five statewide offices and came within six thousand votes of unseating the Republican governor. This, in conjunction with the Democrats' sweep in 1990, suggests that the earlier Republican gains of the 1980s were temporary and that Democratic dominance of state offices is returning.

## TRENDS IN PARTY IDENTIFICATION

The aggregate patterns just described illustrate the longitudinal changes that have developed in Rhode Island politics, but they cannot provide much understanding of the individual-level developments that produced those changes. For greater understanding, one needs survey data on political attitudes and voting behavior. From 1978 to 1983, Alpha Research Associates conducted statewide polls that probed voter sentiments (see Profugi 1988), and since 1984 the A. Alfred Taubman Center for Public Policy and American Institutions at Brown University has conducted a series of surveys that can help us understand some of the developments described earlier.

Table 15.1 describes trends in party identification between 1978 and 1990. The results reveal several interesting things. The biggest cate-

Table 15.1. Trends in Party Identification: Rhode Island, 1978–1990

|  | Democrat (%) | Independent (%) | Republican (%) | N |
|---|---|---|---|---|
| May 1978 | 32 | 60 | 8 | 546 |
| Oct. 1978 | 35 | 56 | 9 | 525 |
| June 1980 | 33 | 58 | 9 | 527 |
| June 1982 | 35 | 55 | 10 | 505 |
| May 1983 | 30 | 61 | 9 | 609 |
| June 1984 | 29 | 57 | 13 | 1,002 |
| June 1986 | 22 | 61 | 17 | 305 |
| Sept. 1987 | 29 | 55 | 16 | 351 |
| June 1988 | 28 | 54 | 18 | 381 |
| Sept. 1988 | 27 | 54 | 19 | 400 |
| Feb. 1990 | 32 | 52 | 16 | 360 |

Sources: Alpha Research Associate polls, 1978–83; the Rhode Island Poll, Brown University, 1984–90.

gory of voters in Rhode Island has been the independents, those individuals who identify with neither party. Throughout this time period, 55 to 60 percent of Rhode Island adults have classified themselves as independents. That finding is consistent with patterns in other states, which also show high levels of independence. For example, Baum and Patterson (1987, 7) find large numbers of independents in Ohio. Although baseline data for Rhode Island from earlier times are lacking, the figures certainly seem to fit with a party decline thesis (see Burnham 1970; Beck 1984). Rhode Islanders do not identify with the major parties, and this helps explain the electoral volatility described in aggregate voting patterns. If a majority of all voters in Rhode Island are political independents, it becomes difficult for either major party to produce consistent victories.

However, that does not mean there is political parity between Republicans and Democrats. Democrats clearly still have a bigger core group of identifiers than Republicans. The Democratic group constituted about a third of the overall electorate during this period. The Republican category meanwhile has risen from 8 to 9 percent to 18 to 19 percent in 1988. With a margin of error of plus or minus 5 percent, it is difficult to know if those over-time changes are significant. But they do suggest some marginal Republican gains in the 1980s that helped popular Republicans successfully win elective office. At the same time, the fact that less than one-fifth of the public identifies with the GOP shows how difficult it is, absent short-term forces favorable to the party, for Republicans to retain offices once they win them.

Table 15.2 reports the composition of Republicans, independents, and Democrats in 1988. Republicans by and large conform to common stereotypes: they were more conservative, had fewer union members, and were more Protestant in their demographic backgrounds than Democrats.

The only surprise fell in the age category, as Republicans also attracted a younger constituency than did Democrats. This creates some long-term opportunities for the GOP if the right circumstances arise (also see chapter 16; Baum and Patterson 1987; Stanley 1987).

In the 1980s, Republicans nationally have attracted more support from young people than traditionally has been the case. Undoubtably because of the successful economy under Reagan and a memory that includes only the Carter presidency, young people have become more sympathetic to the Republican party.

Independents shared a number of characteristics with Democrats. But they were a little more educated and had slightly higher incomes,

Table 15.2. Characteristics of Party Identifiers: Rhode Island, 1988

| | Republican (%) | Independent (%) | Democrat (%) |
|---|---|---|---|
| Ideology | | | |
| Liberal | 11.9 | 10.1 | 20.0 |
| Moderate | 67.8 | 77.3 | 56.7 |
| Conservative | 20.4 | 12.5 | 12.2 |
| Age | | | |
| 18–24 | 27.4 | 7.1 | 16.0 |
| 25–34 | 24.2 | 29.3 | 25.5 |
| 35–44 | 19.4 | 21.2 | 25.5 |
| 45–54 | 11.3 | 15.2 | 14.9 |
| 55–64 | 8.1 | 12.5 | 4.3 |
| 65+ | 9.7 | 14.7 | 13.8 |
| Union Membership | | | |
| Yes | 19.7 | 28.2 | 25.8 |
| No | 80.3 | 71.8 | 74.2 |
| Education | | | |
| 0–8 | 4.8 | 4.9 | 4.1 |
| Some high school | 4.8 | 6.5 | 5.1 |
| High school graduate | 30.6 | 28.1 | 30.6 |
| Some college | 27.4 | 24.9 | 21.4 |
| College graduate | 22.6 | 22.2 | 25.5 |
| Post-Graduate | 9.7 | 13.5 | 13.3 |
| Income | | | |
| $0–7,000 | 7.0 | 5.5 | 3.3 |
| $7,001–12,000 | 7.0 | 6.1 | 7.7 |
| $12,001–20,000 | 12.3 | 18.4 | 15.4 |
| $20,001–35,000 | 24.6 | 26.4 | 28.6 |
| $35,000+ | 49.1 | 43.6 | 45.1 |
| Religion | | | |
| Protestant | 36.1 | 21.8 | 9.8 |
| Catholic | 52.5 | 60.9 | 68.5 |
| Jewish | 0.0 | 3.4 | 4.3 |
| Other | 11.4 | 13.7 | 17.4 |

Source: The Rhode Island Poll, June 1988.

and they also were less likely to be Catholic (71.4 percent of whom were Democrats). Independents furthermore were the most moderate (77.3 percent) of all the groups in the sample.

In short, a cross-sectional look at the composition of party identifiers gives little credence to the idea of an emergent Republican realignment. With the exception of their opportunities among the young, the Rhode Island GOP has made few inroads among groups traditionally thought of as Democratic groups. Republicans instead have

had to forge electoral coalitions around the large group of independents within the state, and this necessity has undermined the possibility for stable margins at the polls over time.

## THE ROLE OF LEADERSHIP

Political leadership has been a critical component of party change in
Rhode Island. Some of the Republican gains in the 1980s emerged
from mistakes and scandals associated with Democratic redistricting
schemes and the resulting bad publicity. Yet there also were several
leadership activities that affected Republican opportunities.

Organizationally, the GOP in Rhode Island during the 1980s became much better funded than in the past. The state adopted a party
checkoff option on income tax forms that allowed residents to contribute money to the Democratic or Republican party. According to Profugi (1988), Democrats in recent years have received approximately
$200,000 and Republicans $70,000 annually from that source.

The parties also have developed more professional staffs and com-
puter operations that allow them to use modern technologies. Training workshops and sponsorship of polls have been services the parties have provided to its recent candidates. These, of course, are
exactly the activities that Gibson et al. (1983) predicted would help
reinvigorate parties at the national level.

In the early 1980s, state Republicans benefited from short-term
forces. President Reagan's popularity, the prosperity of the state economy, and citizen discontent over Democratic redistricting schemes
helped Republicans raise money, get organized, and ultimately contributed to their electoral successes (West 1987).

However, by 1986, Reagan's popularity had nosedived because of
the Iran-*contra* scandal. State surveys showed that Reagan's approval
rating within the state, which had been as high as 78.7 percent in September 1986, before the scandal, dropped to 49.1 percent in February
1988.

In addition, Governor DiPrete suffered his own personal troubles.
Considerable controversy ensued in 1988 when it was revealed that
the governor and some partners had earned $2 million buying and
then reselling in a twenty-four-hour period a small parcel of land in
his home city (receiving a hard-to-obtain zoning variance on the property in the interim). After word of the transaction hit the press, Di-
Prete's approval rating among those expressing an opinion fell from
90.2 to 62.4 percent.

The incident had dramatic consequences for the governor's electoral fortunes. It turned what had been predicted as a runaway landslide into a six-thousand-vote victory over his opponent in 1988. It also slowed what had been Republican momentum in preceding years. In 1990 DiPrete took only 26 percent of the vote.

## CONCLUSION

The results suggest that some of the opportunities available to Republicans in the 1980s have now receded. From time to time they will make gains, such as when popular Republicans run or when Democrats shoot themselves in the foot through corruption or scandals. But the gains that emerge from those situations will be idiosyncratic and temporary, and do not seem likely to produce the types of fundamental and enduring changes associated with party realignments.

Volatility instead seems to be the catchword in Rhode Island. If recent elections are any indication, the electorate displays many of the qualities associated with dealignment: uncertainty, volatility, and fluidity. A post-election survey in 1986, for example, showed that a large percentage of voters made up their minds late in the campaign. In several races 10 to 20 percent of the electorate made up its mind during the last week of the campaign, and in some contests only one-third made up their minds three months or more before the election (figures that are higher than recent national elections). These patterns suggest Rhode Island politics will continue to display the volatility that has made recent elections so dramatic and unpredictable. Unless there is a dramatic breakthrough or cataclysmic event, a Republican realignment is unlikely.

The results also show how difficult it is under conditions of dealignment to forge stable and enduring party coalitions. When short-term forces govern elections, which appears to be the case both in Rhode Island and the nation as well, it is tough to maintain electoral momentum. Temporary conditions always develop that work to the advantage of one or the other party, but those developments almost always change within a short time. Leadership, of course, is very critical to these opportunities. Political leaders can gain or lose possibilities for enduring change by the strategic decisions they make. But because so many of the strategic moves are dictated by short-term forces, enduring change is very difficult.

The only exception to this statement appears to be young people. Both in Rhode Island and the nation, the GOP has developed substantial support among those under thirty-five years of age. Not only is this true in terms of electoral forces, it also characterizes attitudes on policy issues. Recent studies of tax reform, for example, show that young people are more likely than older ones to approve of tax reform and to give credit to President Reagan (West 1990). Republicans, therefore, have combined electoral gains nationally with a policy success among the young. Of course, it is far too early to speculate about the permanence of that development. But it does give Republicans long-term opportunities for party change that otherwise would not be available.

# Party Realignment in America: The View from the States

## PAUL ALLEN BECK

**16**

VIEWED from the perspective of the presidency, the 1980s were a Republican era. Ronald Reagan dominated the nation's political life as few presidents have since Franklin Roosevelt. His two solid electoral victories seemed to secure a Republican lock on the presidency and made him the first president since Dwight Eisenhower to serve two full terms in the White House. His policy activism, dedicated to reversing previous programmatic priorities of the national government and reducing taxes, set the agenda for national politics into the 1990s.

The electorate responded to the Reagan presidency by narrowing the Republican-Democratic gap in party identifications to the point that many observers could claim that the long-awaited Republican realignment had finally arrived. Young voters were especially likely to support GOP presidential candidates and to bring their partisan loyalties in line with their votes, another putative sign of realignment (Norpoth and Kagay 1989). And voters opted for partisan continuity in the presidency by electing George Bush in 1988, for the first time in more than forty years allowing one party to retain that office beyond two terms.

I gratefully acknowledge the assistance of Thomas Little in preparing the state data used in this chapter and of Lawrence Baum, Maureen Moakley, and Samuel C. Patterson for their constructive comments on an earlier draft.

That the only national office was so firmly in Republican hands seemed of great significance for American politics. Only the continuing Democratic strength in the Congress through the 1990 midterm elections, however enfeebled by the relinquishing of political initiative to the White House, has diminished the GOP's ascendancy in Washington in recent years.

The major premise of this volume is that the conventional presidency-centered view provides an inadequate, perhaps even misleading, picture of contemporary partisan change in the American polity. The presidency, to be sure, is America's dominant political prize and a powerful pulpit from which political change can be energized, probably more so than ever before in this media age. Consequently, there is good reason to center study of partisan political change on presidential elections and the electoral reactions they inspire.

Yet there also is a separate electoral politics anchored in the states and localities that must not be forgotten in any full accounting of contemporary changes in the American party system. Subpresidential politics often has a life of its own, nurtured by local personalities and other unique forces, that can insulate it from national trends or at least channel them in unexpected ways.

Viewed from this perspective, a time-honored one in the study of America's decentralized party system, our national electoral politics is a bottom-up aggregation of fifty distinct and varied state politics rather than the top-down imprint of the national contest for the presidency. Therefore, to understand fully the politics of our time, just as in the time of Alexis de Tocqueville more than 150 years ago, it is necessary to leave Washington, D.C., for a journey to the several states.

State politics comes in as many as fifty varieties. Intensive study of the states in this volume leaves the unmistakable impression that no two are exactly alike in their electoral politics. Each has its own dominant figures and forces. Each has manifested individual responses to the politics of the 1980s. In some, there is clear evidence that partisan politics has realigned in recent years. Unlike the aggregated national picture, however, the direction of that realignment is not uniformly pro-Republican. Other states are best characterized by what seems more like dealignment than realignment of the party system. Still others exhibit a constancy that belies national trends.

In spite of their distinctiveness, some important similarities appear across the states. Recent changes in partisan balance have made state politics considerably more competitive than it has been in years—for many states, more competitive than ever before. Along with (and probably contributing to) this greater competitiveness has come an apparent weakening in partisanship as a guide to electoral behavior. The pattern of split results so noticeable in the election of Republican presidents and Democratic Congresses appears to be rooted in the states. Finally, the states have remained remarkably resistant to the pro-Republican tides of the 1980s. It is the Democrats, not the Republicans, who control the governments of most of the states. This may be evidence of the independence of the states from national trends in what Walter Dean Burnham (1970) has called a decomposed party system or a vestige of an earlier era as states lag behind the nation in patterns of political change—two possibilities to be explored later.

These characteristics—vibrant and varied state politics, surprisingly independent of national electoral forces yet exhibiting some ability to shape national politics—will be the themes of this chapter. The raw material from which the themes are developed largely comes from the detailed studies in the preceding chapters, supplemented by some data on all fifty states. With that information as background, it is now possible to gain a broader perspective on party realignment in the American states and on the general nature of electoral politics in America.

## IS THERE A SEPARATE STATE POLITICS?

One cannot read the previous chapters without being impressed by how different national and state politics seem to be. To be sure state and national political patterns show considerable synchronization, although perhaps less so today than at previous times in American history (Key 1956). But electoral politics at those two levels of government are surprisingly independent. The states channel the tides of national politics through their individual practices and traditions, continually reasserting their standing as distinct political arenas in the American federal system.

The first suggestions of state distinctiveness come from Washington, D.C., itself. As Republican presidents Reagan and Bush have looked up Pennsylvania Avenue to Capitol Hill, they have seen, much to their dismay, a House of Representatives dominated by Democrats.

That the most popular house of Congress has been able to resist powerful Republican presidential tides is often attributed to the assets of incumbency. Incumbents possess an arsenal of weapons—the frank; active casework; skilled public relations; more access to financial resources; continuous media coverage—to defend themselves against

serious challenges (Fiorina 1977; Jacobson 1980; Mayhew 1974). In
candidate-oriented contests, as legislative elections increasingly appear to be, those resources seem to give the incumbent an advantage.
Often they are sufficient to discourage serious challengers from running and, as the 1990 midterm contests illustrate, to protect incumbents even when the electorate seems to be in an anti-incumbent
mood.

But the vaunted power of incumbency may be as much result as
cause. It may signify the weakness of the traditional extracandidate
forces that have impinged upon local races—party voting and presidential coattails (Burnham 1975; Calvert and Ferejohn 1983; Ferejohn
and Calvert 1984; Jacobson 1987)—as well as the determination of
local constituencies to judge their representatives on their own terms.
In earlier times, powerful national tides carried by party labels and
national leaders could overwhelm local candidate considerations. It is
rare that they do so today.

Congressional Democrats have been more successful in recent
years for other reasons, of course. The gerrymandering of legislative
districts may have preserved some seats for Democratic incumbents
who otherwise would have been unable to withstand the Republican
tide (Cain 1985). Results from the 1990 contests to elect the legislatures and officials who will do redistricting for the 1990s suggest
that the Democratic advantage will continue. Also, the Republicans
have not proven very adept at challenging vulnerable Democrats with
strong candidates at the right time. They fielded a strong set of challengers in 1982, only to find them swept to defeat in a strongly Democratic national tide. On the other hand, strong Republican challengers
were difficult to recruit in time for the 1984, 1986, and 1988 elections
because early political signs appeared not to favor the GOP (Bibby
1989). GOP recruitment efforts met with little success in 1990 as well,
as Democrats won a majority of the House seats vacated by unsuccessful GOP challengers for the Senate.

Whatever the reasons, the results are split presidential-congressio-
nal vote outcomes in recent years in typically more than one-third,
and sometimes approaching one-half, of the nation's congressional
districts. Since 1956 more than 26 percent of the districts have had
split results in each quadrennial election. Before 1956 such a high percentage of split results was *never* achieved, and only two elections
produced figures above 20 percent.

Once the focus is turned from Washington, the strongest evidence
of resistance within the states to presidential trends appears espe-

cially in contests for state offices. The 1990 election strengthened the Democratic hold on the states. It ensured that they would hold at least twenty-eight of the fifty governorships and majority control of 72 percent of the state legislative houses as the states turned to the critical task of legislative redistricting. Never once in the 1980s did the GOP hold a majority of governorships or state legislatures. The smashing Republican presidential successes in those years did not bring about anything approaching a commensurate party showing in state contests.

The separation of state and national voting patterns is readily apparent in the states analyzed in preceding chapters. Only Arizona produced consistent victories for the Republicans, and even it had Democratic governors part of the time. The modal pattern among the states considered in this volume, as well as among all fifty states, is of Republican support at the presidential level coupled with a strong Democratic presence in most state offices. Even in the southern states considered in this volume (Alabama, Florida, Virginia, and Texas), where GOP gains have been the most impressive, state politics still favors the Democratic party. In Florida and Texas, in fact, the 1990 elections returned control of the governor's office to the Democrats.

It seems reasonable, other things being equal, to expect a closer articulation between national and subnational electoral politics than has existed in recent years. National electoral results, after all, are the aggregation of results from lower units, such as legislative constituencies in parliamentary systems and the states in the American presidential systems. They should reflect local political patterns. With the nationalization of our mass media and its wider penetration into American society (Ranney 1983), as well as a more powerful presence of the national party organizations (Reichley 1985), greater synchronization of national and subnational voting patterns should be promoted from the top down as well.

Signs of increased synchronization between national and state electoral politics are evident. Presidential voting has become more nationalized. State differences in the popular vote for president have narrowed over the years. From standard deviations above twelve from 1892 to 1940, they have dropped to standard deviations below eight from 1972 through 1990 (Beck and Sorauf 1992). Under the unrelenting pressure of a now-nationalized mass media, the island communities that the states and localities once were, which insulated them from national political forces in the presidential races, have been eroded. The South, long resistant to the tides of national politics, also has become less distinctive as a region in the national contests (Beck and Lopatto 1982; Petrocik 1987).

Yet, the nationalization of presidential politics is offset by a decoupling of presidential and subpresidential voting. Powerful countervailing forces, both structural and cultural, have been at work in the American polity to undercut the effects of nationalization at the presidential level. On the cultural side is the staying power of unique state political environments (Erikson, McIver, and Wright 1987) and a stubborn resistance by state political leaders to being captives of national political forces. On the structural side are the persistent insulation of states from national elections, the control of party nominations by state and local constituencies (Key 1956), and of course the easy possibility of divided government.

State officials have not been content to leave the insulation of state politics from national trends to voter choice alone. They have shifted state elections away from presidential election years so that voters cannot vote simultaneously for president and state officials and thereby tie state politics to the swings of the presidential pendulum. Whereas only eighteen states separated gubernatorial from presidential elections as recently as 1952 (Key 1956), this number steadily grew to thirty-eight by 1988. Combined with increases in ticket splitting and the greater attractiveness of state legislative careers that makes incumbents more visible, this has produced a state electoral politics that perhaps is more insulated from national political forces than ever before (Chubb 1987).

Another structural feature that plays an important role in insulating state from national politics is the nature of party nominations. From the beginning, state and local interests have exerted more influence over party choice of candidates in the United States than in most democracies. The adoption of the direct primary by many states in the early 1900s reinforced this localism by placing control of nominations in the hands of voters—usually party voters, except where primaries are open (Epstein 1986, 167–74; Overacker 1926). The primary now has become an almost universal device for selecting candidates for all offices but the presidency, where it must share the billing with caucuses. This means that candidates in most races can win the nomination of their party by appealing solely to voters. To be sure, state and local parties may try to influence voters (and keep out prospective candidates) by making preprimary endorsements and providing slate cards; and many primaries are not competitive. Yet in the end, candidates do not need the approval of local, much less national, party

Table 16.1. Similarities in Presidential and Gubernatorial Outcomes

|  | *Percent of Elections Won by Presidential and Gubernatorial Candidates of the Same Party* |
|---|---|
| 1880–92 | 93.1 |
| 1896–08 | 89.5 |
| 1912–24 | 81.2 |
| 1928–40 | 77.8 |
| 1944–52 | 75.5 |
| 1956–68 | 60.8 |
| 1972–88 | 51.4 |

Source: The 1880–1952 figures come from V. O. Key, *American State Politics: An Introduction* (New York: Knopf, 1956), 49. The 1956–1988 figures were calculated by the author.

leaders to win their party's nomination. The fact that the party ticket in any year can contain a heterogeneous assortment of candidates, each tailoring his or her appeal to local conditions, adds to the separation of national and state politics.

The result is that probably less synchronization exists today between state and national electoral politics than at any time in this century, perhaps even in our history. Walter Dean Burnham (1985) has shown a steady decline in the correlations between state presidential results and Senate, House, and gubernatorial totals for every fifth election since 1900. Table 16.1 demonstrates this declining synchronization in another way: the steadily decreasing tendency for presidential and gubernatorial candidates of the same party to win a state even though they appear on the same ballot.

Now that the major premise of the volume has been established— that state electoral politics is sufficiently independent from national politics—it is time to turn to the nature of this politics as seen from its grass roots.

## PATTERNS OF ELECTORAL CHANGE IN THE AMERICAN STATES

American electoral change as viewed from the states exhibits three important patterns in recent years. First, and perhaps most important, is the increased competitiveness of political life in the states. The one-party politics so dominant just a generation ago has vanished, leaving state politics far more democratic than it once was. Second,

the movement towards competitiveness has carried states in divergent partisan directions. In most states it has improved Republican fortunes, but some states have resisted the powerful GOP tide.
Finally, partially as a result of greater competitiveness, state electoral outcomes are even less predictable than before. Party seems
less important in state voting behavior, as split results have become
increasingly common there as well as at the intersection of state
and nation.

TOWARD A MORE COMPETITIVE STATE POLITICS

Chapter after chapter in this volume has documented the revival, in
some cases actually the arrival, of a competitive party politics in the
states. The convergence of the states upon competitive patterns,
though, is the product of changes in alternative partisan directions—
with some states becoming less Republican and others becoming less
Democratic—within an environment in which party loyalties seem to
be declining as guides to electoral behavior.

The most dramatic changes have occurred in the states of the historically Solid South. Beginning in 1964, then quickening in the 1970s
and especially the 1980s, the Republican party growth in Alabama,
Florida, Texas, and Virginia has been striking. While the authors of
those chapters are cautious about concluding that the change signifies
a pro-GOP realignment of state politics because of the weakened
overall role of party, all agree that the Republicans are more competitive in the South than they have been in more than a hundred years.

Growing competitiveness has been led by a now well-established
Republican presidentialism, which, albeit haltingly, has catalyzed
GOP inroads at other levels of politics. All four of those southern
states now have elected their first Republican governors and senators
since Reconstruction. The Republicans even have made gains, albeit
unevenly, in Democrat-dominated state legislatures. Underlying the
improved Republican fortunes is tremendous growth in Republican
party loyalists. They have risen from being a lonely minority to parity
with the Democrats in the most recent figures. The influx of new residents in those four states has contributed to rising Republican totals,
but the growth of GOP identifiers also is traced by the chapter authors
to the successful mobilization of new generations of native voters into
Republican ranks.

Republican growth has not been confined to those southern states.
The chapters on Arizona, Colorado, and California show that the
West has experienced substantial pro-GOP changes as well (also see

Galderisi et al. 1987). To a degree, the changes are attributed to the same forces that opened the lock on partisan loyalties of southerners created by the Civil War. But the most powerful source of change in the western states is seen as the growth boom that has overlaid large numbers of new residents on the traditional party systems, obliterating old party cleavages in the process. Similar pro-Republican secular changes are found in New Jersey due to a breakdown in the New Deal coalition, the decline of traditional Democratic party machines, and the growing affluence of the population.

At the other pole of change are former GOP strongholds like Iowa, which has realigned in a Democratic direction. Longterm deterioration of the farm economy—a condition localized in a few midwestern states—has undermined GOP strength by depleting those populations that have been its traditional bulwark. Other states (e.g., Kansas) have experienced greater Democratic competitiveness because of a more general decline in partisan fidelity.

This leads to a third type of change that has been manifested in the American states—a decay in the underlying partisan roots of the electoral system. An electoral dealignment along with a rhetorical realignment in the issues that dominate the political agenda have brought an end to the New Deal era in New York without signaling a partisan realignment. In Rhode Island, early 1980s Republican electoral successes were the work of short-term forces that have become more significant in a state electorate that is still more Democratic than Republican in party loyalties but is mostly nonpartisan. Similar changes have taken place in Kansas, although it remains essentially a Republican state. The chapter authors attribute the growing competitiveness there to factional splits within the GOP, the attractiveness of conservative Democratic candidates for governor, and above all the weakened role of partisanship in voting behavior.

Amidst all the change in the last few decades, it is easy to lose sight of the islands of stability. In a few states, the levels of competition remain much the same as they have been for years. The New Deal realignment was slow to arrive in Wisconsin (Epstein 1958) and Ohio (Fenton 1966), and it has been correspondingly slow to leave. Longstanding Republican domination of their politics really did not end until the 1950s. Once a competitive party system was established by the 1960s in states like Wisconsin and Ohio, it resisted the recent forces pressing for change in other states.

The patterns of electoral stability and change exemplified by the states singled out for intensive examination in this volume are so com-

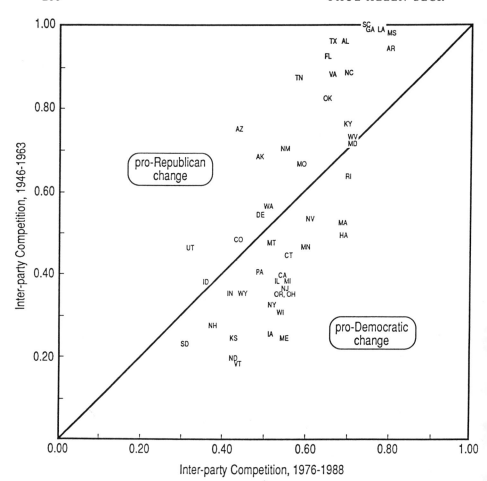

16.1 Changing interparty competition in the states. Note: The Ranney index averages the Democratic percentage of the gubernatorial vote and the percentages of seats held by the Democrats in each house of the state legislature. The index was not calculated for Nebraska, because its legislature was nonpartisan during the time periods under consideration. Based on gubernatorial results alone, however, this state became more Democratic between 1946–63 and 1976–88.

plex that they defy easy summary. Sometimes, though, a single, comparative statistic can capture such complex process of change. For the purpose of fitting the case study states into the general picture, I have calculated such a statistic: the changes in state two-party competition between the immediate post–World War II period (1946–63), before the changes chronicled above were set in motion, and the most recent period of 1976–88. The results are presented in figure 16.1.

The coordinates for each state in figure 16.1 are scores based on the familiar Ranney index, which I have updated for the 1976–88 period. No single quantitative measure can capture the full range of inter-party competition, of course. Even though the Ranney index is biased by district gerrymandering, its state-office focus is an advantage because it insulates the measure from powerful short-term trends in national politics. Only insomuch as they influence partisanship and state voting patterns will those forces be reflected. Consequently, this measure provides a picture of the kinds of electoral change that have engulfed the politics of the states in recent years.

A quick glance at figure 16.1 is sufficient to show that the states overall are much more competitive now than they were in the earlier period. They are more spread out along the vertical 1946–63 axis than they are along the horizontal 1976–88 axis. The range of scores during the recent period is .30 to .80 compared to a range of .18 to 1.00 from 1946 to 1963.

This impression is buttressed by a simple calculation of the mean and standard deviation of the two distributions. The means of the two distributions turn out to be almost exactly the same: .564 for the earlier period, .569 for the more recent period. In spite of pro-Republican forces in recent national politics, the mean Democratic advantage in state politics is unchanged! But the standard deviations are very different: .26 for the earlier period versus .11 for recent years. Many states are more competitive than before! Just eight of the fifty states, including only Colorado of those examined intensively in this volume, are less competitive in 1976–88 than they were in 1946–63.

Figure 16.1 also reflects the divergent partisan directions of the changes, although its focus solely on state offices understates the overall pro-Republican nature of the movement. Between 1946–63 and 1976–88, twenty-three states (the ones above the diagonal) became more Republican in state politics, led by those in the formerly Solid Democratic South. Conversely, twenty-five states (twenty-six if Nebraska is included based on gubernatorial outcomes) became more Democratic between those two time periods, while Maryland stayed in exactly the same position. With these figures in mind, we now can broaden the story line of the nature and causes of partisan change to encompass all fifty states.

Republican growth nationwide is powered by the emergence of the GOP as a viable opposition party in the South for the first time since the brief and anomalous Reconstruction interlude. The pattern is similar from state to state in that region. Emergence of the Democratic party as the vehicle in national politics for expanded civil rights for black Americans has kindled a growing aversion to the Democrats among white southerners, which was fanned by the popularity of Ronald Reagan (Black and Black 1987; Lamis 1984). Even though that aversion has not carried over to state and local politics, it has undermined Democratic loyalties, especially among young voters, which is most ominous for the Democrats. Without their solid southern base in national politics, the Democrats are no longer a majority party.

Complementing the racial-issue realignment of the southern electorate (Carmines and Stimson 1989) is the immigration of northerners into many southern states. They have carried with them disproportionately Republican partisan proclivities, which also have boosted GOP fortunes (Beck 1977). The effects of the massive population movements have been felt outside the South as well. The recent redistribution of Americans among the fifty states, probably even more than the near-record levels of immigration from abroad, has contributed significantly to a reshaping of the partisan map of American politics.

But pro-Republican forces obviously have not been the only ones operating in the American states. The economic prosperity of the 1980s was not shared by all. As much as the economy may have catalyzed GOP success in the boom states, it was a drag on GOP fortunes in those suffering from the ravages of a changing economy. The farm states of the Great Plains and the old industrial heartland were economically troubled in recent years and, consequently, have looked with less favor upon the Republican party. The checkered pattern of economic boom and bust across the land, not unexpectedly, has produced a similarly checkered pattern of political boom and bust for the two major parties.

Other states show more idiosyncratic patterns of change, driven primarily by forces that are local rather than national. The decentralized nature of the party system allows state parties to position themselves in the mainstream of public opinion even if they have to diverge from national party patterns. The conservatism of the Democratic parties in many southern states, as well as in Kansas, for example, has been a source of strength. In other states, it has been the popularity of key political leaders that has played the critical role. Republican growth in New Jersey and Democratic strength in New York during the 1980s owed a great deal to the appeal of Tom Kean and Mario Cuomo, respectively. By the same token, it is possible that an Ann Richards in Texas, a Lawton Chiles in Florida, or a Pete Wilson in California—to name the first big-state governors elected in the 1990s—will leave a similar personal mark on their own states.

An alternative perspective on realignment in the American states may be gained from looking at another summary statistic: registration figures in the twenty-eight states that permit party registration. Party registration is a lagging indicator of partisan change. Because most people do not change their official party designation even after they may have left that party psychologically, it primarily reflects the partisan preferences of newly enrolled voters. This turns registration into a useful barometer of the future if we focus on how much the absolute number of registrants with each party has changed over time. Figure 16.2 presents party registration comparisons between 1976 and 1988 to show changes across the most recent era.

The story told by increases in party registration parallels that shown by changes in the Ranney index. States experiencing pro-Republican net growth appear above the diagonal in figure 16.2, whereas states with pro-Democratic net growth appear below the diagonal. In spite of the caveats about using party registration to measure partisan movement, the figures nonetheless are revealing. Nineteen of the states with party registration have experienced growth in Republican registrants since 1976 that has outstripped, often by a substantial margin, whatever gains might have occurred in Democratic party registrants. In Alabama, Louisiana, Oregon, and Pennsylvania, in fact, the *absolute* number of Democratic registrants actually declined. Overall, it should not be surprising that the greatest GOP growth in party enrollments was concentrated in the South and West.

But registration evidence also shows that some states have resisted the powerful pro-GOP current. Democratic growth outpaced Republican growth in a total of seven states—the middle western farming states of Iowa, Kansas, and South Dakota; industrial giants Ohio and New York; and the New England states of Maine and Massachusetts. Four of those states actually experienced absolute Republican losses. Compared to the huge gains in states showing the greatest Republican growth, the pro-Democratic increases are small. Yet they are real, indicating the ability of some areas of the nation to resist powerful national forces.

The evidence presented here on changes in party competition and party registration essentially corroborates the conclusions drawn from the rich state analyses presented in earlier chapters, while setting them into a fifty-state framework. The American states are far more competitive political environments than they were three de-

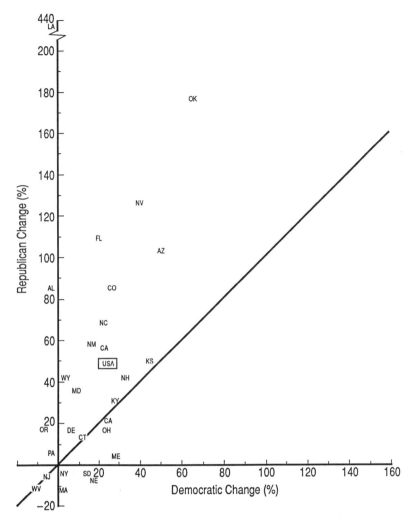

16.2 Changes in party registration, 1976–1988. Note: For Ohio and New Jersey, change is from 1980 to 1988 because there was no party registration in 1976. Because of differences in methods of calculating party registration and in electoral contexts, registration figures are not strictly equivalent across the states. Four of the states use a version of party registration that assigns voters to the party in whose primary contest they last chose to participate. Ohio automatically registers all voters with that party, whereas Massachusetts, New Hampshire, and Rhode Island register independents as partisans in that manner. Registration levels in these states may also be affected by the differential drawing power of their primaries.

cades ago, in the steady-state period before the New Deal party system had begun to decline (Converse 1976). Their enhanced competitiveness results from movement of the most one-party states toward a more balanced electoral politics. That has meant (often tremendous) Republican growth in the South offset by (albeit less extensive) Democratic growth in New England and the Plains. In short, in a sea of change in party electoral prospects, there have been powerful and enduring crosscurrents.

## SPLIT RESULTS AND THE DECLINE OF PARTY IN STATE POLITICS

In one important respect the states have exhibited a common pattern of change in their electoral politics. In chapter after chapter of this volume, as well as in the summary quantitative indicators displayed here, a similar message appears. The same electorate often has chosen candidates from different parties on the same ballot. Split-ticket voting appears to be at an all-time high in American elections, which suggests a reduced role for party as a guide to voting behavior.

The evidence for this phenomenon again is most noticeable in Washington, D.C. This reflects the tremendous growth of split results between congressional and presidential elections (Ornstein, Mann, and Malbin 1990, 62). That the changes are not merely artifacts of close contests in which a few split ballots have large-scale consequences, at least in the modern era, is confirmed by increases in reported ticket-splitting in the Michigan surveys from a range of 13 to 17 percent from 1952 to 1968 to 25 to 30 percent since (Stanley and Niemi 1990, 132).

The presidency is the only office in the United States for which there is a national constituency. Campaigns for the presidency have become nationalized, particularly as television has assumed a more prominent role, and local factors undoubtedly are less important than before in the voter's presidential calculus. The existence of split results, of course, may represent a conscious decision by the voter to check presidential power with a Congress controlled by the other party. More likely than such a sophisticated, strategic posture is that split results are the product of the interaction of national forces impinging most on the presidential choice and local forces, led by a visible incumbent facing an almost invisible challenger, impinging most on the subpresidential choice. Split results, in short, are another strong indicator of the existence of a separate state politics.

But state politics itself is not all of a piece. In state after state, electorates are returning mixed verdicts within state elections as well as between state and national contests. Democratic governors are being elected to face Republican legislatures, and vice versa. Bicameral legislatures often have different parties in control of their two houses. In 1991, for example, in only twenty-one (or 42 percent) of the fifty states will one party exercise complete control of state government and enjoy the unimpeded ability to pursue party policy objectives and to carve out new legislative districts that it brings. A majority of the one-party states, moreover, had experienced split control at some time during the decade of the 1980s.

In the state case studies in this volume, author after author has dwelled on the independence of voters and the weak partisan threads connecting their various votes. Even in states that have experienced striking Republican growth in recent years, state study authors are reluctant to conclude that realignment has occurred because party does not seem to be a reliable guide to voting behavior. Cotter refers to an unsettled electorate in Alabama. Fay and Lawson question whether *party* alignments appear in California at all. Parker favors a dealignment rather than realignment interpretation of Florida politics, even in the face of tremendous GOP growth. Stanley finds that independence and short-term factors have diluted party movements in Texas. Keeter questions how much party identifications matter in Virginia, given the voters' high levels of independence and ticket splitting. McIver and Stone for Colorado and Cigler and Loomis for Kansas trace fluctuations in candidate support for the most visible offices to the importance of candidate over party. Even in states that have moved in a definite partisan direction (e.g., Iowa and New Jersey), similar patterns appear. If there has been a party realignment in those states, it is a strange realignment in which the ascendant party has not been able to turn its advantages into *party* control of state politics.

An intensive focus on electoral politics within the states, then, corroborates inferences about politics on the national stage. In state after state, including states with little apparent partisan change (e.g., New York, Ohio, Rhode Island, and Wisconsin), the electorate seems remarkably independent of strong partisan loyalties as we enter the 1990s. Perhaps the reason is, as some suggest, that voters are more inclined to favor incumbents these days, regardless of party. But we should beware of such facile explanations. Not so long ago, after all, analysts were bemoaning the seeming inability of presidential incumbents to win reelection. Alternatively, it may be that voters simply are influenced more these days by election-specific factors—the nature of a campaign, the relative attractiveness of the candidates, issues that crosscut the normal party cleavages—that exhibit a somewhat random quality. Whatever the explanation, the implication is the same: *Across America, the anchor of party, long heralded as the principal long-term force in voting behavior, has weakened rather than strengthened.* This may be the most significant single fact for party realignment in the states.

## CONCLUSION: IS THERE PARTY REALIGNMENT IN THE STATES?

Partisan realignment has been conceptualized in a variety of ways—as an enduring change in the coalitions of party loyalists (Burnham 1970; Petrocik 1981; Sundquist 1983; Beck 1988), as a long-term alteration in the balance of party strength that produces a new majority party (Pomper 1967), as a change in balance that leads to single-party control of government for a lengthy period (Clubb, Flanigan, and Zingale 1980). At the core of all of the conceptualizations lie the party loyalties of the electorate. The minimum condition for realignment in these conventional treatments is that the loyalties must undergo a significant and lasting change.

That party loyalties have changed in many, although not all, of the American states there can be no doubt. Whether measured indirectly by voting patterns or directly with the familiar party identification index (Campbell et al. 1960), enduring partisan movement is clear. In many states, the changes have produced a shake up in the party coalitions. In the South, for example, the Democratic and Republican parties are significantly different groupings from the parties they were for the one hundred years after Reconstruction. But more characteristic has been the erosion, rather than the replacement, of the New Deal coalition—what Burnham (1982) terms the "collapse of the ancient regime."

Nonetheless, this period does not wear the label of realignment easily, especially when one focuses on the states. In the national politics of presidential elections, the GOP clearly has become the dominant party, displacing the Democratic New Deal majority. And there has been some growth, albeit small, in Republican identifiers nationwide, accompanied by a far larger decline in professed Democrats (Wattenberg 1990). But Republican presidential successes have not been replicated at the state level, where overall the Democratic party remains dominant.

The odd duality of the American electoral response—presidential Republicanism, subpresidential Democraticism—has forced many realignment theorists to apply the concept in modified form to contemporary politics. Wattenberg (1987) speaks of a "hollow realignment" in which party and candidate have been decoupled. Ladd (1985) sees a "two-tiered" realignment produced by public ambivalence on issues and incumbent-centered decision making by voters. Lowi (1985) attributes the present duality to the emergence of a "plebiscitary presidency." Beck (1988), emphasizing state results more than do the others, calls it an "incomplete realignment." All seem to share the notion that, if this is a realignment (and there has been too much change to ignore realignment possibilities), then it is a type of realignment that the United States has never experienced before.

What is missing, from a realignment perspective, is the synchronization of electoral behavior across the various levels of politics that results from voting that is well anchored in partisan loyalties. Previous periods of realignment have exhibited across-the-board patterns of change that clearly favor one party over the other. For example, the tracks of previous realignments appear in parallel changes in presidential and congressional results. Table 16.2 illustrates the synchronization in terms of support for the new majority party during the realignments of 1896 and the New Deal period—juxtaposed against the absence of such synchronization in recent years. Once the two previous realignments had commenced after 1892 and 1930 (shown below the line in each data series in table 16.2), the composition of Congress changed to favor the party winning the presidency. No such change appears in the 1970s and 1980s. While presidential landslides increased the GOP congressional minority somewhat, the effect was neither strong nor enduring. Republican standing in the House remained far below its presidential level.

Nor, as we have seen, does the vote synchronization characteristic of past realignments manifest itself in state politics. Presidential Republicanism stands virtually alone in signaling the emergence of a new majority. It is not matched in the outcomes for state races, even in states with enormous GOP growth. Until such synchronization appears in contemporary times, symbolizing party voting across the ballot, it will be difficult to return a confident verdict of realignment.

Perhaps what we have witnessed in the 1980s and will continue to see as we move into the 1990s is a party system incapable of realignment. What Walter Dean Burnham (1970, 91–134) referred to twenty years ago as the "onward march of party decomposition" may have

Table 16.2. Parallelism of House and Presidential Results for New Majority Party: Comparing Realigning Periods with the Present

| Realignment of 1896 | | | New Deal Realignment | | | Contemporary Period | | |
|---|---|---|---|---|---|---|---|---|
| Year | Pres (%) | House (%) | Year | Pres (%) | House (%) | Year | Pres (%) | House (%) |
| 1884 | 48 | 43 | 1924 | 34 | 42 | 1972 | 61 | 44 |
| 1886 |  | 46 | 1926 |  | 45 | 1974 |  | 33 |
| 1888 | 48 | 52 | 1928 | 41 | 28 | 1976 | 48 | 33 |
| 1890 |  | 26 | 1930 |  | 49 | 1978 |  | 36 |
| 1892 | 43 | 36 | 1932 | 57 | 72 | 1980 | 51 | 44 |
| 1894 |  | 69 | 1934 |  | 74 | 1982 |  | 38 |
| 1896 | 51 | 58 | 1936 | 61 | 77 | 1984 | 59 | 42 |
| 1898 |  | 52 | 1938 |  | 60 | 1986 |  | 41 |
| 1900 | 52 | 56 | 1940 | 55 | 61 | 1988 | 53 | 40 |
|  |  |  |  |  |  | 1990 |  | 38 |

Note: The figures in each column are the percentages of the presidential popular vote and of the congressional seats won by the party that emerged as the majority party at the presidential level after the realignment. Thus, for 1884–1900, Republican percentages are given; for 1924–1940, Democratic percentages are given; and for 1972–1990, the figures are Republican percentages.

progressed to the point of no return. The toll on parties as viable objects of identification imposed by a nominations system that takes the selection of candidates away from party leaders, an electoral system that insulates states from national contests, campaign financing conventions that force candidates to raise their own money, and candidate-centered electoral campaigns, to name but a few of the recent phenomena undermining the political parties' traditional role, finally may have overcome the drag of tradition and locked the American system into a sort of permanent dealignment.

Alternatively, it is conceivable that the lag between party realignment at the presidential level and at lower electoral levels has increased. There was a twenty-year delay, after all, in the penetration of the New Deal realignment into the politics of many states (Sundquist 1983). The forces for party decomposition simply may have slowed the effects of national changes on subpresidential contests. Perceiving what is happening at the national level, candidates may have tailored their appeals to insulate themselves from national forces—something that has become easier to do in an "every candidate for himself or herself" politics. Many observers have seen a critical change in the agenda of American politics in the 1980s (Burnham 1989), as candidates for both parties have scrambled to be on the right side of an electorate resistant to taxes and social welfare spending. Such scrambling, though, may only delay an inevitable party realignment.

Whatever scenario applies, by now there should be no question that the states will play a central role in the future of the American party system. Republican prospects for becoming a new majority party depend critically upon their ability to increase their showings in state elections. Democratic chances to slow the pace of change or to turn it in their direction similarly are tied to their fortunes in state politics. American state politics is now more competitive than probably ever before. But it is a competition that seems to stubbornly resist influence from the national level, thus lending new credence to the familiar aphorism that "all politics is local politics." A focus on party realignment in the states, then, provides a necessary corrective to the often-myopic, Washington-centered perspective on American electoral politics.

# Bibliography

Abramson, Paul R., John H. Aldrich, and David W. Rohde. 1990. *Change and Continuity in the 1988 Elections*. Washington, D.C.: Congressional Quarterly Press.

Adamany, David. 1969. *Financing Politics: Recent Wisconsin Elections*. Madison: University of Wisconsin Press.

Anderson, Kristi. 1979. *The Creation of a Democratic Majority*. Chicago: University of Chicago Press.

Anderson, James E., Richard W. Murray, and Edward L. Farley. 1989. *Texas Politics*. 5th ed. New York: Harper & Row.

Aoki, Elizabeth. 1986. "Which Party Will Harvest the New Asian Votes?" *California Journal* 17 (November): 546.

Asher, Herbert B. n.d. "The Emergence of the Democratic Party in Ohio." Unpublished paper.

Averyt, Ronald A. 1970. "The Minority Party in a Non-Competitive State: The Case of Kansas." (Ph.D. diss., University of Kansas).

Babbit, Bruce. Interview by David R. Berman, 4 March 1989.

Barnard, W. D. 1974. *Dixiecrats and Democrats: Alabama Politics, 1943–1950*. Tuscaloosa: University of Alabama Press.

Barnes, Fred. 1985. "Meet Mario the Moderate." *New Republic* 8 April: 17–20.

Barone, Michael, and Grant Ujifusa. 1983. *The Almanac of American Politics*. Washington, D.C.: National Journal.

———. 1987. *The Almanac of American Politics*. Washington, D.C.: National Journal.

Bartley, N. V., and H. D. Graham. 1976. *Southern Politics and the Second Reconstruction*. Baltimore: Johns Hopkins University Press.

Bass, J. and W. DeVries. 1976. *The Transformation of Southern Politics*. New York: Basic Books.

Baum, Lawrence, and Samuel C. Patterson. 1987. "Is There Party Realignment in Ohio?" Paper presented at the annual meeting of the American Political Science Association, Chicago, 3–6 September.

Beck, Paul Allen. 1976. "A Socialization Theory of Partisan Realignment." In *Controversies in American Voting Behavior*. edited by Richard G. Niemi and Herbert Weisberg.

———. 1977. "Partisan Dealignment in the Post-War South." *American Political Science Review* 71:477–96.

———. 1982. "Realignment Begins? The Republican Surge in Florida." *American Politics Quarterly* 10:279–304.

―――. 1984. "The Dealignment Era in America." In *Electoral Change in Advanced Industrial Democracies*, edited by Russell J. Dalton, Scott Flanagan, and Paul Beck. Princeton, N.J.: Princeton University Press.

―――. 1988. "Incomplete Realignment: The Reagan Legacy for Parties and Elections." In *The Reagan Legacy*, edited by Charles O. Jones. Chatham, N.J.: Chatham House.

Beck, Paul Allen, and Paul Lopatto. 1982. "The End of Southern Distinctiveness." In *Contemporary Southern Political Attitudes and Behavior*, edited by Laurence W. Moreland, Tod A. Baker, and Robert P. Steed. New York: Praeger.

Beck, Paul Allen, and Frank J. Sorauf. 1992. *Party Politics in America*. New York: Harper Collins.

Berman, David. 1985. *Parties and Elections in Arizona: 1863–1984*. Morrison Institute: Arizona State University.

―――. 1986. "Voters, Candidates, and Issues in the Progressive Era: The 1912 Presidential Election in Arizona." *Social Science Quarterly* 67:255–66.

―――. 1987. "Arizona's Political Culture. In *Culture and Values in Arizona Life*, edited by John Hall and Larry Mankin. Phoenix: Arizona Town Hall.

Beyle, Thad. 1983. "Governors." In *Politics in the American States*, edited by Virginia Gray, Herbert Jacob, and Kenneth Vines. Boston: Little, Brown.

Bibby, John F. 1989. "Party Realignment in the Midwest." Paper presented at the annual meeting of the American Political Science Association, Atlanta.

Black, Earl. 1976. *Southern Governors and Civil Rights*. Cambridge: Harvard University Press.

Black, Earl, and Merle Black. 1987. *Politics and Society in the South*. Cambridge: Harvard University Press.

Bowen, Lewis, William E. Hulbary, Anne E. Kelley. 1987. "Party Organization and Behavior in Florida: Assessing Grassroots Organizational Strength." Paper presented at the annual meeting of the American Political Science Association.

Brewer, Daniel Chauncey. 1926. *The Conquest of New England by the Immigrant*. New York: G. P. Putnam and Sons.

Bullock, Charles. 1988. "Regional Realignment from an Officeholding Perspective." *Journal of Politics* 50:553–74.

Burnham, Walter Dean. 1964. "The Alabama Senatorial Election of 1962: Return of Inter-Party Competition." *Journal of Politics* 26:798–829.

―――. 1970. *Critical Elections and the Mainsprings of American Politics*. New York: Norton.

―――. 1975. "Insulation and Responsiveness in Congressional Elections." *Political Science Quarterly* 90:411–35.

―――. 1982. "Into the 1980s with Ronald Reagan." In *The Current Crisis in American politics*, edited by Walter Dean Burnham. New York: Oxford University Press.

―――. 1985. "The 1984 Elections and the Future of American Politics." In *Election 1984: Landslide Without a Mandate?*, edited by Ellis Sandoz and Cecil V. Crabb, Jr. New York: Mentor.

————. 1989. "The Reagan Heritage." In *The Election of 1988,* edited by Gerald M. Pomper. Chatham, N.J: Chatham House, 1–32.

Byrkit, James. 1982. *Forging the Copper Collar.* Tucson: University of Arizona Press.

Cain, Bruce E. 1985. "Assessing the Partisan Effects of Redistricting." *American Political Science Review* 79:320–33.

Calvert, Randall L., and John A. Ferejohn. 1983. "Coattail Voting in Recent Presidential Elections." *American Political Science Review* 77:407–19.

Campbell, Angus, Philip E. Converse, Warren E. Miller, and Donald E. Stokes. 1960. *The American Voter.* New York: Wiley.

Carey, Hugh D. 1981. *The New York State Economy in the 1980s: A Program for Economic Growth.* Albany: Governor's Office of Development Planning.

Carlson, J. 1981. *George Wallace and Politics of Powerlessness.* New Brunswick, N.J.: Transaction Books.

Carmines, E. G. and J. A. Stimson. 1986. "On the Structure and Sequence of Issue Evolution." *American Political Science Review* 80:901–20.

————. 1989. *Issue Evolution: Race and the Transformation of American Politics.* Princeton, N.J.: Princeton University Press.

Chubb, John E. 1987. "Institutions, the Economy, and the Dynamics of State Elections." *American Political Science Review* 82:133–54.

Cigler, Allan J., and James W. Drury. 1981. "Kansas." In *Reapportionment Politics: The History of Redistricting in the 50 States,* edited by Leroy Hardy, Alan Heslop, and Stuart Anderson. Claremont, Calif.: Rose Institute of State and Local Government.

Clubb, Jerome, William Flanigan, and Nancy Zingale. 1980. *Partisan Realignment: Voters, Parties, and Government in American History.* Beverly Hills, Calif.: Sage.

Colburn, David R., and Richard Scher. 1980. *Florida's Gubernatorial Politics in the Twentieth Century.* Tallahassee: University of Florida.

Colby, Peter W., and John K. White, eds. 1989. *New York State Today: Politics, Government and Public Policy.* Albany: State University of New York Press.

Converse, Philip E. 1966. "On the Possibility of Major Political Realignment in the South." In *Elections and the Political Order,* edited by A. Campbell et al. New York: Wiley.

Converse, Philip E. 1972. "Change in the American Electorate." In *The Human Meaning of Social Change,* edited by Angus Campbell and Philip E. Converse. New York: Russell Sage.

Converse, Philip E. 1976. *The Dynamics of Party Support.* Beverly Hills, Calif.: Sage.

Copper, James. 1964. "Arizona: The State Primeval." In *States of Crisis,* edited by James Reichley. Chapel Hill: University of North Carolina Press.

Cotter, Cornelius, James L. Gibson, John F. Bibby and Robert J. Huckshorn. 1984. *Party Organizations in American Politics.* New York: Praeger.

Cotter, P. R., and J. F. Kline. 1987. "George Wallace and Leadership in Alabama." Paper presented at the Southern Political Science Association, Charlotte, N.C.

Cotter, P. R. and J. G. Stovall. 1987. "The 1986 Election in Alabama: The Beginning of the post–Wallace Era." *PS* 20:655–66.

Cuomo, Mario M. 1986. "Acceptance Speech to the New York State Democratic Convention." 3 June.

Dennis, Jack. 1975. "Trends in Public Support for the American Party System." *British Journal of Political Science* 5:187–230.

———. 1980. "Changing Public Support for the American Party System." In *Paths to Reform*, edited by William J. Crotty. Lexington, Mass.: Lexington Books.

*Des Moines Register.* 8 June 1986. "Voters Not Swayed by Mingo Stag Party."

———. 5 November 1988a. "Democrats the Winners in Registering Iowans."

———. 10 November 1988b. "Democratic Surge in Iowa: The Implications Are Many."

———. 14 November 1988c. "What Iowa GOP Must Do Now to Survive."

———. 15 December 1988d. "Take that, Census Bureau: Firm Predicts More Iowans in 2010."

Drury, James W., and James E. Titus. 1960. *Legislative Apportionment in Kansas: 1960.* Lawrence, Kans.: Government Research Center, University of Kansas.

Dye, Thomas R. 1989. *Public Policy in Florida: A Fifty State Perspective.* A Policy Sciences Program Publication: Florida State University.

Dyer, James A., Arnold Vedlitz, and David B. Hill. 1988. "New Voters, Switchers and Political Party Realignment in Texas." *Western Political Quarterly* 41:155–67.

Dykstra, Robert R., and David R. Reynolds. 1978. "In Search of Wisconsin Progressives, 1904–1952: A Test of the Rogin Scenario." In *The History of American Electoral Behavior*, edited by Joel H. Silbey, Allan G. Boque and William Flanigan. Princeton, N.J.: Princeton University Press.

Echols, Margaret Thompson, and Austin Ranney. 1976. "The Impact of Interparty Competition Reconsidered: The Case of Florida." *Journal of Politics* 38:142–52.

Ehrenhalt, Alan, ed. 1985. *Politics in America.* Washington, D.C.: Congressional Quarterly Press.

Ehrenhalt, Alan. 1989. "How a Party of Enthusiasts Keep Its Hammerlock on a State Legislature." *Governing* (June): 28–33.

Elazar, Daniel J. 1972. *American Federalism: A View from the States,* 2d ed. New York: Thomas Crowell.

Epstein, Leon D. 1958. *Politics in Wisconsin.* Madison: University of Wisconsin Press.

———. 1982. "Party Confederations and Political Nationalization." *Publius* 12:67–102.

———. 1986. *Political Parties in the American Mold.* Madison: University of Wisconsin Press.

Erikson, Robert S., John P. McIver, and Gerald C. Wright. 1987. "State Political Culture and Public Opinion." *American Political Science Review* 81:797–814.

Erikson, Robert S., and Kent L. Tedin. 1981. "The 1928–1936 Partisan Realignment: The Case for the Conversion Hypothesis." *American Political Science Review* 75:951–62.

Fenton, John H. 1966. *Midwest Politics*. New York: Holt, Rinehart and Winston.

Ferejohn, John A., and Randall L. Calvert. 1984. "Presidential Coattails in Historical Perspective." *American Journal of Political Science* 28:127–46.

Field Institute. 1986. "A Survey of 1986 General Election Voters." *California Opinion Index* 6.

———. 1987. "Economic Well-Being." *California Opinion Index* 7.

———. 1988. "Political Demography." *California Opinion Index* 8.

Fiorina, Morris P. 1977. "The Case of the Vanishing Marginals: The Bureaucracy Did It." *American Political Science Review* 71:177–81.

Flinn, Thomas A. 1973. "Ohio." In *Explaining the Vote: Presidential Choices in the Nation and the States*, edited by David M. Kovenock and James W. Prothro, 209–43. Chapel Hill, N.C.: Institute for Research in Social Science, University of North Carolina.

Flinn, Thomas A. 1962. "Continuity and Change in Ohio Politics." *Journal of Politics* 24:521–44.

Flinn, Thomas A. 1960. "The Outline of Ohio Politics." *Western Political Quarterly* 13:702–21.

Forsythe, Dall W. 1977. *Taxation and Political Change in the Young Nation, 1781–1833*. New York: Columbia University Press.

Franklin, C. H. and J. E. Jackson. 1983. "The Dynamics of Party Identification." *American Political Science Review* 77:957–73.

Freedberg, Louis. 1987. "Latinos: Building Power from the Ground Up." *California Journal* 18 (January): 16.

Galderisi, Peter, Michael Lyons, Randy Simmons, and John Francis. 1987. *The Politics of Realignment: Party Change in the Mountain West*. Boulder, Colo.: Westview.

Garrow, D. J. 1978. *Protest at Selma*. New Haven: Yale University Press.

Gatlin, D. S. 1975. "Party Identification, Status, and Race in the South, 1952–1972." *Public Opinion Quarterly* 39:39–51.

Germond, Jack, and Jules Witcover. 1989. *Whose Broad Stripes and Bright Stars? The Trivial Pursuit of the Presidency 1988*. New York: Warner Books.

Gibson, James, Cornelius Cotter, John Bibby, and Robert Huckshorn. 1983. "Assessing Party Organizational Strength." *American Journal of Political Science* 27:193–222.

Grantham, Dewey W. 1988. *The Life and Death of the Solid South*. Lexington: University of Kentucky Press.

Gold, David, and John R. Schmidhauser. 1960. "Urbanization and Party Competition: The Case of Iowa." *Midwest Journal of Political Science* 4:62.

Gunther, John. 1947. *Inside U.S.A.* New York: Harper and Brothers.

Hahn, Harlan. 1971. *Urban-Rural Conflict*. Beverly Hills: Sage Publications.

Hamilton, V. V. 1987. *Lister Hill: Statesman from the South*. Chapel Hill: University of Kentucky Press.

Harder, Marvin A. 1959. "Party Factionalism in Kansas." Ph.D. diss., Columbia University.

———. 1989. "Electoral Politics in Kansas: A Historical Perspective. In *Politics and Government in Kansas,* edited by Marvin A. Harder. Topeka: Capitol Complex.

Harder, Marvin A., and Carolyn Rampey. 1972. *The Kansas Legislature: Procedures, Personalities and Problems.* Lawrence, Kans.: The University Press of Kansas.

Hardt, Bill. Interviewed by David R. Berman, 28 May 1985.

Heil, Richard P. 1983. "Indices of Party Strength: The Case of kansas," Ph.D. diss., University of Kansas.

Hunker, Henry L. 1984. "Changing Patterns of Business and Industry in Ohio." Paper presented at conference, Ohio in Our Times, Ohio Historical Society, Columbus.

Intertribal Council of Arizona. "The History of Arizona Indian Voting Rights." Reprint, *Congressional Record* 14 May 1986, E1676–77.

Ippolito, Dennis. 1986. "Texas." In *The 1984 Presidential Elections in the South: Patterns of Southern Party Politics,* edited by Robert Steed, Lawrence Moreland, and Tod Baker, 303–35. New York: Praeger.

Jacobson, Gary C. 1980. *Money in Congressional Elections.* New Haven: Yale University Press.

———. 1987. *The Politics of Congressional Elections.* Boston: Little, Brown.

Jennings, M. K., and R. Niemi. 1975. "Continuity and Change in Political Orientations." *American Political Science Review* 69:1316–35.

Jewell, Malcolm E., and David Breaux. 1988. "The Effect of Incumbency on State Legislative Elections." *Legislative Studies Quarterly* 13:495–514.

Jewell, Malcolm E., and David M. Olson. 1988. *Political Parties and Elections in the American States.* Chicago: The Dorsey Press.

Kelly, George C. 1926. *Legislative History: Arizona 1864–1912.* Phoenix: Manufacturing Stationers, Inc.

Key, V. O. 1949. *Southern Politics in State and Nation.* New York: Alfred A. Knopf.

———. 1955. "A Theory of Critical Elections." *Journal of Politics* 17:198–210.

———. 1956. *American State Politics: An Introduction.* New York: Alfred A. Knopf.

———. 1959. "Secular Realignment and the Party System." *Journal of Politics* 21:198–210.

Kraft Corporation. "Voter Attitudes Toward Candidates and Issues." September 1961, Hayden Papers, Arizona Collection, Arizona State University.

Krauthammer, Charles. "How Does Liberal Dukakis Seek Reagan Democrats? In Disguise." *The Providence Journal* 1 August 1988.

Ladd, Everett Carll. 1985. "On Mandates, Realignments and the 1984 Presidential Election." *Political Science Quarterly* 11:1–25.

Ladd, Everett Carll. 1989a. "The 1988 Elections: Continuation of the Post-New Deal System." *Political Science Quarterly* 104:1–18.

Ladd, Everett Carll. 1989b. "Like Waiting for Godot: The Uselessness of Realignment for Understanding Change in Contemporary American Politics." Paper presented at the annual meeting of the American Political Science Association.

Ladd, Everett Carll, and Charles Hadley. 1975. *Transformations of the American Party System*. rev. ed. New York: Norton.

Lamis, Alexander P. 1984. *The Two-Party South*. New York: Oxford University Press.

Larew, James C. 1980. *A Party Reborn*. Iowa City: Iowa State Historical Department.

Larson, David R. 1982. "Ohio's Fighting Liberal: A Political Biography of John J. Gilligan." Ph.D. diss., The Ohio State University. Columbus.

Lowi, Theodore. 1985. *The Personal President: Power Invested, Promise Unfilled*. Ithaca, N.Y.: Cornell University Press.

MacRae, Duncan, and James E. Meldrum. 1960. "Critical Elections in Illinois: 1888–1958." *American Political Science Review* 54:669–83.

Marcus, Robert. 1983. "How Many New Yorks?" *Empire State Report* April.

Marist Institute for Public Opinion. 1990. *Survey of New Yorkers*. 31 January–4 February.

Markusen, Ann. 1987. *Regions: The Economics and Politics of Territory*. Totowa, N.J.: Rowman & Littlefield.

Martin, Curtis, and Rudolph Gomez. 1972. *Colorado Government and Politics*. 3d ed. Boulder, Colo.: Pruett Press.

Mayhew, David R. 1974. *Congress: The Electoral Connection*. New Haven: Yale University Press.

———. 1986. *Placing Parties in American Politics*. Princeton, N.J.: Princeton University Press.

McGlennon, John J. 1988. "Virginia's Changing Party Politics, 1976–1986." In *The New South's New Politics*, edited by Robert H. Swansbrough and David M. Brodsky. Columbia, S.C.: University of South Carolina Press.

McLoughlin, William. 1986. *Rhode Island: A History*. New York: Norton.

Miller, Arthur H. 1987. "Public Opinion and Regional Political Realignment." In *The Politics of Realignment*, edited by P. Galderisi et al. Boulder, Colo.: Westview.

Miller, Warren E. 1990. "The Electorate's View of the Parties." In *The Parties Respond: Changes in the American Party System*, edited by L. Sandy Maisel. Boulder, Colo.: Westview.

Mireles, Valerie. 1987. "Surging Toward a Latino State." *California Journal* 18 (January): 19.

Miringoff, Lee, and Barbara Carvalho. 1986. *The Cuomo Factor: Assessing the Political Appeal of New York's Governor*. Poughkeepsie, N.Y.: Marist Institute for Public Opinion.

Moakley, Maureen. 1985. "New Jersey." In *The Political Life of the American States*, edited by Alan Rosenthal and Maureen Moakley. New York: Praeger.

———. 1986. "Political Parties." In *The Political State of New Jersey*, edited by Gerald M. Pomper. New Brunswick, N.J.: Rutgers University Press.

Morehouse, Sarah McCally. 1981. *State Politics, Parties and Policy.* New York: Holt, Rinehart and Winston.

Mueller, J. E. 1973. *War, Presidents and Public Opinion.* New York: Wiley.

Nelson A. Rockefeller Institute of Government. 1987. *New York State Statistical Yearbook, 1985–1986.* Albany: Nelson A. Rockefeller Institute of Government.

*New York Times.* 6 November 1980. "New York GOP Sees Power Shift within the Party."

———. 16 June 1985a. "Buchanan Labels Cuomo a 'Reactionary Liberal.'"

———. 20 October 1985b. "This Liberal Party's Over."

———. 6 November 1986. "Cuomo's Solo Campaign Drive Leaves Undercurrent of Discontent in Party."

———. 2 October 1990a. "Criminal Justice: Elusive Priority in the Cuomo Years."

———. 8 November 1990b. "Most Incumbents Win in Races for Legislature."

Nie, Norman H., Sidney Verba, and John R. Petrocik. 1976. *The Changing American Voter.* Cambridge: Harvard University Press.

Norpoth, Helmut. 1987. "Under Way and Here to Stay: Party Realignment in the 1980s?" *Public Opinion Quarterly* 51:376–91.

Norpoth, Helmut, and Jerrold Rusk. 1982. "Partisan Dealignment in the American Electorate: Itemizing the Deductions Since 1964." *American Political Science Review* 76:522–37.

Norpoth, Helmut, and Michael R. Kagay. 1989. "Another Eight Years of Republican Rule and Still No Partisan Realignment?" Paper presented at the annual meeting of the American Political Science Association, Atlanta.

Ohio Bureau of Employment Services. 1989. *Ohio at Work: 1988 Chartbook.* Columbus: Ohio Bureau of Employment Services.

Ornstein, Norman J., Thomas E. Mann, and Michael J. Malbin. 1990. *Vital Statistics on Congress: 1989–1990.* Washington, D.C.: Congressional Quarterly Press.

Osmond, Marie, and Eliza Pavalko. 1987. "Attitudes Toward Abortion Challenge Dichotomous Positions." *Florida Public Opinion* 2:6–12.

Overacker, Louise. 1926. *The Presidential Primary.* New York: Macmillan.

Parker, Suzanne L. 1988a. "Shifting Party Tides in Florida: Where Have All the Democrats Gone?" In *The South's New Politics: Realignment and Dealignment,* edited by Robert H. Swansborough and David M. Brodsky. Columbia, S.C.: University of South Carolina Press.

———. 1988b. "How Strong is Republicanism in Florida?" *Election Politics* 5:6–10.

Parsons, Malcolm B. 1950. "Party and Pressure Politics in Arizona's Opposition to Colorado River Development." *Pacific Historical Review* 19:47–58.

Patterson, Samuel C. 1984. "Iowa." In *The Political Life of the American States,* edited by Alan Rosenthal and Maureen Moakley. New York: Praeger.

Patterson, Samuel C., and Thomas W. Kephart. 1991. "The Case of the Wayfaring Challenger: The 1988 Senate Election in Ohio." *Congress & the Presidency* 18:105–20.

Persico, Joseph E. 1982. *The Imperial Rockefeller: A Biography of Nelson A. Rockefeller*. New York: Simon and Schuster.

Petrocik, John R. 1981. *Party Coalitions*. Chicago: University of Chicago Press.

―――. 1987. "Realignment: New Party Coalitions and the Nationalization of the South." *Journal of Politics* 49:347–75.

Pierce, Neal R. 1973. *The Great Plains States of America*. New York: Norton.

Pierce, Neal R., and Jerry Hagstrom. 1984. *The Book of America*. New York: Warner Books.

Pomper, Gerald. 1967. "Classification of Presidential Elections." *Journal of Politics* 29:535–66.

Pomper, Gerald. 1989. "The Presidential Nominations." In *The Election of 1988*, edited by Gerald Pomper. Chatham, N.J.: Chatham House.

Profugi, Victor. 1988. "Rhode Island: A Party Rebirth." Paper presented at the annual meeting of the New England Political Science Association, 16 April.

Raimundo, Jeff. 1986. "The New Republican Party." *California Journal*, 17 (July): 546.

Ranney, Austin. 1983. *Channels of Power*. New York: Basic Books.

Redwood, Anthony, and Charles Krider. 1986. *Kansas Economic Development Study: Findings, Strategy, Recommendations*. Lawrence, Kans.: Institute for Public Policy and Business Research, University of Kansas.

Reichley, A. James. 1985. "The Rise of National Parties." In *The New Direction in American Politics*, edited by John Chubb and Paul Peterson, 175–200. Washington, D.C.: Brookings.

Republican National Committee. *Republican Almanac*. 1989. Washington, D.C.: Republican National Committee.

Rice, Ross R. 1964. "Recent Legislative Politics in Arizona." *Western Political Quarterly* (Supplement) 17:69–70.

*Richmond Times–Dispatch*. 3 January 1988. "Population Changes Stamping New Character on Old Dominion."

Riordan, William L. 1963. *Plunkitt of Tammany Hall*. New York: E. P. Dutton.

Rosenthal, Alan. 1986. "The Legislature." In *The Political State of New Jersey*, edited by Gerald M. Pomper. New Brunswick, N.J.: Rutgers University Press.

Ryan, Thomas G. 1981. "The Early Years of the Iowa Democratic Revival, 1950–1956." *The Annals of Iowa* 46:43–63.

Salmore, Stephen. 1986. "Voting, Election and Campaigns." In *The Political State of New Jersey*, edited by Gerald M. Pomper. New Brunswick, N.J.: Rutgers University Press.

Sample, Herbert. 1987. "Black Political Party." *California Journal* 18 (May): 232–39.

Schlesinger, Joseph. 1966. *Ambition and Politics*. Chicago: Rand McNally.

Shafer, Byron E. 1989. "The Notion of an Electoral Order: The Structure of Electoral Politics at the Accession of George Bush." Paper presented at the annual meeting of the American Political Science Association, Atlanta.

Silbey, Joel. 1989. "Beyond Realignment and Realignment Theory: American

Political Eras, 1789–1989." Paper presented at the annual meeting of the American Political Science Association, Atlanta.

Sinding, Rick. 1989. "Tom Kean's Legacy." *New Jersey Reporter* 5:8–29.

Smith, Eric R. A. N., and Peverill Squire. 1987. "State and National Politics in the Mountain West." In *The Politics of Realignment*, edited by Peter F. Galderisi, et al. Boulder, Colo.: Westview.

Sorauf, Frank J. 1954. "Extra-Legal Parties in Wisconsin." *American Political Science Review* 48:692–704.

Sorauf, Frank J., and Paul Allen Beck. 1988. *Party Politics in America*, 6th ed. Glenview, Ill.: Scott, Foresman and Company.

Spitzer, Robert J. 1989. "The Tail Wagging the Dog: Multi-Party Politics." In *New York State Today: Politics, Government and Public Policy*, edited by Peter W. Colby and John K. White. Albany: State University of New York Press.

Squire, Peverill. 1989. "Iowa and the Nomination Process." In *The Iowa Caucuses and the Presidential Nominating Process*, edited by Peverill Squire. Boulder, Colo.: Westview.

Squire, Peverill, Raymond E. Wolfinger, and David P. Glass. 1987. "Residential Mobility and Voter Turnout." *American Political Science Review* 81:46–65.

Stanley, Harold W. 1985. "The 1984 Presidential Election in the South: Race and Realignment." In *Patterns of Southern Party Politics*, edited by R. Steed, L. W. Moreland, and R. A. Baker. New York: Praeger.

———. 1988. "Southern Partisan Changes: Dealignment, Realignment or Both?" *Journal of Politics* 50:64–89.

Stanley, Harold W., and Richard G. Niemi. 1990. *Vital Statistics on American Politics*. Washington, D.C.: Congressional Quarterly Press.

Stanley, Jeanie R. 1986. "Women in Texas Politics." In *Practicing Texas Politics*, edited by Eugene Jones et al. Boston: Houghton Mifflin.

———. 1987. "Party Realignment in the States: Texas in the 1980s." Paper presented at the annual meeting of the American Political Science Association, Chicago, 3–6 September.

Sternlieb, George, and James W. Hughes. 1986. "Demographic and Economic Dynamics." In *The Political State of New Jersey*, edited by Gerald M. Pomper. New Brunswick, N.J.: Rutgers University Press.

Stone, Walter J. 1987. "Regional Variation in Partisan Change: Realignment in the Mountain West." In *The Politics of Realignment*, edited by P. Galderisi et al. Boulder, Colo.: Westview.

Sundquist, James L. 1983. *Dynamics of the Party System: Alignment and Realignment in the United States*. Washington, D.C.: Brookings.

Tedin, Kent L. March, 1987a. "The Transition of Electoral Politics in Texas: Voting for Governor in 1978–1986." Paper presented at the annual meeting of the Southwest Social Science Convention, Houston.

———. 1987b. "The Transition of Electoral Politics in Texas: Voting for Governor in 1978–1986." In *Perspectives on American and Texas Politics*, edited by Donald Lutz and Kent Tedin, 233–51. Dubuque, Iowa: Kendall/Hunt Publishing Company.

Terkel, Studs. 1984. *The Good War*. New York: Pantheon Publishers.

U.S. Bureau of the Census. 1988. *Current Population Reports,* series P-25, no. 957.

———. 1987. *State Government Finances in 1987,* series GF-87-3.

U.S. Department of Commerce. 1989. *Survey of Current Business.* "State Personal Income, 1986–1988: Revised Estimates." 71 (August): 33–46.

Valentine, Richard. 1968. "Arizona and the Great Depression." Master's thesis, Northern Arizona University.

Voss, Paul R. 1988. "A Demographic Portrait of Wisconsin's People." In *State Policy Choices: The Wisconsin Experience,* edited by Sheldon Danziger and John F. Witte. Madison: University of Wisconsin Press.

Waltz, Waldo E. 1940. "Arizona: A State of New–Old Frontiers." In *Rocky Mountain Politics,* edited by Thomas C. Donnelly. Albuquerque: University of New Mexico Press.

Wattenberg, Martin P. 1987. "The Hollow Realignment: Partisan Change in a Candidate-Centered Era." *Public Opinion Quarterly* 51:58–74.

———. 1990. *The Decline of American Political Parties: 1952–1988.* Cambridge: Harvard University Press.

West, Darrell. 1990. "Tax Reform and Credit-Claiming." *Western Political Quarterly* September: 647–59.

West, Darrell. 1987. *Congress and Economic Policymaking.* Pittsburgh: University of Pittsburgh Press.

White, John C. 1988. *The New Politics of Old Values.* Hanover, N.H.: University Press of New England.

Whittemore, Katharine. 1988. "Rise and Fall." *New England Monthly* December: 61–70.

Wirls, Daniel. 1986. "Reinterpreting the Gender Gap." *Public Opinion Quarterly* 50:316–30.

Wolfinger, Raymond E., and R. A. Arseneau. 1978. "Partisan Change in the South, 1952–1976." In *Political Parties: Development and Decay,* edited by L. Maisel and J. Cooper. Beverly Hills, Calif.: Sage.

Wolfinger, Raymond E., and Steven J. Rosenstone. 1980. *Who Votes?* New Haven: Yale University Press.

Wolfinger, Raymond E., and Michael G. Hagan. 1985. "Republican Prospects: Southern Comfort." *Public Opinion* 8:8–13.

Wright, Gerald C., Robert S. Erikson, and John P. McIver. 1985. "Measuring State Partisanship and Ideology with Survey Data." *Journal of Politics* 47: 469–89.

# Contributors

MAUREEN MOAKLEY is assistant professor of government at Connecticut College. She coedited *The Political Life of the American States* (1984) and is writing a book on Rhode Island politics.

LAWRENCE BAUM is professor of political science at The Ohio State University. His primary research interest is judicial politics, although his current research includes analysis of voting behavior in contests for state offices. He is the author of two books on judicial politics: *The Supreme Court* (1989) and *American Courts* (1990).

PAUL ALLEN BECK is professor of political science at The Ohio State University and author of numerous articles in leading journals and several books on the topics of electoral behavior, political parties, and realignment. One of his current research interests is voting in American subpresidential elections, supported by a National Science Foundation grant to study voting across the ballot.

DAVID R. BERMAN is professor of political science, Arizona State University, where he specializes in state and local politics. Among his publications are *State and Local Politics* (1991) and articles in several professional journals.

JOHN BIBBY is professor of political science at the University of Wisconsin-Milwaukee and a specialist in party politics. He is the coauthor of *Party Organizations in American Politics*, a longitudinal and comparative study of state party organizations in the fifty states, and the author of *Politics, Parties, and Elections in America*, as well as articles for professional journals and symposia.

ALLAN J. CIGLER is a professor in the Department of Political Science at the University of Kansas. His research focuses on interest groups and political parties. He coedited *Interest Group Politics* (1990) and *U.S. Agriculture Groups* (1990) and is the author of numerous articles and book chapters.

PATRICK R. COTTER is associate professor of political science at the University of Alabama. He also is a codirector of Southern Opinion Research. He has conducted research in the areas of political behavior, southern politics, and survey research methodology.

JAMES FAY is professor of political science at California State University, Hayward. He has written a number of articles on politics and election law and is the editor of the *California Almanac*.

SCOTT KEETER is an associate professor of political science and the former director of the survey research laboratory at Virginia Commonwealth University. He is the author of *Uninformed Choice: The Failure of the New Presidential Nominating System* and is working on a book about the U.S. public's knowledge of politics.

KAY LAWSON is professor of political science at San Francisco State University. Her recent works include *When Parties Fail: Emerging Alternative Organizations* (coedited with Peter Merkl) and *The Human Polity* (1989). She is cofounder of the California Committee for Party Renewal.

BURDETT A. LOOMIS is professor of political science at the University of Kansas. His research specialties include congress, interest groups, and public policy. He is the author of *The New American Politician* (1988) and a coeditor of *Interest Group Politics* (1990). He is researching and writing a book dealing with politics and policy making in Kansas.

JOHN P. MCIVER is associate professor of political science at the University of Colorado, Boulder. He is coauthor of *Unidimensional Scaling* (with Edward G. Carmines) and is at work on a book to be published by Cambridge University Press titled *Public Opinion, Politics, and Policy in the American States* (with Gerald Wright and Robert Erikson).

SUZANNE PARKER is the director of the survey research laboratory at The Florida State University. She has written extensively on public opinion and politics in Florida. Her recent work includes "Interest Groups and Public Opinion: Special Interests and the Publics' Interests in Florida" in *Florida Politics and Government*, edited by Robert J. Huckshorn, University Presses of Florida, 1991.

SAMUEL C. PATTERSON is professor of political science at The Ohio State University and managing editor of the *American Political Science Review*. In addition to conducting research on American state political parties and elections, he is the author of many research articles on state legislatures and the U.S. Congress.

PEVERILL SQUIRE is associate professor of political science at the University of Iowa. He has written extensively on congressional elections and state legislatures.

JEANIE R. STANLEY is associate professor of political science at The University of Texas at Tyler. She has written extensively on women and politics and state politics, including a recent study of gender differences in legislative effectiveness to be published by the Center for the American Woman and Politics.

WALTER J. STONE is professor of political science and faculty research associate at the Institute of Behavioral Science, University of Colorado, Boulder. He is author of *Republic at Risk: Self-Interest in American Politics* and coauthor (with Alan Abramowitz) of *Nomination Politics: Party Activists and Presidential Choice*. He is editor of the *Western Political Quarterly*.

DARRELL M. WEST is associate professor of political science and director of the public opinion laboratory at the A. Alfred Taubman Center for Public Policy and American Institutions at Brown University. He is the author of *Making Campaigns Count* and *Congress and Economic Policymaking* as well as numerous articles on public opinion and voting behavior.

JOHN KENNETH WHITE is associate professor of politics at the Catholic University of America and the author of *The New Politics of Old Values* and co-editor of *New York State Today: Politics, Government, and Public Policy*.

# Index